Overreach

OVERREACH

LEADERSHIP IN THE OBAMA PRESIDENCY

GEORGE C. EDWARDS III

TEXAS A&M UNIVERSITY

PRINCETON UNIVERSITY PRESS

PRINCETON AND OXFORD

Copyright © 2012 by Princeton University Press

Published by Princeton University Press, 41 William Street, Princeton, New Jersey 08540

In the United Kingdom: Princeton University Press, 6 Oxford Street, Woodstock, Oxfordshire OX20 1TW

press.princeton.edu

Jacket Photograph: *U.S. President Barack Obama speaks at a Democratic National Committee (DNC) fundraiser in Washington, DC, on Monday, May 16, 2011.* © Joshua Roberts/Pool/Corbis

Library of Congress Cataloging-in-Publication Data

Edwards, George C.

   Overreach : leadership in the Obama presidency / George C. Edwards III.

     p. cm.

   Includes bibliographical references and index.

   ISBN-13: 978-0-691-15368-1 (alk. paper)

   ISBN-10: 0-691-15368-X

1. Obama, Barack. 2. United States—Politics and government—2009- 3. Leadership—United States—Case studies. 4. Presidents—United States—Case studies. 5. Political leadership—United States—Case studies. 6. Executive power—United States—Case studies. I. Title.

   E907.E39 2012

   973.932092—dc23   2011031837

British Library Cataloging-in-Publication Data is available

This book has been composed in Minion Pro

Printed on acid-free paper. ∞

Printed in the United States of America

10 9 8 7 6 5 4 3 2 1

to Richard Neustadt
who taught us to think strategically about the presidency

CONTENTS

PREFACE

IN MY EARLIER BOOK, *The Strategic President: Persuasion and Opportunity in Presidential Leadership*, I offered a challenge to the conventional understanding of presidential leadership. Near the time of the book's publication, Barack Obama was elected president, presenting a fascinating test of my theory that presidents do not succeed by persuading others to support them but rather by recognizing and exploiting effectively the opportunities already present in their environments. In other words, presidents cannot create opportunities for change. Instead, they are dependent on exploiting the opportunities that already exist.

Obama possesses a first-class intellect, is a gifted communicator, and in the 2008 election attracted a devoted following. He and his aides concluded that he could move a highly polarized public to support his initiatives, several of which were of historic proportions. They also felt they could obtain bipartisan backing in Congress for these proposals. Many bright and politically experienced people agreed with them.

My view was quite different. It follows from my theory of presidential leadership that the president would fail to move both the public and congressional Republicans. Moreover, I argued that by asking the right questions, i.e., making accurate strategic assessments, we could predict these outcomes on the first day of the Obama presidency. In this volume, we will see which view was correct.

This book builds on *The Strategic President* and applies the ideas and discussion therein to predicting and explaining the politics of the Obama presidency. Because this volume is in important ways a test of the ideas presented in *The Strategic President*, I have included some text from that book in this one to provide the necessary introduction to my ideas for the reader who has not read *The Strategic President*.

I began my work on the Obama presidency during a sojourn at Oxford in the first half of 2009. Nuffield College once again extended its hospitality and provided me with a scholar's most valuable resource—the time to focus on research. I am most grateful for the productive relationship I have enjoyed with Nuffield. Special thanks go to my good friend Desmond King, the Mellon Chair of American Government at Oxford, who provided essential support for my stay.

I am also appreciative of the Department of Political Science at Texas A&M University, which for many years has provided me with an environment conducive to research. As always, I am indebted to my wife, Carmella, for making life so enjoyable and affording me the luxury of quality time for working.

My friend Chuck Myers has been an exceptional editor. Intelligent, knowledgeable, insightful, and supportive, he has played an essential role in this project. Karen Verde once again did a skilled and sensitive job editing the manuscript. Karen Fortgang was an efficient and skilled production editor.

Overreach

Introduction

IN 2008, AMERICA SUFFERED FROM WAR and economic crisis. Partisan polarization was extraordinarily high while faith in government was exceptionally low. In such times, the reflexive call is for new—and better—leadership, especially in the White House. Barack Obama answered the call, presenting himself as a transformational leader who would fundamentally change the policy and the politics of America.

Even though both the public and commentators are frequently disillusioned with the performance of individual presidents and recognize that stalemate is common in the political system, Americans eagerly accept what appears to be the promise of presidential leadership to renew their faith in the potential of the presidency. Many Americans enthusiastically embraced Obama's candidacy and worked tirelessly to put him in the White House. Once there, the new president and his supporters shared an exuberant optimism about the changes he would bring to the country.

There is little question that Obama was sincere in wanting to bring about change. So were his followers. Yet a year into his administration, many were frustrated—and surprised—by the widespread resistance to his major policy proposals. The public was typically unresponsive to the president's calls for support. Partisan polarization and congressional gridlock did not disappear. As a result, the promised transformation in energy, environmental, immigration, and other policies did not occur. When the president succeeded on health care reform, it was the result of old-fashioned party leadership, ramming the bill through Congress on a party line vote. Even worse, from the Democrats' perspective, the 2010 midterm elections were a stunning defeat for the president's party that would undermine the administration's ability to govern in the succeeding years.

How could this bright, articulate, decent, and knowledgeable new president have such a difficult time attaining his goals? Did the president fumble the ball, making tactical errors in his attempts to govern? Although no president is perfect, the Obama White House has not been severely mismanaged, politically insensitive, or prone to making avoidable mistakes. Ineffective implementation of a strategy is not the explanation for the lack of progress in transforming policy and politics.

Instead, the problem was in the strategies themselves—in the belief that they could succeed. A common premise underlying the widespread emphasis on political leadership as the wellspring of change is that some leaders have the capability to transform policy by reshaping the influences on it. As we will see, the Obama White House believed in the power of the bully pulpit. The president and his advisors felt that he could persuade the public to support his program. They also believed that the president could obtain bipartisan support in Congress through efforts to engage the opposition. As a result of these premises, the White House felt comfortable advancing an extraordinarily large and expensive agenda.

These premises were faulty, however. There is not a single systematic study that demonstrates that presidents can reliably move others to support them. Equally important, we now have a substantial literature showing that presidents typically fail at persuasion.[1]

In *The Strategic President*, I challenged the conventional understanding of presidential leadership, arguing that presidential power is *not* the power to persuade. Presidents cannot reshape the contours of the political landscape to pave the way for change by establishing an agenda and persuading the public, Congress, and others to support their policies.[2]

The point is not that presidents do not matter. Of course they do. The question is *how* they matter—how do they bring about change? The answer I offer is that successful presidents facilitate change by recognizing opportunities in their environments and fashioning strategies and tactics to exploit them. In other words, presidents who are successful in obtaining support for their agendas have to evaluate the opportunities for change in their environments carefully and orchestrate existing and potential support skillfully.[3]

Overreach

The stakes of understanding the potential of persuasiveness are especially high for the White House. If the conventional wisdom is wrong and presidents are not able to persuade, much less mobilize, the public or Congress, then presidents may be wasting their time and resources and adopting governing styles that are prone to failure. Presidents—and the country—often endure self-inflicted wounds when they fail to appreciate the limits of their influence.

The concept of overreach refers to presidents proposing policies that lack substantial support in the public or Congress, expecting to create opportunities for change by persuading a majority of the public and the Congress to support their policies. As a result of their risky behavior, they suffer heavy political losses that undermine their ability to govern. The best way to elucidate the concept is to examine some prominent examples of overreach.

FDR's Court-Packing Plan

In February 1937, shortly after his landslide reelection and at the height of his powers, Franklin D. Roosevelt surprised the nation by proposing a plan to increase the size of the Supreme Court. His motivation was transparent: to add members who would support New Deal policies. It is telling that after the election, the president was so confident of his public support and his ability to channel it to sustain his initiatives that he did not consult with major groups of supporters, such as leading liberals or leaders of labor unions and farm organizations, on his proposal and ignored information on the public's fundamental support for the Court.[4]

The story of the battle is a complicated one, and Roosevelt claimed success (a more responsive Court) even though his bill failed to pass. However we interpret the White House's success in achieving its immediate goal, there is little doubt that the entire episode was a costly one for the president. The Court battle became a rallying point around which latent opposition to the New Deal coalesced and helped to weld together a bipartisan coalition of anti–New Deal senators into a conservative bloc composed of the irreconcilable Democrats, Republicans, and, most important, previously loyal moderate Democrats. The battle over the Court also deeply divided the Democratic Party, precipitating factional wars in the states.[5]

Similarly, the dispute produced divisions among reformers of many types, undermining the bipartisan support for the New Deal and confirming for Republican progressives their suspicions that New Dealers were interested in self-aggrandizement and concentrating power in Washington. In addition, the attempt to pack the Court helped to cause the middle-class backing Roosevelt had mobilized in the 1936 campaign to ebb away.

As a result, the Court struggle helped to blunt the most important drive for social reform in American history and squandered the advantage of Roosevelt's triumph in 1936. As William Leuchtenburg put it, "Never again would FDR be as predominant, either on Capitol Hill or at the polling places, as he was when 1937 began."[6] Years later, Henry Wallace reflected: "The whole New Deal really went up in smoke as a result of the Supreme Court fight." At the end of the 1937 session of Congress, one reporter inquired, "How did the President slide so far—so fast?"[7]

Bill Clinton's Health Care Reform

Bill Clinton declared health care reform as the cornerstone of his new presidency. In November 1993, he sent a 1,342-page proposal to Congress. The administration based its massive health care reform plan on the underlying, and unquestioned, assumption within the White House that the president could sell his plan to the public and thus solidify congressional support. Because the administration believed it could persuade the public, Clinton and his aides felt they could focus on developing their preferred option in health care policy in 1993. In the process, they discounted centrist opinion and underestimated how opponents could criticize their plan as big government. The president was not able to sustain the support of the public for health care reform, however.[8]

Moreover, even as the bill's fortunes soured, the White House refused to compromise. As Lawrence Jacobs and Robert Shapiro put it, "The White House's unquestioned faith that the president could rally Americans produced a rigid insistence on comprehensive reforms." In the end, Clinton's proposal did not pass—or even come to a vote in either house of Congress. The president and his aides had greatly overestimated their ability to persuade the public to support their proposal.[9]

This is not the lesson that Clinton learned, however. Indeed, the premise of the power of the presidential pulpit was so strong that each downturn in the bill's progress prompted new schemes for going public rather than a reconsideration of the fundamental framework of the bill or the basic strategy for obtaining its passage.[10] Ultimately, the president concluded that health care reform failed because "I totally neglected how to get the public informed. . . . I have to get more involved in crafting my message—in getting across my core concerns."[11] In other words, it was not his strategy that was inappropriate, only his implementation of it. The premise of the potential of presidential persuasion seems to be nonfalsifiable.

In the 1994 midterm elections, the Democrats lost majorities in both the House and the Senate for the first time in four decades, undermining the president's ability to move his agenda. The administration's health care proposal was the prime example of the Republicans' charge that the Democrats were ideological extremists who had lost touch with the wishes of Americans. Summing up the health care reform debacle, Jacobs and Shapiro concluded that the "fundamental political mistake committed by Bill Clinton and his aides was in grossly overestimating the capacity of a president to 'win' public opinion and to use public support as leverage to overcome known political obstacles—from an ideologically divided Congress to hostile interest groups."[12]

George W. Bush's Social Security Reform

On November 4, 2004, two days after the presidential election, George W. Bush painted his second-term vision in bold, aggressive strokes during a press conference at the White House. A central thrust of his second term would be to spend the political capital he felt he had earned in the election to reform Social Security. Rather than winding down its 2004 campaign effort, the administration launched an extensive public relations effort to convince the public, and thus Congress, to support the president's reform proposal.

Even before the inauguration, the White House announced plans to reactivate Bush's reelection campaign's network of donors and activists to build pressure on lawmakers to allow workers to invest part of their Social Security taxes in the stock market. As Treasury Secretary John W. Snow put it, the "scope and scale goes way beyond anything we have done."[13] The same architects of Bush's political victories, principally political strategists Karl Rove at the White House and Ken Mehlman, who was the Bush-Cheney campaign manager, at the Republican National Committee (RNC), would be masterminding the new campaign. As Mehlman put it, the "whole effort will be focused on the legislative agenda."[14]

At the end of President Bush's "60 Stops in 60 Days" campaign to promote his Social Security proposals, the Treasury Department reported on its Web site that 31 administration officials had made 166 stops outside the beltway, visiting 40 states and 127 cities, and had given more than 500 radio interviews in 50 states. Administration officials also placed opinion columns in newspapers with circulation totaling 7.94 million during this period, and they participated in 61 town hall meetings with 30 members of Congress in their constituencies.[15]

All this effort did not succeed in convincing the public to support the president or his Social Security proposal. What was probably the largest and best-organized public relations effort to sell a policy in the history of the Republic ended with a whimper—and in failure. Neither the public nor Congress supported the president's plan.[16] Instead, the president's efforts contributed to the unraveling of Republican cohesiveness in Congress and reinforced the growing perception among the public that he was not up to the job of president.

Franklin D. Roosevelt, Bill Clinton, and George W. Bush overestimated the prospects for change on Supreme Court appointments, health care policy, and Social Security, respectively, overreached, and failed to achieve their goals. (In his memoirs, Clinton admits that he overestimated the pace and amount of change Americans could digest.)[17] In each case, the president's assumption that he could achieve his goals through persuasion led to much greater problems than the failure to achieve his immediate policy goals. Their strategic choices also weakened their administrations in the long term.[18]

The dangers of overreach and debilitating political losses alert us that it is critically important for presidents to assess accurately the potential for obtaining support. Moreover, the success of a strategy for governing depends on the opportunities for it to succeed. Adopting strategies for governing that are prone to failure waste rather than create opportunities.[19]

Strategic Assessments

Before a president can fashion a strategy for accomplishing his goals and avoid the consequences of overreach, he must understand the environment in which he is operating. Because presidents are not in strong positions to *create* opportunities for legislative success by persuading others to support their policies, recognizing the opportunities that already exist is particularly significant. Indeed, it may be the most important skill of all. Ideally, such appraisals will influence how much and what types of change presidents seek and the strategies they choose for achieving it.

Although accurately assessing the possibilities for change in the president's environment is a key to success, the context of any presidency is complex, making such assessments difficult. Public support is a critical political resource. Indicators of the potential for public support for a president seeking to expand the scope of government include a mandate from the voters favoring specific policies, a broad public predisposition for government activism, and opposition party identifiers open to supporting the president's initiatives.

All politicians claim to know what the public wants, but the facts that it is rare to test such claims and that there are typically contradictory claims on the same issue ought to give one pause about their accuracy. In truth, it is not easy to decipher public opinion or to predict public response to specific proposals. Moreover, it is possible that presidential success at altering public policy will create a backlash against further change. Future currents of public opinion, which are inherently difficult to gauge, will influence the support the president receives from members of Congress, especially those in vulnerable seats.

Supportive majorities in Congress and an opposition party open to compromise are also critical factors in presidential success. Equally useful to the White House is a weakened, or even reeling, opposition party attempting to find its footing after electoral setbacks. Moreover, the size and nature of the president's legislative agenda will strongly influence how representatives and senators respond to his proposals and affect the resources available to fund and implement them. The nature of the opposition to the president is also critical—and difficult to assess. It is one thing to count the number of opposition party members in Congress. It is something else to predict the party's resiliency in response to defeat, the effectiveness of its leaders, and the issues on which it may find its voice.

A range of political and financial resources can be useful for engendering widespread, non-incremental change. Slack budgetary resources or minimal resistance to expanding budgets can be crucial for many programs. The availability of public funds, and the tolerance for spending them, can change quickly, however.

It will be rare for a presidency to enjoy all the most useful resources simultaneously, and effecting change does not require such an unusual confluence of favorable forces. Every president requires some of these resources to succeed, however. Equally important, no chief executive can properly assess the opportunity structure of his administration without rigorously analyzing the most significant features of his environment. As I show in chapters 1 and 4, it was possible to assess the president's strategic position accurately and make predictions about what strategies would and would not work. These predictions, of course, are premised on asking the right questions about the likely success of presidential leadership efforts.

Two weeks into the Obama presidency, I gave a presentation covered by C-SPAN in which I predicted that the administration would not be able to rally the public behind its initiatives and would not obtain significant bipartisan support in Congress. If the president succeeded on his major initiatives, it would be a result of mobilizing his party in Congress.[20] The next month, I answered five questions about the new administration for *CQ Weekly*, making similar arguments.[21]

I savored no schadenfreude in predicting that the Obama administration would be less transformative than either the president or his supporters hoped. However, the accuracy of the predictions shows the value of thinking rigorously about the strategic level of power. According to Richard Neustadt:

> There are two ways to study "presidential power." One way is to focus on the tactics . . . of influencing certain men in given situations. . . . The other way is to step back from tactics . . . and to deal with influence in more strategic terms: what is its nature and what are its sources? . . . Strategically, [for example] the question is not how he masters Congress in a peculiar instance, but what he does to boost his chance for mastery in any instance.[22]

To think strategically about power, we must search for generalizations. Influence is a concept that involves relationships between people. To understand relationships, we must understand why people respond to the president as they do. We cannot assume that they will respond positively to the president's requests for support. Nor can we evaluate the promise of a presidency simply by examining its aspirations. Instead, we have to adopt a skeptical posture and carefully analyze the patterns of public and congressional behavior. Once we can explain relationships, we are in a better position to evaluate both the opportunities for a president and the utility of potential strategies for governing.

Plan of the Book

In this volume, I apply the lessons of *The Strategic President*—that the essential presidential leadership skills are recognizing and exploiting opportunities, not creating them—to the first years of the Obama presidency. I want to explain why the president found it so difficult to engender change. I proceed by asking two core questions about his administration. The first deals with the opportunities for public and congressional support. What were these opportunities and how did the administration understand them? And what does our analysis lead us to expect about the likely success of the strategies it pursued? Chapter 1 focuses on assessing the potential for public support, while chapter 4 examines the potential for support in Congress.

Like most presidents, Obama was not content to exploit existing opportunities for change. As we will see, the White House thought it could create new opportunities. Thus, the second fundamental question deals with the ability of the White House to create such opportunities. Could the president move the public in the direction of support for his policies? Could he obtain bipartisan support in Congress? Chapter 2 analyzes Obama's efforts to lead the public, while chapter 3 evaluates his success in doing so. Similarly, chapter 5 examines the president's efforts to lead Congress, and chapter 6 presents his success in gaining congressional support, especially from the opposition.

In chapter 7, I examine lessons for both presidents and students of politics that we can learn from studying the Obama presidency. I particularly stress the importance of strategic assessments in presidential leadership and the leverage they give us to evaluate the likely success of strategies for governing.

CHAPTER 1

Assessing Opportunities

PUBLIC SUPPORT

PUBLIC SUPPORT IS A KEY POLITICAL RESOURCE, and modern presidents have typically sought public support for themselves and their policies that they could leverage to obtain backing for their proposals in Congress. It is natural for a new president, basking in the glow of an electoral victory, to focus on creating, rather than exploiting, opportunities for change. After all, if he convinced voters and party leaders to support his candidacy—and just won the biggest prize in American politics by doing so—why should he not be able to convince the public or members of Congress to support his policies? Thus, presidents may not focus on evaluating existing possibilities when they think they can create their own.

Yet it is a mistake for presidents to assume they can lead the public. There is nothing in the historical record to support such a belief. In earlier work, I focused on the opinion leadership of Bill Clinton and Ronald Reagan on a wide range of policies and efforts to defend themselves against scandal. I found that public opinion rarely moved in the president's direction. On most of Clinton's and Reagan's policy initiatives, pluralities, and often majorities, of the public *opposed* the president. Moreover, movement in public opinion was typically *against* the president.[1] An analysis of Franklin D. Roosevelt's efforts to lead the public also found that the president typically experienced frustration and failure.[2] Like Barack Obama, George W. Bush sought far-reaching changes in public policy across a broad range of issues. To achieve his goals, he went public as much as any of his predecessors, but from tax cuts and immigration to Social Security and the war in Iraq, he was not able to move the public in his direction.[3]

The success of a strategy for governing depends on the opportunities for it to succeed. Relying on going public to pressure Congress when the public is unlikely to be responsive to the president's appeals is a recipe for failure, so it is critically important for presidents to assess accurately the potential for obtaining public support. Moreover, adopting strategies for governing that are prone to failure wastes rather than creates opportunities.[4]

There are two fundamental components of the opportunity for obtaining public support. First is the nature of public opinion at the time a president takes office. Does it support the direction in which the president would like to move? Is there a mandate from the voters in support of specific policies? Is there a broad public predisposition for government activism? Are opposition party identifiers open to supporting the president's initiatives? A second facet of the potential for public leadership focuses on the long run. What are the challenges to leading the public that every president faces?

After outlining the White House's view of the opportunities for change in its environment, I explore both facets of public opinion in this chapter. We will see that by analyzing the opportunity for obtaining public support for Obama's initiatives, it is possible to understand and predict the challenges President Obama faced in going public and the relative utility of this strategy for governing.

The View from the White House

Barack Obama is all about change. Calling for change was at the center of his campaign strategy, and he spoke tirelessly of fundamental reforms in health care, energy, the environment, and other policy areas. Once in office, the president and his aides embraced the view that the environment offered a rare opportunity for the changes they espoused. They reasoned that the crisis atmosphere would galvanize the country, perhaps even generating bipartisan support for the president's initiatives. Thus, they viewed the economic crisis as an opportunity, a catalyst for action, rather than as a constraint. White House Chief of Staff Rahm Emanuel articulated this strategy most succinctly when he declared that one should "Never let a serious crisis go to waste."[5] In other words, the new administration concluded that the economic crisis had heightened the desire for change that voters expressed in November, creating a once-in-a-generation opportunity for bold policy shifts.[6]

On the surface, it seemed reasonable to conclude that in a time of severe economic crisis that touched many aspects of everyday life such as housing, banking, and consumer credit, Americans were seeking reassurance from the White House and the president would have both the public's ear and its good wishes. More importantly, Obama's team felt the recession had left public opinion malleable and highly responsive to bold leadership. Thus, even during the transition, the president-elect launched a full-scale marketing blitz to pass his massive stimulus package, including delivering a major speech at George Mason University.

The new president quite sensibly concluded that he had to promote economic recovery as his first order of business. Moreover, his proposal for recovery called for massive subsidies to keep the banking and automobile industries afloat and a staggeringly expensive program to stimulate the economy. These expenditures and tax cuts produced by far the largest deficits in American history. In addition, passing them required the president to spend his political capital in the early days of his presidency, in difficult legislative battles in which he could not attract bipartisan support. A politically costly battle over his budget followed directly, with similar legislative results.

An alternative analysis of the policy environment might have viewed the economic crisis as a constraint. Obama could have justifiably argued that he would have to scale back his agenda, that the economy was in such a fragile state that he should focus all his attention on nursing it back to health as soon as possible. He also could have explained that, given the amount of money the government would be pouring into the economy, at the moment the country could not afford a costly overhaul of health care or an ambitious initiative to combat global warming that included a controversial cap-and-trade system and energy taxes. Instead, he would work to overhaul the financial services industry, whose excesses triggered the crisis.

Obama realized that dealing with a severe recession was not at the core of his campaign for the presidency. He later recalled, "The last thing I would have liked to do as an incoming President is figure out how to save GM and Chrysler from bankruptcy. That wasn't on my list of to-dos when I was running for office."[7] Moreover, the White House was aware of the challenge it faced in dealing with the economy. According to senior advisor David Axelrod, "We came to office and immediately walked into a fiscal crisis, a financial crisis, and an economic crisis. It required some very difficult decisions, and it required everyone to spend some political capital."[8] The president knew it was "political suicide" to ask for freeing up the second portion of the Troubled Asset Relief Program (TARP) funds, and later reflected that he knew his "political capital would go down pretty rapidly."[9]

Nevertheless, the administration moved aggressively to propose the most ambitious domestic agenda since Lyndon Johnson's Great Society. Obama decided that he would convey the idea that the nation's problems, from the retreating economy to falling student test scores, were intertwined as he pressed for action on a host of fronts simultaneously.[10] The president often argued, for example, that the country had to address the cost and availability of health care and lessen its dependence on foreign oil before there could be a real economic recovery. From a policy analytic standpoint, the White House had a good case. Politics rarely defers to analysis, however.[11]

Even after the frustrations of his first year in office, Obama declared in his State of the Union message in January 2010:

> From the day I took office, I've been told that addressing our larger challenges is too ambitious; such an effort would be too contentious. I've been told that our political system is too gridlocked, and that we should just put things on hold for a while.
>
> For those who make these claims, I have one simple question: How long should we wait? How long should America put its future on hold?[12]

After the Republican success in the 1994 elections, Bill Clinton felt that he needed to get ahead of the political passions of the moment and turned toward the center of the political spectrum with his triangulation strategy. Barack Obama had a different response to the setbacks of his first year. He kept to his agenda, only altering its timing.[13]

The President's Mandate

New presidents traditionally claim a mandate from the people, because the most effective means of setting the terms of debate and overcoming opposition is the perception of an electoral mandate, an impression that the voters want to see the winner's programs implemented. Indeed, major changes in policy, as in 1933, 1965, and 1981, rarely occur in the absence of such perceptions.

Mandates can be powerful symbols in American politics. They accord added legitimacy and credibility to the newly elected president's proposals. Concerns for representation and political survival encourage members of Congress to support the president if they feel the people have spoken.[14] As a result, mandates change the premises of decision. Perceptions of a mandate in 1980, for example, placed a stigma on big government and exalted the unregulated marketplace and large defense budgets, providing Ronald Reagan a favorable strategic position for dealing with Congress.

Barack Obama won the presidency with nearly 53 percent of the popular vote, the first time a Northern Democrat had won a majority of the popular vote for president since Franklin D. Roosevelt's victory in 1944—and only the third time any Democrat had won a majority of the vote in those sixty-four years. Democrats won additional seats in both houses of Congress, and the historic nature of the election of the first black president generated an enormous amount of favorable press coverage. Furthermore, the new president had emphasized change, not continuity, in his campaign and promised bold new initiatives.[15] Thus, it was easy for Democrats to overinterpret the new president's mandate for change.

Obama seemed to have a realistic interpretation of the nature of his victory, however, as we can see from his response to a question about his mandate in a press conference on November 25, 2008.

> **Q:** Thank you, Mr. President-elect. Given the election results, what sort of mandate do you have from the voters, do you believe? And does the large Democratic majority in Congress present an opportunity to pass your agenda, or is there a danger, in this environment, of overreach?

> **PRESIDENT-ELECT OBAMA:** Well, first of all, we had, I think, a decisive win because of the extraordinary desire for change on the part of the American people. And so I don't think that there's any question that we have a mandate to move the country in a new direction and not continue the same old practices that have gotten us into the fix that we're in.

> But I won 53 percent of the vote. That means 46 or 47 percent of the country voted for John McCain. And it's important, as I said on election night, that we enter into the new administration with a sense of humility and a recognition that wisdom is not the monopoly of any one party.

> In order for us to be effective, given the scope and the scale of the challenges
> that we face, Republicans and Democrats are going to have to work together.[16]

The president-elect had it about right. An ABC News/*Washington Post* poll taken shortly before his inauguration found that although most people felt Obama had a mandate to work for major policy changes, 46 percent of the public felt he should compromise with Republicans in doing so.[17]

By Inauguration Day, however, the new president took a more expansive view.

> Now, there are some who question the scale of our ambitions, who suggest that our system cannot tolerate too many big plans. Their memories are short, for they have forgotten what this country has already done, what free men and women can achieve when imagination is joined to common purpose, and necessity to courage. What the cynics fail to understand is that the ground has shifted beneath them, that the stale political arguments that have consumed us for so long no longer apply.[18]

Apparently, he concluded that the contours of the political landscape had shifted in a way to expand the opportunities for major liberal change.

Support for Government Activism

Major expansions in public policy also require public support for, or at least toleration of, government activism in the form of new programs, increased spending, and additional taxes. It appears as though the White House concluded that Obama's victory indicated the electorate had turned in a more liberal direction and that the economic crisis had increased the public's demand for more government. Its allies agreed. "The center has moved," declared Robert Borosage, president of the liberal Institute for America's Future and co-director of the Campaign for America's Future.[19]

There was even some evidence from the right that times had changed. Republican Governor Arnold Schwarzenegger of California supported new federal spending on infrastructure and urged lawmakers to "get off of their rigid ideologies." Former Federal Reserve chairman Alan Greenspan revealed that the financial crisis caused him to reexamine his free market views. Martin Feldstein, a top economic advisor to Ronald Reagan, was advocating large increases in federal spending. George W. Bush himself had proposed a $700 billion bailout for financial institutions.[20]

There was reason for skepticism, however—if one were to look for it. The country's partisan balance had shifted more than its ideological balance. The broad repudiation of President George W. Bush propelled the Democrats to their widest advantage over Republicans in party identification in decades, but the public's ideological alignment did not change nearly as much. More Ameri-

TABLE 1.1.
Trends in Ideological Identification

Year	% Conservative	% Moderate	% Liberal
1992	36	43	17
1993	39	40	18
1994	38	42	17
1995	36	39	16
1996	38	40	16
1997	37	40	19
1998	37	40	19
1999	38	40	19
2000	38	40	19
2001	38	40	20
2002	38	39	19
2003	38	40	20
2004	38	40	19
2005	38	39	20
2006	37	38	21
2007	37	37	22
2008	37	37	22
2009	40	36	21
2010	40	35	21

Source: Gallup Poll.

cans identified as conservatives than as liberals, for example (table 1.1). In both 2009 and 2010, 40 percent of Americans described their political views as conservative and only 21 percent as liberal. Thirty-six and thirty-five percent, respectively, identified as moderates. The number of conservatives increased since 2008, reaching its highest level in the entire time series. The 21 percent calling themselves liberal was in line with findings throughout the decade. Equally significant, the number of moderates, potential supporters of Obama's agenda, was at its lowest point since the time series began in 1992 (when moderates made up 43 percent of the public).

Despite the Democratic Party's political strength in representation in Congress, a significantly higher percentage of Americans in most states, even some solidly Democratic ones, called themselves conservative rather than liberal. No state in 2009 had a majority or even a plurality of people who called themselves liberal, with the conservative advantage ranging from 1 percentage point in Vermont, Hawaii, and Massachusetts to 35 percentage points in Alabama. (Washington, DC has a plurality of liberals, 36 percent.)[21]

We can also see the dominance of conservatism if we disaggregate opinion by political party. While 72 percent of Republicans in 2009 called themselves conservative, only 37 percent of Democrats identified as liberal. Thirty-nine percent of Democrats said they were moderates and another 22 percent saw themselves as conservative. Among Independents, 35 percent said they were conservative, and only 18 percent identified as liberal. Between 2008 and 2009, there was an increase of 5 points in the percentage of Independents calling themselves conservative.[22]

Ideological identification is not determinative, of course, and there is a well-known paradox of the incongruity between ideological identification and issue attitudes.[23] Scholars have long known that only a fraction of the public exhibits the requisite traits of an "ideologue."[24] Nevertheless, many more Americans are able to choose an ideological label and use it to guide their political judgments than in previous decades.[25] Scholars have found that ideological self-placements are influential determinants of vote choice,[26] issue attitudes,[27] and views toward government spending.[28]

There are other indicators of conservatism aside from ideological identification. For example, in December 2009, Pew found that Americans had become more conservative on abortion, gun control, and climate change.[29] Similarly, Gallup found that at the end of August 2009, 53 percent of Americans said the government should promote "traditional values," while 42 percent disagreed and believed the government should not favor any particular set of values. The previous year, Americans were divided down the middle, with 48 percent taking each position. (The poll did not define the term "traditional values." Gallup found that when it disaggregated the results by party and ideology, it appeared that respondents understood traditional values to be those generally favored by the Republican Party.) The shift in attitudes came primarily from Independents, whose views showed a dramatic turnaround, from a 55 percent to 37 percent split against government-promoted morality in 2008 to a 54 percent to 40 percent division in favor of it in 2009.[30]

The public also increased its traditional skepticism about expanding government's role. For example, in November 2008, 54 percent of the public said it was the responsibility of the federal government to make sure all Americans had health care coverage. A year later, this figure had decreased to 47 percent, while 50 percent said it was not the government's responsibility. At the same time, there was an increase of 12 percentage points in the number of people rating health care coverage in the United States as good or excellent.[31]

More broadly, when asked whether it preferred smaller government offering fewer public services or larger government offering more services, the public chose the former. Support for larger government was modest when Obama took office, and was down to 38 percent support a year later (table 1.2).[32] Meanwhile support for smaller government grew somewhat during his first two years in the White House.

The general state of the economy encouraged caution about bold innovation in public policy. With unemployment around 10 percent and a stock market plunge that threatened retirement savings, Americans started spending less,

TABLE 1.2.
Support for Larger Government

Poll Dates	% Smaller Government, Fewer Services	% Larger Government, More Services	% No Opinion
October 29–November 1, 20007	50	44	5
June 12–15, 2008	50	45	5
January 13–16, 2009	53	43	4
June 18–21, 2009	54	41	4
January 12–15, 2010	58	38	4
April 22–25, 2010	56	40	4

Source: ABC News-Washington Post Poll.
Question: "Generally speaking, would you say you favor (smaller government with fewer services), or (larger government with more services)?

saving more,[33] and adopting a more measured approach to change. Expectations of a weak economy typically move the country to the right.[34]

In March 2009, Gallup found that only 13 percent of Americans both approved of the government's expansion to address the economic crisis *and* wanted that expansion to be permanent. Another 39 percent favored the expansion but wanted it to be cut back once the crisis was resolved. Finally, a plurality—44 percent—of Americans opposed the expansion from the beginning.[35]

Overwhelming Republican opposition to government activism should surprise no one. But by July 2009, 66 percent of Independents thought Obama's proposals for addressing the country's major problems called for too much government spending and 60 percent said his agenda called for too much government expansion.[36] The public supported fiscal discipline over economic stimulus by 56 percent to 41 percent.[37]

Another obstacle to change was paying for it, which is especially problematic in bad economic times. In August 2009, Gallup found that 68 percent of Americans expected their federal income taxes would be higher by the end of Barack Obama's first term as president. Nearly half of these people (35 percent) expected their taxes would be "a lot higher."[38] The rise in expectations that taxes would increase probably was a reflection of Obama's ambitious domestic agenda, which began with a $787 billion economic stimulus plan and then focused on a roughly $1 trillion health care reform bill. Although Obama regularly reiterated his pledge not to raise taxes except for the wealthiest, most Americans remained skeptical that the administration could pay for health care reform and its other programs without raising their taxes.

Americans were also markedly cynical about the amount of waste in federal spending. At the end of the summer of 2009, on average, Americans believed 50 cents of every tax dollar that went to the government in Washington, DC, was wasted, an increase from 40 cents in 1979.[39]

The public's resistance to government activism should not be surprising. In their sweeping "macro" view of public opinion, Robert Erikson, Michael MacKuen, and James Stimson show that opinion always moves contrary to the president's position. They argue that a moderate public always gets too much liberalism from Democrats and too much conservatism from Republicans. Because public officials have policy beliefs as well as an interest in reelection, they are not likely to calibrate their policy stances exactly to match those of the public. Therefore, opinion movement is typically contrary to the ideological persuasion of presidents. Liberal presidents produce movement in the conservative direction and conservatives generate public support for more liberal policies.[40]

The public continuously adjusts its views of current policy in the direction of a long-run equilibrium path as it compares its preferences for ideal policy with its views of current policy to produce a policy mood.[41] Thus, the conservative policy period of the 1950s produced a liberal mood that resulted in the liberal policy changes of the mid-1960s. These policies, in turn, helped elect conservative Richard Nixon. In the late 1970s, Jimmy Carter's liberal policies paved the way for Ronald Reagan's conservative tenure, which in turn laid the foundation for Bill Clinton's more liberal stances. Negative reaction to the conservatism of George W. Bush encouraged the election of the more liberal Barack Obama. Stuart Soroka and Christopher Wlezien have reached similar conclusions with their thermostat model of public opinion.[42]

Public Polarization

A primary reason for the difficulty of passing major changes in public policy is the challenge of obtaining support from opposition party identifiers among the public. We know that partisan polarization reached record levels during the presidency of George W. Bush.[43] The election of Barack Obama did not diminish this polarization and presented an obstacle to the new president obtaining support from Republicans. We can start with the election results to better understand this dimension of the context of the Obama presidency.

The 2008 Election

In 2008, party line voting was 89.1 percent, the second highest level in the history of the American National Election Studies (ANES), which go back to 1952. This level was surpassed only by the 89.9 percent level in 2004. Moreover, Obama's electoral coalition contained the smallest share of opposite-party identifiers of any president elected since the advent of the ANES time series, just 4.4 percent.[44]

Republicans and Republican-leaning Independents not only did not support Obama. By Election Day, they perceived a huge ideological gulf between themselves and the new president and viewed him as an untrustworthy radical leftist with a socialist agenda. Forty-one percent of McCain voters judged Obama to be an "extreme liberal," further left than Republican voters had placed any previous Democratic candidate. Moreover, they placed him further to the left of their own ideologies than they had placed any previous Democratic candidate.[45]

Thus, the Republicans' campaign to brand Obama as a radical socialist[46] out of touch with American values resonated with many McCain voters. An African American candidate was also likely to exacerbate right-wing opposition,[47] as was his Ivy League education and somewhat detached manner. The fact that he spent part of his childhood in Muslim Indonesia and that his middle name was "Hussein" provided additional fodder for those willing or even eager to believe that he was outside the mainstream. Republican voters did not simply oppose Obama; they despised and feared him.

Jay Cost calculated both unweighted and weighted (where each state is factored according to its share of the nationwide popular vote) averages of Obama's share of the vote in each state plus the District of Columbia to calculate the standard deviation of votes (the greater the standard deviation, the more the states varied around the average, the more accentuated were their differences, and so the more polarization there was). He found the highest level of partisan polarization in the past sixty years.[48]

Similarly, identifying the states that deviated from Obama's share of the nationwide vote (about 52.9 percent) by 10 percentage points or more reveals that there were more "polarized" states than in any election in the past sixty years.[49] A few states (figure 1.1)—Vermont, Rhode Island, Hawaii, and the District of Columbia—were polarized in favor of Obama. Most of the polarized states, however, voted for Republican John McCain. The majority of these states form a belt stretching from West Virginia, Kentucky, and Tennessee through Alabama, Mississippi, Louisiana, and Arkansas over to Oklahoma, Kansas, and Nebraska. In addition, Wyoming, Idaho, Utah, and Alaska were strongly in the Republican camp. Never before had many of these states voted so heavily against a victorious Democrat.

The electoral polarization of the Bush years persisted in the 2008 presidential election, indicating that it represents more than a reaction to George W. Bush (although he certainly exacerbated it).[50] The crucial point, however, is that Obama would have his work cut out for him to reach the public in states that are turning increasingly red.

Polarization of the electorate has increasingly taken place along ideological lines. Partisans are more likely to apply ideological labels to themselves, and a

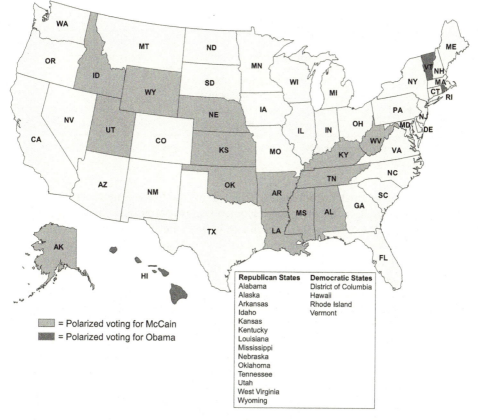

Figure 1.1.
States with Polarized Election Results in the 2008 Presidential Election.
Light gray indicates polarized voting for McCain; dark gray indicates polarized voting for Obama.

declining number of them call themselves moderate. Strong party identifiers are the most likely to define politics in ideological terms while the differences in the ideological self-placements of Republicans and Democrats have grown dramatically since the 1980s. This polarization of partisans has contributed to much more ideological voting behavior.[51]

In addition, people now live in communities where their neighbors are likely to agree with them politically and share the same tastes,[52] and migrants are more likely to move into a congressional district that matches their ideological preferences (even after controlling for the partisanship in the district of origin).[53] Nearly half of the 2008 presidential vote came from counties that either Obama or McCain won by 20 percentage points or more. Education levels reinforce this partisan polarization (table 1.3). Among the 96 percent of

TABLE 1.3.
Education and 2008 Presidential Vote in Counties

Winner	Size of Victory in Counties	% Population with BA, BS Degree or Higher
Obama	> 20 percentage points	33
Obama	< 20 percentage points	28
McCain	< 20 percentage points	24
McCain	> 20 percentage points	20

Source: Adapted from David Nather, "Now, to Bridge A Deep Divide," CQ Weekly, December 15, 2008, p. 3319.

voters who graduated from high school, Obama did best (58 percent) among those with postgraduate degrees.[54] Homogeneous communities make it even more difficult for the president to change people's views. When Obama's supporters seek support for him, they are likely to be asking those who already agree with them.

The polarization of the 2008 campaign and the nature of the opposition to Obama laid the groundwork for the intense aversion to Obama and his policies that appeared shortly after he took office. His initial actions of seeking the release of additional TARP funds and promoting an historic economic stimulus bill confirmed for conservatives that he was indeed a left-wing radical who needed to be stopped at all costs and, along with the president's support of health care reform, fueled the emergence of the Tea Party movement.

Party and Ideological Divisions in the Public

The polarization evident in the 2008 election results did not end on Inauguration Day. Instead, it persisted in the underlying partisan and ideological divisions of the country. Indeed, there has been an increase in partisan-ideological polarization as Americans increasingly base their party loyalties on their ideological beliefs rather than on membership in social groups,[55] and they align their policy preferences more closely with their core political predispositions.[56]

When President Obama took office, he enjoyed a 68 percent approval level, the highest of any newly elected president since John F. Kennedy. For all of his hopes about bipartisanship, however, his early approval ratings were the most polarized of any president in the past four decades. By February 15, less than a month after taking office, only 30 percent of Republicans approved of his performance in office, while 89 percent of Democrats and 63 percent of Independents approved.[57] The gap between Democratic and Republican approval had already reached 59 percentage points—and Obama never again reached even 30 percent approval among Republicans. By the 100-day mark of his tenure, 92 percent of Democrats but only 28 percent of Republicans approved of his performance, a difference of 64 percentage points.[58]

The wide partisan divide in presidential approval ratings was not in itself new. From his first days in office, George W. Bush was a polarizing president, eventually the most polarizing in the history of public opinion polling. The first Gallup poll of his tenure found that he had the highest level of *disapproval* of any new president since polling began.[59] Similarly, Gary Jacobson reported that the public's initial reception of Bush reflected the widest partisan differences for any newly elected president in polling history. In the twenty-eight Gallup and CBS/*New York Times* polls taken before September 11, 2001, Bush's approval ratings averaged 88 percent among self-identified Republicans but only 31 percent among Democrats (Independents averaged 50 percent). This 57-point difference indicates an extraordinary degree of polarization.[60] Yet this gap between the assessments of Democrats and Republicans was just the beginning. In the May 21–23, 2004, Gallup poll, the difference between his approval among Republicans (89 percent) and Democrats (12 percent) was an astounding 77 percentage points! That gap of 70 points or higher became common starting with Bush's fourth year in office.[61]

These were extreme and unprecedented levels of polarization.[62] No president, dating back to Harry Truman, has had a partisan gap above 70 points in any Gallup poll in a reelection year. Moreover, Gallup had never before found such a high proportion of partisans with such strongly opposing views of a president. In the May 21–23, 2004, poll, 64 percent of Republicans said they strongly approved of the job Bush was doing as president, while 66 percent of Democrats strongly disapproved. As Gallup put it, "Bush is the only president who has had more than 6 in 10 of his party's identifiers strongly approving of him at the same time that more than 6 in 10 of the other party's identifiers strongly disapprove of him." The only other president to have more than 60 percent of a partisan group disapproving of him was Richard Nixon in the year of his resignation, when 61 percent of Democrats strongly disapproved of him. At that time, Nixon had overall job approval ratings below 30 percent.[63]

The fact that the public had been polarized under his predecessor was of little comfort to Obama. It merely showed the stability of the partisan divide and indicated the difficulty of reaching those identifying with the opposition party. Gallup reported that there was an average gap of 65 percentage points between Democrats' and Republicans' evaluations of the president in his first year, greatly exceeding the prior high of 52 percentage points for Bill Clinton.[64] Obama's second year was even worse, with a 68-percentage point gap between Democrats and Republicans. Once again, this polarization was the highest for any president during his second year, 12 percentage points higher than the prior high of Ronald Reagan's 56 percentage points in 1982.[65]

Moreover, ideological division reinforced partisan polarization. At the midpoint of the new president's first year in office, nearly half of Americans

TABLE 1.4.
Polarized Job Approval

Group	% Approval
All	56
White conservative Democrats	70
White moderate/liberal Democrats	88
White conservative Republicans	11
White moderate/liberal Republicans	32
White Independents	36
Blacks	94
Hispanics	74

Source: Gallup Daily tracking polls, July 1–August 17, 2009.

identified themselves as moderate or liberal white Democrats or conservative white Republicans, the poles of the political spectrum. Those in the middle, on the other hand, were a much smaller group. Only 6 percent of the public said they were conservative white Democrats, and only 11 percent moderate/liberal white Republicans.[66] Table 1.4 shows that in averaging its daily tracking polls over the July 1–August 17, 2009, period, Gallup found that the difference between white conservative Republicans and white moderate and liberal Democrats in evaluating the president's performance in office was 77 percentage points.

We can also see the confounding influence of race in support for the president. While 94 percent of blacks, almost all of whom are Democrats, approved of Obama's handling of his job, only 11 percent of white conservative Republicans did so—an 83-percentage point difference. There is evidence that predispositions to opposing the president combined with the salience of race contributed to the acceptance of smearing labels such as Obama was Muslim or a socialist.[67] There is also reason to believe that negative stereotypes about blacks significantly eroded white support for the president,[68] as did racial resentment.[69]

The Democratic political organization Democracy Corps concluded from its focus groups that those in the conservative GOP base believed that Obama "is ruthlessly advancing a secret agenda to bankrupt the United States and dramatically expand government control to an extent nothing short of socialism."[70] By June 2010, Democracy Corps found that 55 percent of the public found Obama to be "too liberal" and the same percentage thought "socialist" was a reasonably accurate way of describing him.[71] In July 2010, 41 percent of Republicans clung to the false belief that Obama was not born in this country.[72] A poll the next month found that 31 percent of Republicans thought he was a Muslim.[73] Another poll in the same month found that 52 percent of the Republican respondents said it was definitely (14 percent) or probably (38 percent) true that "Barack Obama sympathizes with the goals of Islamic fundamentalists who want to impose Islamic law around the world."[74] These views represented a profound sense of alienation.[75]

Contributing to this polarization was the insulation of the opposition. Sixty-three percent of Republicans and Republican leaners reported that they received most of their news from Fox News, which is known for its conservative reporting and commentators.[76] The president's initial actions were grist for commentators on the right, especially those on radio and cable television. They aggressively reinforced the fears of their audiences and encouraged active opposition to the White House.

The impact of elite discourse is important, as it clarifies where parties stand. Members of the public use the cues of elites to align their partisanship and ideology, usually bringing their issue attitudes in line with the stances of their party's elites. Thus, party and ideology are now more closely aligned than in previous decades.[77]

Public Perspectives on Issues

As the Obama administration and Congress wrestled with how to fix the country's economic problems while at the same time dealing with the longer-term impact of those efforts, tensions between the two were inevitable. Differences in party and ideology inevitably result in different policy priorities and tradeoffs between policies among the public. By June 2010, 63 percent of Democrats thought the government should do more to solve the country's problems, but only 13 percent of Republicans (and 32 percent of Independents) agreed.[78]

In mid-2009, Gallup reported that Republicans and Democrats viewed the economic issues facing the country from substantially different perspectives (table 1.5). Republicans were much more likely than Democrats to express worry about issues that represented *consequences* of attempting to fix economic problems: the federal government's expanding ownership and regulation of private business and industry, increasing federal and state taxes, and the increasing federal budget deficit. Democrats, on the other hand, were much more likely to be worried about the societal problems that the increased spending and regulation were designed to address, including the increasing numbers of Americans without health insurance, and, to a lesser degree, about the rising unemployment rate, the increasing cost of health care, and decreasing pay and wages for the average worker.[79]

Another poll, conducted at the end of July 2009, also showed the differences between the parties on their priorities in making tradeoffs between spending and reducing the budget deficit (see table 1.6). The biggest partisan difference—40 points—was over health care. Nearly three-quarters (72 percent) of Democrats saw spending more on health care as the priority, while 23

TABLE 1.5.
Partisan Concerns about Economic Issues

Issue	% Concerned		Democrats minus Republicans (percentage points)
	Democrats/ Leaners	Republicans/ Leaners	
Increasing numbers of Americans without health care insurance	90	65	25
The rising unemployment rate	91	82	9
The increasing cost of health care	89	82	7
Decreasing pay and wages for the average worker	81	74	7
Increasing problems Americans have with personal debt and credit cards	74	75	-1
The increasing price of gas	76	79	-3
Increasing problems state governments have funding their budgets	79	84	-5
The increasing federal budget deficit	75	90	-15
Increasing state income taxes	59	78	-19
Increasing federal income taxes	62	86	-24
The federal government's increasing regulation of business and industry	40	78	-38
The federal government's expanding ownership of private corporations	42	82	-40

Source: Gallup poll, June 23–24, 2009.
Question: "Please tell me whether you, personally, are worried about each of the following:"

percent placed a higher priority on deficit reduction. By contrast, 63 percent of Republicans put deficit reduction ahead of increased health care spending, while 32 percent favored such spending over trimming the deficit. Just over half (54 percent) of Independents placed a higher priority on health care spending, while 42 percent said deficit reduction was more important. Partisan views were similar, though less polarized, when it came to education. Most Democrats (69 percent) and Independents (56 percent) saw increased spending on education as more important than deficit reduction, while most Republicans (54 percent) disagreed. Democrats stood apart from both Republicans and Independents in saying that stimulus spending was a higher priority than deficit reduction. By a 68 percent to 23 percent margin, Democrats saw spending to help the economy recover as more important than reducing the deficit. By contrast, Independents were split about evenly (47 percent placed a higher priority on economic stimulus, 43 percent on deficit reduction), and a slim

TABLE 1.6.
Budget Tradeoffs by Party

Higher Priority	%			Percentage Points Democrats– Republicans
	Democrats	Republicans	Independents	
Spending more on health care	72	32	54	40
Reducing the budget deficit	23	63	42	-40
Spending more on education	69	43	56	26
Reducing the budget deficit	26	54	40	-28
Spending more on new energy technology	48	29	42	19
Reducing the budget deficit	43	67	53	-24
Spending more on economic recovery	68	43	47	25
Reducing the budget deficit	23	52	43	-29

Source: Pew Research Center for the People and the Press poll, July 22–26, 2009.

majority (52 percent) of Republicans saw deficit reduction as the bigger priority. No partisan group prioritized spending on new energy technology over deficit reduction.

In March 2010, the public said it was more important to develop U.S. energy supplies than to protect the environment by a 50 percent to 43 percent margin. Several weeks after the massive oil spill resulting from the explosion of a BP oil rig in the Gulf of Mexico produced the biggest oil spill in American history, priorities shifted in favor of environmental protection, by a 55 percent to 39 percent margin. Support for the environmental protection option increased by 15 percentage points among both Democrats and Independents. By contrast, Republicans' opinions did not change at all in response to the environmental disaster and continued to prioritize energy production over environmental protection by a 2-to-1 margin.[80]

The Opportunity for Health Care Reform

After the stimulus package passed in February, the president's highest priority legislation in 2009 was health care reform. In addition to the broad challenges to policy change discussed above, there were policy-specific aspects of public opinion that presented a complex and challenging context in which to win the public's support. Although it was in favor of the principle of reform, there was plenty of potential for resistance. Many people were concerned about losing existing benefits. Even more worried about the cost of expanding insurance coverage, especially in light of the historic deficits the government was running in response to the economic crisis.

Comparing 1993 and 2009

One way to understand Obama's strategic position regarding health care reform is to compare public opinion in 1993, when Bill Clinton launched his effort to overhaul the health care system, with opinion in mid-2009, as Congress was completing its health care bill. We can see in table 1.7 that Clinton had a somewhat more advantageous environment in which to work. In early 1993, the sense of a health care crisis was far more widespread than it was in 2009. Fully 55 percent of the public felt the health care system needed to be "completely rebuilt," compared with only 41 percent in 2009. (However, in 2009, an additional 30 percent of the public thought the health care system needed "fundamental changes.") Similarly, in 1993 a larger percentage of the public (83 percent to 75 percent) felt that it was important to provide health insurance for all Americans, although the view was widespread in both years.

In addition, the public was more likely to see the cost of health care as a problem in 1993—63 percent of Americans said paying for the cost of a major illness was a "major problem" for them, compared with 48 percent in 2009. About 40 percent of American said paying for routine medical care was a major

TABLE 1.7.
Views on Reforming Health Care, 1993 and 2009

	% Agree/Favor	
Issue	April 1993	June 2009
Health care system needs to be completely rebuilt?	55	41
Health care system needs fundamental changes?	26	30
Changing the health care system so that all Americans have health insurance that covers all medically necessary care?	83	75
Cost of a major illness a major problem?	63	48
Cost of routine health care a major problem?	40	34
Very important to change the health care system to limit the overall annual increase in health care costs?	69	61
Do we spend too much on health care?	36	38
Do we spend too little on health care?	49	40
More important to expand care than limit costs?	74	56
More important to limit costs than expand care?	20	36

Source: Pew Research Center for the People and the Press.

problem in 1993, while this figure declined to 34 percent in 2009. By a 69 percent to 61 percent margin, Americans in 1993 were also more likely to think it was very important to limit the increase in health care costs. There was no significant difference between the years on the issue of spending too much on health care, but in 1993, people were more likely to believe we spent too little. Similarly, in 1993 people were much more likely to believe it was more important to expand health care than limit costs (by a 74 percent to 56 percent margin) than in 2009, while the share who rated costs as the more important concern in 2009 was nearly double what it was in 1993.

Anxiety about Change

Beyond somewhat less demand for health care reform than in 1993, Obama faced a strategic problem in attempting to reform the health care system without igniting fears that people could lose what they like about their own health care. Although there was widespread agreement that substantial change in the health care system was necessary, most people were reasonably satisfied with the quality of their own medical care and were anxious about government involvement, including its impact on their own care. Majorities of respondents said they worried that if the government guaranteed health coverage, they would see declines in the quality of their own care and in their ability to choose doctors and get needed treatment.[81]

As the *Washington Post* reported in late June, "Most respondents are 'very concerned' that health-care reform would lead to higher costs, lower quality, fewer choices, a bigger deficit, diminished insurance coverage and more government bureaucracy."[82] Part of the reason so many were nervous about changes in the health care system was a fear they might lose what they currently had. Five out of six Americans had health insurance, more than eight in ten said they were satisfied with the quality of care they currently received, and about three in four were satisfied with their health insurance coverage.[83]

In July, Gallup found that whether the focus was access to health care or the quality of care, less than a majority of Americans were convinced that health care reform would be beneficial either to the country or to their own personal situations. Only 44 percent felt reform would improve medical care in the United States, and only 26 percent believed it would improve their personal medical care (34 percent felt it would worsen it). Although 47 percent predicted that health care reform would expand access to health care nationally, only 21 percent felt it would increase their personal access to health care. The public also expected health care reform to increase costs rather than lower them, both nationally and for themselves. Thirty-four percent of the public anticipated their personal costs would increase, nearly twice the 18 percent who believed their personal costs would be reduced.[84]

The numbers did not improve for the White House as the year progressed. In August, one poll found that only 19 percent of the public said that Obama's plan would improve the quality of their health care, and the same percentage thought it would lower their health care costs. Conversely, 33 percent believed the quality of their health care would deteriorate under the Democrats' proposal, and 41 percent predicted it would cause their health care costs to rise. Thus, fully half (50 percent) opposed the changes Congress and Obama were proposing.[85] Another poll found that 40 percent of the respondents felt Obama's plan would make the quality of their health care worse (only 24 percent had the opposite view), and the sample opposed the plan by a 47 to 43 percent margin.[86] In December, 50 percent of the public said they would have better quality health care with the status quo, as opposed to 37 percent who responded that reform would increase the quality of their care. Fifty-three percent expected reform to increase their personal health care costs.[87]

Seniors, a significant percentage of voters, were the least likely of all age groups in the United States to say that health care reform would benefit their personal health care. By a margin of three to one, 36 percent to 12 percent, adults sixty-five and older were more likely to believe health care reform would reduce rather than expand their access to health care. In addition, by 39 percent to 20 percent, they were more likely to say health care reform would worsen rather than improve their own medical care, and by 35 percent to 13 percent, they felt it would increase their health care costs.[88]

The public displayed conflicting impulses and confusion about health care reform. For example, in late July, 75 percent of respondents said they were concerned that the cost of their own health care would eventually go up if the government did not create a system of providing health care for all Americans, but 77 percent said they were concerned that the cost of health care would go up if the government did create such a system.[89]

On the one hand, there appeared to be a strong desire to get something done. Most people favored the principle of Congress passing major health care reform legislation in 2009.[90] Pew found that 43 percent of Americans said paying for health insurance posed a major problem for them and their family.[91] Large majorities said they supported fundamental changes or completely rebuilding the health care system.[92] Sixty-six percent of respondents were concerned that they might eventually lose their insurance if the government did not create a new health care system, and 80 percent said they were concerned that the percentage of Americans without health care would continue to rise if Congress did not act.[93]

At the same time, Americans were concerned that revamping the health care system would reduce the quality of their care, increase their out-of-pocket health costs and tax bills, and limit their options in choosing doctors, treatments, and tests. When in doubt, people tend to lean against change.

Cost

Yet another problem bedeviling Obama's effort to obtain the public's support for health care reform was the cost of the policy, estimated at $1 trillion over a decade. The president proposed sweeping policy changes in an environment characterized by high levels of concern about the expansion of government, fiscal responsibility, government spending, and the rapidly expanding federal deficit.

At the end of July 2009, most Americans believed the U.S. health care system had major problems, but fewer than 20 percent believed the system was in a state of crisis. The economy greatly outweighed health care as the most pressing problem facing the country and Americans' personal lives.[94] It is not surprising that when Pew asked those who opposed health care reform to explain their opinion, the two concerns offered most often were the cost and the impact on the budget and taxes and the potential for too much government involvement and bureaucracy.[95]

Democrats claimed that the plan would be budget-neutral, while Republicans argued the cost savings and tax increases being used to fund new programs would be better spent if put toward reducing the fast-growing federal budget deficit. The president had trouble making the case that his health plan would have the teeth necessary to eliminate the waste that he blamed for driving up costs. A key moment in the debate came on July 16, when Congressional Budget Office director Douglas Elmendorf told a congressional committee, "We do not see the sort of fundamental changes that would be necessary to reduce the trajectory of federal health spending by a significant amount." He added, "on the contrary, the legislation significantly expands the federal responsibility for health care costs."[96]

Interestingly, in 2008 Obama did not campaign on promising universal coverage, except for children. Then, and in 2009, he more often cited as potential beneficiaries not the mostly poor uninsured but the working and middle classes, people like his mother, who had insurance but fought her insurance carrier all the while she was dying of cancer. When he spoke of covering the uninsured, he argued that doing so would also help the insured because hospitals, doctors, and insurers would no longer have to pass on unpaid expenses in higher premiums and prices to paying patients. He emphasized that insured Americans would see lower costs, more choices, and better coverage.

Nevertheless, when Congress began writing legislation and its analysts priced the various proposals in the summer of 2009, the sticker shock drew taxpayers' attention to the main expense, which was covering the uninsured. Democrats' plans would expand Medicaid for the poor and subsidize both low-income workers buying insurance and small businesses seeking coverage for employees. In December, 55 percent of the public predicted that reform would cause the overall cost of the national health care system to increase sharply.[97]

In sum, rather than a public primed for reforming health care, Barack Obama faced a citizenry skeptical about change. Thus, he was not in a position in which he could easily exploit favorable support. So he took his case to the public to try to convince it that his proposals were good for them and for the country. In other words, he went public to try to *create* an opportunity for change.

Constraints on Opinion Change

The contexts of individual presidencies vary, but there are some features of the political landscape that every president faces. What is the fundamental nature of public opinion? Just how malleable is it? What obstacles does every president have to overcome to move the public to support his policies?[98]

Commentators often refer to Barack Obama's charisma, but there is no magic associated with certain leaders, and the "charisma" and personality of leaders are not the keys to successfully leading the public. Even George Washington, who was better positioned than any of his successors to dominate American politics because of the widespread view of his possessing exceptional personal qualities, did not find the public particularly deferential.

The first step in the president's efforts to lead the public is focusing its attention. Despite the enormous total volume of presidential public statements, they are dispersed over a broad range of policies, and wide audiences hear only a small portion of the president's remarks. The president rarely focuses a televised address on an issue before Congress and actually makes few statements on even significant legislation. In addition, the president faces strong competition for the public's attention from previous commitments of government, congressional initiatives, opposing elites, and the mass media. Even more importantly, the president often provides competition for himself as he addresses other issues, some on his own agenda and others that are forced upon him.

Presidents make a substantial effort to frame issues in ways that will favor their preferred policy options and to place their own performance in a favorable light. However, there are many limitations on successful framing, including the presence of competing frames. Committed, well-organized, and well-funded opponents inhabit the president's world. Intense disagreement among elites generates conflicting messages. In addition, for the president to frame issues for the public, people must perceive accurately the frame offered by the White House. There is reason to believe, however, that different people perceive the same message differently. With all his personal, ideological, and partisan baggage, no president can assume that all citizens hear the same thing when he speaks. Partisanship is especially likely to bias processing perceptions, interpretations, and responses to the political world.[99] Again, there is little reason to believe that Barack Obama would be any more successful than his predecessors.

A related matter of perception is the credibility of the source. Experimental evidence supports the view that perceived source credibility is a prerequisite for successful framing.[100] The president is likely to be more credible to some people (those predisposed to support him) than to others. Many people are unlikely to find him a credible source on most issues, especially those on which opinion is divided and on which he is the leader of one side of the debate. We have seen that polarization is high, pointing toward severe credibility problems for the chief executive.

If the president is going to lead the public successfully, it must *receive* and *understand* his messages. Yet the White House finds it increasingly difficult to obtain an audience for its views—or even airtime on television to express them. Those who are unaware of a message are unlikely to know the president's positions. Moreover, many people who do pay attention miss the president's points. Because the president rarely speaks directly to the American people as a whole, the White House is dependent on the press to transmit its messages. The media are unlikely to adopt consistently either the White House's priorities or its framing of issues. Although the Obama White House had the potential to supplement its press operation with other means of communicating with the public, the administration was largely preaching to the converted, who composed its mailing list.

Perhaps most significantly, the president must overcome the predispositions of his audience if he is to change people's minds about his policies or his performance. Yet a series of related psychological mechanisms often bias perceptions of both facts and evaluations of them. Most people seek out information confirming their preexisting opinions and ignore or reject arguments contrary to their predispositions. When exposed to competing arguments, they typically uncritically accept the confirming ones and dismiss or argue against the opposing ones.[101]

Those who pay close attention to politics and policy are likely to have well-developed views and thus be less susceptible to persuasion. Better-informed citizens possess the information and sophistication necessary to identify the implications of messages. They are best able to construct ostensibly reasonable counterarguments and rebuttals to evidence that they are emotionally inclined to resist and thus reject communications inconsistent with their values. In the typical situation of competing frames offered by elites, reinforcement and polarization of views are more likely than conversion among attentive citizens.[102]

Thus, partisan biases may significantly skew the public's perceptions, and motivated reasoning, skepticism, and information gathering present an increasing obstacle to the president's efforts to persuade the public. Even the most basic facts are often in contention. Larry Bartels found that in 1988 a majority of respondents who described themselves as strong Democrats said that inflation had "gotten worse" over the eight years of the Reagan administration, although it had actually fallen by about 70 percent.[103] Similarly, he and Christopher Achen found that a majority of Republicans in 1996 thought the federal budget deficit had increased under Bill Clinton, whereas it had in fact shrunk by over 90 percent.[104]

Studies have also found that partisan leanings have significantly influenced perceptions—and contributed to misperceptions—of the war with Iraq (including the possession of weapons of mass destruction, Iraqi relationships with al Qaeda, and world opinion about the war).[105] As Gary Jacobson put it, "Consistent with the theories of cognitive dissonance and mass opinion formation, partisan differences in prior beliefs were thus reinforced by partisan differences in reactions to events and revelations in Iraq."[106] Other studies have reached similar findings regarding Watergate,[107] the Lewinsky scandal,[108] and presidential approval more generally.[109]

Such misperceptions are often most prevalent among those who are generally well informed about politics. Political knowledge neither corrects nor mitigates partisan bias in perception of objective conditions. Instead, it enhances it.

It may seem that those with less interest and knowledge present the most potential for presidential persuasion. Such people cannot resist arguments if they do not possess information about the implications of those arguments for their values, interests, and other predispositions. However, these people are also less likely to be aware of the president's messages, limiting the president's influence. To the extent that they do receive the messages, they will also hear from the opposition how the president's views are inconsistent with their predispositions. In addition, even if their predispositions make them sympathetic to the president's arguments, they may lack the understanding to make the connection between the president's arguments and their own underlying values. Moreover, the more abstract the link between message and value, the fewer people who will make the connection.[110]

In addition, people are frequently *misinformed* (as opposed to uninformed) about policy, and the less they know, the more confidence they have in their beliefs. Thus, they resist correct factual information. Even when others present them with factual information, they resist changing their opinions.[111] The increasing array of media choices means that individuals are less likely to encounter information that would correct misperceptions. Moreover, the tendency to process information with a bias toward their preexisting views means that those who are most susceptible to misinformation may reject the corrections that they receive.[112]

Other psychological factors also increase the likelihood that corrections will fail to undo the effects of misperceptions. Negations (i.e., "I am not a crook") often reinforce the perception they are intended to counter.[113] In addition, even if people initially accept corrections debunking a false statement, they may eventually fall victim to an "illusion of truth" effect in which people misremember false statements as true over time.[114] Finally, misleading statements about politics continue to influence subjects' beliefs even after they have been discredited.[115]

John Zaller argues that those in the public most susceptible to presidential influence are those attentive to public affairs (and thus who receive messages) but who lack strong views (and thus who are less likely to resist messages).[116] At best, such persons are a small portion of the population. In addition, these persons receive competing messages. There is no basis for inferring that they will be most likely to find the president's messages persuasive. Such a conclusion is especially suspect when we recognize that most attentive people have explicit or latent partisan preferences. The president is leader of one of the parties, and those affiliated with the opposition party must overcome an inherent skepticism about him before he can convert them to support his position.

The media play a large role in creating misperceptions. The Internet, cable television, and talk radio convey and amplify the strident differences among partisan elites. They facilitate selective exposure to information through "narrowcasting" to particular audiences. They create a distrust of information from other sources. And the highly charged nature of discourse on these venues magnifies the impression of partisan conflict, heightening viewers' and listeners' emotional engagement with politics and lessening the accuracy of their political perceptions.[117]

Loss Aversion

Research in psychology has found that people have a broad predisposition to avoid loss[118] and place more emphasis on avoiding potential losses than on obtaining potential gains. In their decision making, they place more weight on information that has negative, as opposed to positive, implications for their interests. Similarly, when individuals form impressions of situations or other people, they weigh negative information more heavily than positive. Impressions formed on the basis of negative information, moreover, tend to be more lasting and more resistant to change.[119]

Risk and loss aversion and distrust of government make people wary of policy initiatives, especially when they are complex and their consequences are uncertain. Since uncertainty accompanies virtually every proposal for a major shift in public policy, it is not surprising that people are naturally inclined against change.[120] Further encouraging this predisposition is the media's focus on political conflict and strategy, which elevates the prominence of political wheeling-dealing in individuals' evaluations of political leaders and policy proposals. The resulting increase in public cynicism highlights the risk of altering the status quo.

The predisposition for loss aversion is an obstacle for presidential leadership of the public. Most presidents want to leave some substantial change at the core of their legacies. Yet those proposing new directions in policy—and Barack

Obama is all about change—encounter a more formidable task than advocates of the status quo. Those opposing change have a more modest task of emphasizing the negative to increase the public's uncertainty and anxiety to avoid risk.[121] Michael Cobb and James Kuklinski found in an experimental study of opinion change on NAFTA and health care that arguments against both worked especially well. They found people to be both risk- and loss averse, and arguments against change, which accentuate the unpleasant consequences of a proposed policy, easily resonated with the average person. In addition, they suggest that fear and anger, which negative arguments presumably evoke, are among the strongest emotions and serve as readily available shortcuts for decision making when people evaluate an impending policy initiative.[122]

Conclusion

Despite the historic and decisive nature of his election, Barack Obama did not enjoy an especially favorable environment for making major changes in public policy. The election results did not signal a mandate for change, an increase in support for government activism, or an end to extreme partisan polarization. In addition, the long-term constraints on opinion change remained firmly in place.

It is difficult to interpret public opinion and to predict what forces may arise to influence it in the months ahead. It is even more difficult to predict public response to specific proposals, since candidates generally avoid delving into details on the campaign trail. Moreover, it is possible that presidential success at altering public policy will create a backlash against further change.

Nevertheless, it is critical that presidents carefully evaluate their opportunity structure regarding obtaining public support for their policies. If they do not ask the right questions, they certainly will not arrive at the right answers. To answer the questions requires, first, *not* assuming that opinion is malleable. Rejecting the *assumption* of opinion leadership leads one naturally to examine the nature of existing opinion. It also leads one to ask whether one can rely on going public to accomplish policy change.

Analyzing the opportunity structure of the Obama presidency reveals that the nature of a president's opportunity structure is dynamic. The new administration quite reasonably felt it had to devote its initial attention to the crisis in the economy before moving to the issues, such as health care reform, energy, and environmental protection, on which Obama had campaigned for the previous two years. Doing so cost vast sums of money, however, and required unparalleled government intervention in the economy. The scope of the response to the recession discouraged rather than encouraged demand for government services.

Shortly before the 2010 midterm elections, Gallup found that 49 percent of the public thought there was too much government regulation of business and industry, as opposed to 21 percent who felt there was the right amount and 27 percent who thought there was too little. In 2008, only 38 percent of the public felt there was too much regulation. In 2010, 58 percent felt the federal government was doing too much to solve nation's problems, and 59 percent thought it had too much power, up from 52 percent near the time of Obama's election in 2008.[123]

Despite voting for a presidential candidate espousing change, the public had not changed its basic skepticism of government or its resistance to paying for it. For some, these policies triggered serious anxiety about the future and were a catalyst for mobilization into intense opposition that manifested itself in both mass protests and hostile confrontations at meetings in congressional constituencies. In sum, by taking dramatic and sweeping action to stem the economy's slide, the president narrowed the prospects for change in other areas of public policy. Political analyst Charlie Cook termed the effort to pass a large agenda rather than focusing on the economy "a colossal miscalculation."[124]

> What Obama and Democrats failed to realize was that the escalation of spending under Bush, the bailouts and the implementation of TARP, created a political environment that made significant climate change and health care reform ring up "no sale" in the minds of voters. It was too much for them to handle when all they [the public] wanted was a focus on job creation and the economy.[125]

The public did not see health care reform as an element of economic recovery. It is not surprising that after a year of Obama's tenure, Americans said they preferred smaller government and fewer services to larger government with more services by 58 percent to 38 percent.[126]

Near the midpoint of his term, Obama himself acknowledged that the succession of so many costly initiatives wore on the public.

> That accumulation of numbers on the TV screen night in and night out in those first six months I think deeply and legitimately troubled people. They started feeling like: Gosh, here we are tightening our belts, we're cutting out restaurants, we're cutting out our gym membership, in some cases we're not buying new clothes for the kids. And here we've got these folks in Washington who just seem to be printing money and spending it like nobody's business. And it reinforced the narrative that the Republicans wanted to promote anyway, which was "Obama is not a different kind of Democrat—he's the same old tax-and-spend liberal Democrat."[127]

The analysis of Barack Obama's opportunities for obtaining public support leads us to predict that he would have difficulty obtaining the public's backing for his initiatives—even allowing for his impressive public relations skills. In other words, a strategy of governing by going public was unlikely to succeed. In chapter 2, I focus on his efforts to sell his policies to the public, and in chapter 3, I test the prediction by examining public support for his policies.

CHAPTER 2

Creating Opportunities?

GOING PUBLIC

BARACK OBAMA ENTERED THE PRESIDENCY with an impressive record of political success, at the center of which were his rhetorical skills. In college, he concluded that words had the power to transform: "with the right words everything could change—South Africa, the lives of ghetto kids just a few miles away, my own tenuous place in the world."[1] It is no surprise, then, that Obama followed the pattern of presidents seeking public support for themselves and their policies that they can leverage to obtain backing for their proposals in Congress.

Moreover, it was commonplace at the beginning of his term for commentators to suggest that the president could exploit the capacity for social networking to reach people directly in a way that television and radio could not and harness this potential to overcome obstacles to legislative success. In theory, the new president could mobilize his legions of supporters and use their support to transform public policy.

In this chapter, I examine the Obama White House's efforts to lead the public. I focus on its press relations and other aspects of going public and pay particular attention to the classic challenges that every administration faces in focusing the public's attention, reaching the public with its messages, framing issues to its advantage, and mobilizing supporters.

Aggressive Advocacy

The White House was aggressive in its public advocacy. The president-elect requested a communications strategy right after the election,[2] and the White House communications staff swelled from forty-seven members under Bill Clinton and fifty-two under George W. Bush to sixty-nine under Barack Obama.[3] Even during the transition, the president began a full-scale marketing blitz to pass his massive stimulus package, including delivering a major speech at George Mason University. The president delivered 989 speeches, comments, and remarks in his first two years in office.[4] He also conducted twenty-three town hall meetings (including one in Strasbourg, France, and another in Shanghai, China) in his first year.[5] He was the first sitting president to appear on the Jay Leno and David Letterman shows, and he talked to ESPN and *People* magazine.

When he was sworn in, Obama told friends he was eager to tackle the rigors of the Oval Office without the drudgery of shuttling to a different part of the country every other day during his two-year campaign for the presidency. In addition, the president was reluctant to be too far away from Washington, aides said, because he was juggling economic proposals, meeting with military commanders, trying to fill his cabinet, and meeting with a series of agencies for an early look at his administration. After three weeks in office, however, the president found the public's support for his economic recovery package was eroding as Republicans intensified their criticism of the plan. So his advisors told him he had no choice but to use *Air Force One* and take his case to the public.[6]

The president pledged to leave Washington every week. On February 9, 2009, he visited Indiana. The next day he was in Florida, and then on to Virginia and Illinois in the next two days. He has never let up his travel schedule.[7]

Often the travel provided helpful backdrops for making his case. When Obama announced a plan to slow mortgage foreclosures by reducing troubled homeowners' monthly payments, he traveled to Mesa, Arizona, a community hit hard by the subprime crisis, where median home prices had fallen 35 percent over the past year. In signing the economic stimulus package, he dispensed with customary settings like the Oval Office or Rose Garden and held the ceremony in Denver so he could be out West in an area that had been hit hard economically, away from the politics of Washington.

The same principles applied to foreign policy. When it came time for the president to offer a time line for withdrawing troops from Iraq, he journeyed to Camp Lejeune, North Carolina, to deliver the news before thousands of U.S. Marines. When he ordered 30,000 additional troops to Afghanistan, he did so in a prime-time speech to the cadets at West Point.

The primary intermediary between the president and the public is the press, and the White House has been attentive to servicing the press. Obama appointed Robert Gibbs, a close associate who had his ear, as press secretary. Being in the inner circle of the White House gave Gibbs high credibility as a White House spokesman. (There were some complaints from reporters, however, that Gibbs spent so much time with the president that he did not have enough time to talk to reporters.)[8]

The president hosted lunches and dinners for TV anchors and columnists; held off-the-record sessions with liberal columnists and historians; and ate dinner with conservative writers at columnist George Will's house. In addition, White House Chief of Staff Rahm Emanuel was unusually active in working the media, cajoling, lobbing, berating, and trading information with reporters. The White House pays particular attention to the *New York Times*, which Gibbs believes has the ability to drive the news.[9]

Equally important, Obama made a concerted effort to tap into alternatives to the mainstream national media, including Spanish-language magazines, newspapers, and television and radio stations and those oriented to African Americans.[10] As we will see, the White House is also oriented toward blogs,

Internet videos, Facebook, and Twitter. The press pool that takes turns covering the president up close now includes Web-only publications like Talking Points Memo, the Huffington Post, and the Daily Caller. The president also submits to interviews with regional newspapers.

At the same time, the president has tried to deal with the press in a different way from that of his predecessors. Obama held forty-six news conferences in his first two years, of which eleven were formal, solo White House question-and-answer sessions. Four were in prime time. He went for seven months before holding a full-scale press conference on February 9, 2010.[11] When he did hold his formal press conferences, the White House decided the day before each one who the president would call on, and sometimes notified the reporters in advance. This procedure miffed some reporters, who felt they were being reduced to the role of mere extras. Past presidents have generally worked their way around the room, starting with the wire services, networks, and major newspapers.[12]

In his first daytime news conference, held on June 23, 2009, the president declared, "I know Nico Pitney is here from the Huffington Post." Obama knew this because White House aides had called Pitney the day before to invite him, and they had escorted him into the room. The aides told him the president was likely to call on him, with the understanding that he would ask a question about Iran. Pitney said that although the White House was not aware of the question's wording, it asked him to come up with a question about Iran proposed by an Iranian. Later, Obama passed over representatives from major U.S. news outlets to call on Macarena Vidal of the Spanish-language EFE news agency. The White House called Vidal in advance to see whether she was coming and arranged a seat for her. She asked about Chile and Colombia.[13]

In addition, the president has chosen not to answer reporters' questions at most day-to-day events, such as those with foreign leaders, as other presidents have done. During his first two years in office, Obama took questions in such venues 75 times, compared with the 243 times George W. Bush and 390 times for Bill Clinton did in the comparable periods. Instead of open-ended sessions with multiple reporters, he prefers one-on-one interviews, particularly on television.[14]

The president sits for far more interviews than his two most recent predecessors did, reflecting the fact that he feels the interview format is a more effective means for getting his message through. In his first two years, he gave 269 interviews, compared with 83 by Bush and 136 by Clinton in comparable periods. One hundred and forty of the sessions were TV interviews, and forty-four were for radio. Another sixty-nine were for print organizations, fourteen were for mixed media, and two were for solely online organizations.[15] Among the attractions of television interviews for Obama are that they tend to be played in full and serve as a useful vehicle for reaching a large number of people.

The White House has displayed some skill in using the press to serve its purposes. After the protracted decision-making process that climaxed with the president's December 1, 2009, announcement of sending an additional 30,000 U.S. troops to Afghanistan, the White House briefed the *New York Times*, the *Washington Post*, and the *Los Angeles Times* on the policy discussions. In early December, each newspaper carried behind-the-scenes stories on the process, all reflecting Obama as a deliberative and tough-minded manager.[16]

When the president faced strong Democratic opposition to the extension of the Bush-era tax cuts during the 2010 lame-duck session of Congress, the White House launched a public relations blitz. Presidential press secretary Robert Gibbs instructed his staff to send out an e-mail every time a prominent politician backed the deal—even those of governors, mayors, and state legislators who had no power to directly influence the outcome. Obama even escorted former President Bill Clinton into the White House briefing room on December 10, where the former president praised the deal as the best compromise possible during a memorable thirty-minute exchange with reporters.[17]

The White House has also shown some deftness at catering to a nonstop, Internet- and cable-television-driven news cycle. For example, the White House went to great lengths to project an image of competence in U.S. relief efforts in Haiti, in implicit contrast to the way the Bush administration mishandled Hurricane Katrina and its aftermath. The administration and the military set up a busy communications operation with twenty-five people at the American Embassy and in a cinder-block warehouse at the airport in Port-au-Prince, Haiti's capital. The White House released a torrent of news releases, briefings, fact sheets, and statements, including "ticktock" (a newspaper term of art for a minute-by-minute reconstruction of how momentous events unfolded), a link to a Flickr photo of a meeting on Haiti in the Situation Room, presided over by the president, a video of American search teams rescuing a Haitian woman from a collapsed building, and a list of foreign leaders he had telephoned.[18]

The administration has been less successful when wielding the stick. It soon grew weary of Fox News's unrelenting and often vitriolic criticism and limited the appearances of some top officials on some Fox News shows. More visibly, it excluded *Fox News Sunday with Chris Wallace*—which it had previously treated as distinct from the network—from a round of presidential interviews with Sunday morning news programs in mid-September 2009. In late October, the White House tried to exclude Fox from a round of interviews with the executive-pay czar Kenneth R. Feinberg. When Fox's television news competitors refused to go along, the White House relented.[19] Fox's access soon returned to normal.[20]

Focusing Attention

The first step in the president's efforts to lead the public is focusing its attention. The president is unlikely to influence people who are not attentive to the issues on which he wishes to lead. If the president's messages are to meet his coalition-building needs, the public must sort through the profusion of communications in its environment, overcome its limited interest in government and politics, and concentrate on the president's priority concerns. Even within the domain of politics, political communications bombard Americans every day (many of which originate in the White House). The sheer volume of these communications far exceeds the attentive capacity of any individual.

In recent decades, presidents have had the goal of a disciplined communications strategy, at the core of which is a consistent message of the day. Shortened news cycles have made such strategies obsolete, however. Obama wanted to focus on winning the week rather than the day,[21] but achieving even this goal was to prove a major challenge.

Obama's team earned a reputation for skill and discipline in dominating the communications wars with his opponents on the road to winning the White House. Governing is considerably more difficult, however. Campaigns are tightly focused on one goal: winning elections. Governing requires attention to multiple goals, many of which are thrust upon the White House. Thus, the president must speak on many issues and to many audiences simultaneously. As White House senior advisor David Axelrod put it, the challenge of managing and controlling messages in a campaign and in the White House is "the difference between tick-tack-toe and three-dimensional tick-tack-toe. It's vastly more complicated."[22]

Presidents must cope with an elaborate agenda established by their predecessors.[23] The president's choices of priorities usually fall within parameters set by prior commitments of the government that obligate it to spend money, defend allies, maintain services, or protect rights.[24] As Kennedy aide Theodore Sorensen observed, "Presidents rarely, if ever make decisions . . . in the sense of writing their conclusions largely on a clean slate."[25]

Moreover, every administration must respond to unanticipated or simply overlooked problems, including international crises. These issues affect simultaneously the attention of the public and the priorities of Congress and thus the White House's success in focusing attention on its priority issues.[26] Administration officials also cannot ignore events, as campaigns often do. "You can pick and choose what you want to discuss and what you don't want to discuss," said Axelrod. "When you're president of the United States, you have a responsibility to deal with the problems as they come." Communications director Daniel Pfeiffer added: "In the White House, you have the myriad of challenges on any given day and are generally being forced to communicate a number of complex subjects at the same time."[27] Thus, according to Axelrod, the sheer volume of crises overwhelmed the message.[28]

In September 2009, the president was engaged in a major public relations effort to turn around public opinion on health care reform. The effort to sustain a focus on health care came to a screeching halt after September 21, however. In the period of September 22–25, 2009, Obama addressed the UN General Assembly, chaired a meeting of the UN Security Council, and spoke at a UN Climate Change Summit and former President Clinton's Global Initiative conference. He also attended multiple meetings of the G-20 countries, a Friends of Pakistan meeting, and a meeting of countries contributing peace-keeping troops, and held bilateral meetings with British Prime Minister Gordon Brown, Japanese Prime Minister Hatoyama, President Medvedev of Russia, Israeli Prime Minister Netanyahu, Palestinian Authority President Abbas, and Chinese President Hu. In addition, the president hosted a reception for heads of state and government and a lunch for Sub-Saharan African heads of state and held a news conference focused on foreign affairs. It is not surprising, then, that Pew found that international issues and events dominated news coverage in the week of September 21–27, with health care coverage constituting only 9 percent of the news hole.[29]

At the beginning of May 2010, the president's top advisors thought they had a public relations plan for the week: a focus on jobs and the White House's efforts to boost the economic recovery.[30] That agenda lost focus, however, when three unanticipated events with which Obama had to deal dominated the news. First, the BP oil spill and possible environmental crisis in the Gulf of Mexico required a presidential visit to the area and regular commentary from the White House. Then, a terrorist's bomb found in New York's Times Square provided yet another distraction. There was no way the president could not comment on such an event, and there was no way it would not dominate the news. Finally, Arizona passed a controversial immigration law, focusing attention on yet another issue.

In addition to prior commitments and unanticipated events, there are competitors for the public's attention. Successful campaigns maintain control of their message most of the time. Once in office, the president communicates with the public in a congested communications environment clogged with competing messages from a wide variety of sources, through a wide range of media, and on a staggering array of subjects.[31] A year into the president's term, communications direction Dan Pfeiffer declared, "It was clear that too often we didn't have the ball—Congress had the ball in terms of driving the message."[32]

To be effective in leading the public, the president must focus the public's attention on his policies for a sustained period of time. This requires more than a single speech, no matter how eloquent or dramatic it may be. The Reagan White House was successful in maintaining a focus on its top-priority economic policies in 1981. It molded its communication strategy around its legislative priorities and focused the administration's agenda and statements on economic policy to ensure that discussing a wide range of topics did not diffuse the president's message.[33] Sustaining such a focus is difficult to do, however. After 1981, President Reagan had to deal with a wide range of noneconomic policies. Other administrations have encountered similar problems.

Focusing attention is more difficult as an administration proceeds. The White House can put off dealing with the full spectrum of national issues for several months at the beginning of a new president's term, but it cannot do so for four years; eventually it must make decisions. By the second year, the agenda is full and more policies are in the pipeline as the administration attempts to satisfy its constituencies and responds to problems it has overlooked or that arose after the president's inauguration.

Focusing attention on priorities is considerably easier for a president with a short legislative agenda, such as Ronald Reagan, than it is for one with a more ambitious agenda, such as Barack Obama's. Obama began proposing his large agenda immediately after taking office. Moreover, Democrats had a laundry list of initiatives that George W. Bush had blocked, ranging from gender pay equity and children's health insurance to tougher tobacco regulations and a new public service initiative. In addition, there were recession-related efforts to provide mortgage relief and curb predatory banking practices to complement the president's economic stimulus measure.

The president and his fellow partisans believed in activist government and were predisposed toward doing "good" and against husbanding leadership resources. But no good deed goes unpunished. The more the White House tried to do, the more difficult it was to focus the country's attention on priority issues. Once the administration had put in place policies to deal with the worst of the crises Obama inherited, it moved on to health care, climate change, Afghanistan, and other major initiatives. The result was a perception in the public about a loss of focus on unemployment, prompting a shift back to the economy at the beginning of the president's second year in office.

Former White House communications director Anita Dunn said the administration had always seen health care reform as a central part of its economic message. "Our lack of success at doing that . . . is one of the reasons that people feel there wasn't the focus" on the economy, she said. Another White House official asserted that on the economy, "We've got a better story to tell than we've told."[34]

Distractions

There were many challenges to the Obama White House focusing on its priorities. One challenge was not being distracted by peripheral issues. When the Republicans began characterizing the president's economic stimulus bill as wasteful "pork" spending, the president launched a media blitz to counteract this image. Wary of selecting one favored network and alienating the others, the White House arranged for interviews with NBC's Brian Williams, CBS's Katie Couric, ABC's Charles Gibson, CNN's Anderson Cooper, Fox's Chris Wallace, and on ABC's *Nightline* on February 3.

There was a problem with this strategy, however, because the interviews took place only hours after former senator Tom Daschle withdrew as Obama's nominee to become secretary of Health and Human Resources over his belated payment of back taxes. This embarrassing situation became the dominant story in the interviews, with the president telling one anchor after another that he had "screwed up." Although by admitting what he called "self-inflicted wounds," the president preempted days of stories about whether the administration was playing down the magnitude of the mess, the issue distracted from the White House's principal purpose in granting the interviews.

In May, the president's commencement speech at the University of Notre Dame, in Indiana, and his choice of a candidate to replace Justice David H. Souter raised the issue of abortion to higher levels of visibility. This prominence counteracted Obama's effort to "tamp down some of the anger" over abortion, as he said in a news conference in April, and to distract from his other domestic priorities, like health care.[35]

On July 16, Professor Henry Louis Gates Jr. returned to his Cambridge, Massachusetts home to find the door stuck. A neighbor reported that someone might be trying to break into the house, and the police responded. Although the arresting police officer, Sgt. James Crowley, became aware that Professor Gates was in his own home, the police said Gates was belligerent and arrested him for disorderly conduct. (The charge was later dropped.)

A reporter asked Obama for his reaction to the incident as the last question in his July 22 prime-time press conference, a session that was otherwise largely devoted to health care reform. The president replied that the police had "acted stupidly" in hauling Professor Gates from his home in handcuffs. Obama's choice of words generated angry responses from the Cambridge police. Worse, media attention spiked in response to the president's comments. Thirty percent of the public reported that they followed the story very closely, and 17 percent said it was the story they followed most closely. The media devoted 12 percent of the news hole to the incident, tying it for the second-most covered story of the week. More significantly, the story filled only 4 percent of the news hole on Wednesday, before the president's press conference that evening, but the figure rose to 19 percent on Thursday and 31 percent on Friday.[36] The president had become a distraction from his high-priority policy initiative and his attempt to focus attention on it with a televised prime-time press conference.

In an attempt to move beyond the controversy that had dominated the previous two days of press coverage, the president made a surprise visit to the White House Briefing Room on July 24. He admitted that he "could have calibrated" his words more carefully in his press conference response, and told the press of his phone call that afternoon to Officer Crowley, whom he complimented as an outstanding police officer. The controversy, Obama acknowledged, overshadowed his attempt to explain the effort to overhaul the nation's health care system. As he put it, "over the last two days as we've discussed this issue . . . nobody has been paying much attention to health care."[37]

The Gates issue still had legs, however. The president invited the professor and Crowley for a beer at the White House on July 30, producing yet another round of stories. The controversy composed 8 percent of the news hole the week of July 27.[38]

Yet another distraction for the president were protests organized by a loose-knit coalition of conservative voters and advocacy groups at meetings held by congressional Democrats and administration officials to discuss health care. The conservative groups, including FreedomWorks, Americans for Prosperity, Right Principles, and Americans for Limited Government, harnessed social networking Web sites to organize and encourage their supporters to flood events and heckle and generally disrupt discussion.[39]

The eruption of anger at town hall meetings on health care became a cause célèbre on television. The louder the voices and the fiercer the confrontation, the more coverage the controversy received, obscuring the substantive arguments in favor of what producers love most: conflict. As Fox News broke away from the president's town meeting in New Hampshire, for example, anchor Trace Gallagher promised his audience, "Any contentious questions, anybody yelling, we'll bring it to you."[40] When those who became known as the Tea Partyers marched on Freedom Plaza in downtown Washington three days after the president's address on health care reform to a joint session of Congress on September 9, 2009, they displaced the image of Obama addressing Congress with one of marchers, placards, and populist rage.

Interestingly, anger about the legislative proposals under consideration was not especially widespread. Only 18 percent of the public reported they would be "angry" if health care legislation proposed by the president and Congress was to pass; only half as many (9 percent) said they would be angry if it did not pass. Conservative Republicans were paying more attention than those with other ideological or partisan leanings, and they had the most intense reactions. Thirty-eight percent said they would be "angry" if Congress enacted the Democrats' reform proposals, while just 13 percent of Democrats said they would be angry if the legislation did not become law. While 19 percent of Independents said they would be angry if the health care bills passed, just 8 percent said they would be angry if the bills did not pass.[41]

The White House recognized its problems with distractions. In February 2010, aides said the administration was returning to the message discipline that marked the 2008 campaign. It had to filter out unhelpful topics in favor of those that advanced the president's goals. For example, the plan was for a tighter focus on Obama's commitment to the economy and jobs for average Americans.[42] The administration created a "White House to Main Street" tour, giving Obama a forum to see and feel America's pain, and offer his plan for relief. Yet because the president refused to give up on health care, a policy not popular with voters, it kept dominating the news and undermining his broader public relations strategy.[43]

On August 13, 2010, the president entered the fray over the issue of a mosque being built in the vicinity of Ground Zero in New York City, which should have been a local issue. In remarks at a White House Iftar dinner (marking the beginning of the Moslem holy month of Ramadan Kareem), Obama made a strong statement about religious freedom. The next day he appeared to backtrack on the issue, saying he was not advocating a location for the mosque. The day after that, he reaffirmed his original point. These statements were grist for the talk show and cable television mill. Republicans seized upon the issue of the unpopular mosque, increasing the prominence of the president's words. Many Democrats openly wondered why the White House was wasting news cycles on unimportant skirmishes when it should have been focusing on the economy and jobs in the run-up to midterm elections.

Minimizing Attention and Distractions

The White House did know how to minimize the president's media exposure when the topic was one he would rather avoid or that would distract from his media strategy. When Obama lifted travel, gift, and telecommunication restrictions on Cuba on April 13, 2009, the White House deftly limited the visibility of the announcement by leaving the president in the Oval Office and having a mid-level official from the National Security Council make the announcement in the briefing room—in Spanish.

In his first week in office, the president was promoting his economic stimulus package. The White House wanted to discourage coverage of a divisive issue, which ran counter to the week's message of bipartisanship. Thus, on Friday afternoon, Obama quietly signed an order repealing restrictions on federal money for international organizations that encourage or provide abortions overseas. He acted a day after the anniversary of the *Roe v. Wade* decision establishing a constitutional right to abortion, rather than on the day, which would have attracted considerable attention. He held the signing away from reporters and cameras, issued his comments only in writing, and released the order after 7 p.m. Friday.[44] His strategy worked, as the order received little attention.

Staying on Message

Another aspect of focus is consistency in message. "Campaign speech is all part of one narrative, but now you are making a series of arguments," said Obama speechwriter Ben Rhodes. "An argument is a lot clearer to a listener if there is a structure that they can follow. Structure is what allows you to build a case."[45]

When the president nominated Sonia Sotomayor to a position on the Supreme Court, the White House sent word to its allies that the last thing the administration needed was a war with conservatives such as Rush Limbaugh and Newt Gingrich over whether the judge was a racist. Stay on message, the president's aides counseled, and they would offer a clear case about her credentials and legal experience.[46]

The administration found it difficult to project a consistent message on health care reform. Dan Pfeiffer, the White House communications director, argued, "you can draw a straight line substantively and rhetorically" through all of Obama's major speeches on health care. Nevertheless, he added, because of the complexity of the issue, "there have been a number of fronts" in the message war that have required the administration's engagement.[47]

The White House sought to sell health care reform as a way to make coverage affordable and accessible to middle-class families. Yet at various times it also presented reform as a cost-containment measure, a restraint on greedy insurance companies, a moral imperative to cover the uninsured, a cornerstone of economic recovery, and, to Democratic lawmakers, an enterprise at which the party could not afford to fail. The president and his aides sent mixed signals on the "public option" as well, voicing support for a government-run plan while signaling their willingness to see it die to get a bill passed. The president also abandoned his opposition to a requirement that everyone have insurance, known as an individual mandate, and signaled a willingness to consider financing schemes, including tax increases, that originally were not on his agenda. Moreover, perhaps to lower expectations, administration officials began speaking of putting the nation on a "glide path" to universal coverage rather than the insurance-for-all trumpeted by many Democrats.[48]

It is also difficult to coordinate supporters around a message.[49] A campaign team has near-total control over its message. A White House does not. "When it's either legislative strategy or regulatory strategy, you have to cede a considerable amount of control to people who don't share your interest, even if they're in your party," said Dan Bartlett, communications director in George W. Bush's White House.[50]

Through most of the summer, opposition to the president's health care initiative came almost entirely from the right. By mid-August, however, there was a growing concern among Obama's progressive allies that he was prepared to deal away the public insurance option to win passage of a health care bill. Obama insisted that he still preferred the public option as part of any legislative package, but many on the left doubted his resolve. Liberal commentators, progressive bloggers, and grassroots activists raised their concerns about Obama's health care policy and the deals he appeared to be striking with the health care industry—as well as on his increased troop commitment in Afghanistan and his stances on detainees and torture policy. The president's advisors acknowledged that they were unprepared for this intraparty rift. Rather than selling middle-class voters on how insurance reforms would benefit the public, the White House instead found itself mired in a Democratic Party feud over an issue it never intended to spotlight.[51]

Reaching the Public

There is little the White House can do to limit the overall volume of messages that citizens encounter or to make the public more attentive to politics, and it has limited success in influencing the media's agenda. Yet it still must try to reach the public with its message and break through the public's disinterest in politics and the countless distractions from it.

It is likely that reaching the public will require frequent repetition of the president's views. According to George W. Bush, "In my line of work you got to keep repeating things over and over and over again for the truth to sink in, to kind of catapult the propaganda."[52] Given the protracted nature of the legislative process, and the president's need for public support at all stages of it, sustaining a message can be equally important as sending it in the first place. As former White House public relations counselor David Gergen put it, "History teaches that almost nothing a leader says is heard if spoken only once." Administrations attempt to establish a "line of the day" so that many voices echo the same point.[53]

The lack of interest in politics of most Americans, as evidenced by the low turnouts in elections, compounds the challenge of reaching the public. Policymaking is a complex enterprise, and most voters do not have the time, expertise, or inclination to think extensively about most issues. In fact, people generally have only a few issues that are particularly important to them and to which they pay attention.[54] The importance of specific issues to the public varies over time and is closely tied to objective conditions such as unemployment, inflation, international tensions, and racial conflict. In addition, different issues are likely to be salient to different groups in the population at any given time. For example, some groups may be concerned about inflation, others about unemployment, and yet others about a particular aspect of foreign policy or race relations.[55]

A hallmark of the contemporary presidency is the White House's failure to draw impressive audiences for nationally televised speeches. Although wide viewership was common during the early decades of television, when presidential speeches routinely attracted more than 80 percent of those watching television, recent presidents have seen their audiences decline to the point where less than half of the public—often substantially less—watch their televised addresses.[56] Paradoxically, developments in technology have allowed the president to reach mass audiences, yet further developments have made it easier to for these same audiences to avoid listening to the White House. Cable televi-

TABLE 2.1.
Audiences for Obama Nationally Televised Speeches and Press Conferences

Date	Venue	Topic	Audience Size
February 9, 2009	White House	Press conference	49.5 million
February 24, 2009	Joint Session of Congress	Overview of administration	52.4 million
March 24, 2009	White House	Press conference	40.4 million
April 29, 2009	White House	Press conference	28.8 million
July 22, 2009	White House	Press conference	24.7 million
September 9, 2009	Joint Session of Congress	Health care reform	32.1 million
December 1, 2009	USMA, West Point	Afghanistan	40.8 million
January 27, 2010	Joint Session of Congress	State of the Union Message	48 million
June 15, 2010	Oval Office	Gulf of Mexico oil spill	32.1 million
August 31, 2010	Oval Office	End of Iraq War	29.2 million
January 12, 2011	Tucson, Arizona	Memorial for shooting victims	30.8 million
January 25, 2011	Joint Session of Congress	State of the Union Message	42.8 million
March 28, 2011	National Defense University	Libya	25.6 million
May 1, 2011	White House	Death of Osama bin Laden	56.7 million
June 22, 2011*	White House	Troop cuts in Afghanistan	25.4 million

Source: Nielsen Company.
*Univision did not carry the speech

sion[57] and news networks provide alternatives that make it easy to tune out the president. The average home received 118 channels in 2009.[58]

Table 2.1 shows the audiences for President Obama's nationally televised prime-time formal events. Although many people did choose to watch the president speak, the great majority of people did not—even for major addresses. Moreover, as the novelty of the new president wore off, the audiences for his prime-time televised addresses (except for his State of the Union messages) and press conferences steadily declined.

Less formal events drew smaller audiences. His March 19, 2009, appearance on the *Tonight Show* drew 12.8 watchers; and an interview on *60 Minutes* drew 16.2 million viewers.[59] These were good ratings for the programs, but reached a small fraction of the public. By June 24, 2009, ABC's *Primetime* special featuring a town hall discussion about health care with the president attracted just 4.7 million viewers.[60] A presidential appearance on the daytime talk show, *The View*, in July 2010, drew 6.6 million viewers.[61] Nevertheless, the president felt he had to exploit a range of venues to reach the public. As he put it in an interview on *60 Minutes*, "it used to be a President could call a press conference, and the three major networks would come, and he'd talk to 'em, and you pretty much reached everybody in America. . . . But there are a whole bunch of folks . . . who watch *The Daily Show*, or watch *The View*. And so I've got to adapt the presidency to reach as many people as possible in as many settings as possible so that they can hear directly from me."[62]

Commentary cascades from the White House. One official estimated that the White House produces as many as five million words a year in the president's name in outlets such as speeches, written statements, and proclamations.[63] Wide audiences hear only a small proportion of the president's statements, however. Comments about policy proposals at news conferences and question and answer sessions and in most interviews are also usually brief and made in the context of a discussion of many other policies. Written statements and remarks to individual groups may be focused, but the audience for these communications is modest. In addition, as David Gergen puts it, nearly all of the president's statements "wash over the public. They are dull, gray prose, eminently forgettable."[64]

The public can miss the point of even the most colorful rhetoric. In his 2010 State of the Union address, President Obama declared that as part of their economic recovery, his administration had passed twenty-five different tax cuts. "Now, let me repeat: We cut taxes," he said. "We cut taxes for 95 percent of working families. We cut taxes for small businesses. We cut taxes for first-time homebuyers. We cut taxes for parents trying to care for their children. We cut taxes for 8 million Americans paying for college." In his Super Bowl Sunday interview with Katie Couric, he touted the tax cuts in the stimulus package: "we put $300 billion worth of tax cuts into people's pockets so that there was demand and businesses had customers." (The only tax increases passed in 2009 were on tobacco.)

Shortly afterward, a major polling organization asked, "In general, do you think the Obama Administration has increased taxes for most Americans, decreased taxes for most Americans or have they kept taxes the same for most Americans?" Twenty-four percent of the public responded that the administration had *increased* taxes, and 53 percent said it kept taxes the same. Only 12 percent said taxes were decreased.[65] In July, that figure dwindled to 7 percent of the public.[66] Misperceptions only grew as the midterm elections approached. In September, 33 percent of the public thought that Obama had raised taxes for most Americans.[67] By the end of October, 52 percent of likely voters thought taxes had gone up for the middle class.[68]

On the other hand, only 34 percent of the public knew the unpopular bailout of banking and financial institutions (known as TARP) was passed under George W. Bush. Nearly half (47 percent) thought it passed during Obama's presidency.[69] Even though the White House announced in October 2010 that the federal government would actually turn a profit on these funds, 60 percent of likely voters at the end of the month thought most of the money was lost. Despite the fact that the economy had been growing for over a year, 61 percent thought it had been shrinking.[70]

David Axelrod lamented, "For me, the question is, why haven't we broken through more than we have? Why haven't we broken through?"[71] But the problems continued. Perceptions of the president's religion were closely linked to his job approval, and those who did not know Obama was a Christian were highly unlikely to approve of his job performance. In August 2010, 18 percent of the public thought the president was a Muslim, up from 11 percent in March 2009. Another 43 percent did not know Obama's religion (an increase from 32 percent in March 2009). Only 34 percent of the public knew he was a Christian, down from 48 percent in March 2009.[72]

It is important not only to reach the public, but also to reach it in a timely fashion. As Anita Dunn, the first director of communications in the Obama White House, put it, once a story gains traction, the administration needs to respond quickly or "rumors become facts."

In the summer of 2009, Betsey McCaughey voiced the false claim that the health care legislation in Congress would result in seniors being directed to "end their life sooner."[73] Numerous conservative pundits and Republican members of Congress quickly parroted her claim, including Rush Limbaugh, Glenn Beck, Sean Hannity, Fred Thompson, Laura Ingraham, the *New York Post*, *Wall Street Journal*, *Washington Times*, and Fox News. The myth reached its peak after Sarah Palin embellished it on her Facebook posting on August 7, 2009, denouncing government "death panels." Palin's comments created a media frenzy. In the ten days after her initial statement, *Washington Post* media critic Howard Kurtz counted 18 mentions of "death panels" in the *Post*, 16 in the *New York Times*, and more than 154 on network and cable news shows.[74]

The White House did not respond to Palin until four days after her Facebook posting, when Obama addressed the issue in a town hall meeting in New Hampshire. At the same time, the White House established a "Reality Check" blog on which officials challenged assertions they considered to be false. One prominent media observer termed this a "tepid" means of responding.[75]

In the meantime, the false charge of the fictitious death panels had gained traction in the conservative media and received widespread attention. By mid-

August, fully 86 percent of the public reported hearing either a lot (41 percent) or a little (45 percent) about "death panels." Among those who had heard about death panels, 50 percent said correctly that the claim was not true, but a sizable minority (30 percent) believed that health care legislation would create such organizations (20 said they did not know). Nearly half of Republicans (47 percent) were misinformed, as were 45 percent of those who reported regularly receiving their news from Fox News.[76] Another mid-August poll found that 45 percent of those surveyed believed the Democrats' bill would "allow the government to make decisions about when to stop providing medical care to the elderly," a figure that rose to 75 percent among Fox News viewers.[77]

Health Care Reform

A good example of the problems of reaching the public is health care reform, the president's highest legislative priority in his first year in office. The White House was aggressive in its public advocacy of reform. The president alone made fifty-two public addresses or statements specifically on his health care proposals during his first year in office.[78]

SUMMER AWAKENING   Mindful of the failures of former President Bill Clinton, who produced an extraordinarily specific plan for health care in 1993, Obama insisted he would leave the details of health care reform to Congress. He set forth broad principles and concentrated on bringing disparate factions— doctors, insurers, hospitals, pharmaceutical companies, labor unions—to the negotiating table. By June, however, the president grew concerned that he was losing the debate over certain policy prescriptions he favored, like a government-run insurance plan to compete with the private sector. With Congress beginning serious work on the measure, the president concluded that he had to exert greater control over the health care debate.[79]

Worried about the lack of public support for health care reform, the White House arranged with ABC News for a prime-time program on June 24, 2009, *Questions for the President: Prescription for America* (with a follow-up session on *Nightline*) that allowed the president to explain his health care proposal to the public yet again. Only 4.7 million viewers tuned in, however, nearly 3 million fewer than a competing repeat of CBS's crime series, *CSI: New York*.[80] On July 1, Obama held a town hall–style meeting on health care in Virginia—his second town hall meeting in two weeks.

Yet the polls kept getting worse for the administration. With skepticism about the president's health care reform effort mounting on Capitol Hill—even within his own party—the White House moved its public relations effort into high gear in late July. In the words of the *Washington Post*, it was "all Obama, all the time." Senior White House aides promised an aggressive public and private

TABLE 2.2.
Going Public on Health Care: Mid-Summer 2009

Date	Location	Event
July 15	White House	Statement on health care
July 16	White House	Statement on AMA's support for health care reform
July 18	White House	Weekly radio address: health care
July 20	Washington, DC	Statement on health care at children's hospital
July 21	White House	Statement on health care and F-22
July 22	White House	Prime-time press conference
	White House	Interview with *Washington Post* editorial page editor
July 23	Cleveland, OH	Tour of Cleveland Clinic
	Shaker Heights, OH	Town hall meeting on health care
	Chicago, IL	Remarks on health care at fund-raiser
July 24	White House	Release of Report on Economic Effects of Health Care Reform on Small Businesses and Their Employees
July 25	White House	Weekly radio address: health care
July 28	Washington, DC	Town hall-style session on health care at the AARP's Washington headquarters
July 29	Raleigh, NC	Town hall meeting on health care
	Bristol, VA	Discussion on health care with Kroger employees
	White House	Statement on Health Insurance Reform Efforts in Congress
August 1	White House	Statement on House Energy and Commerce Committee Passage of Health Insurance Reform

schedule for Obama as he pressed his case for reform. "Our strategy has been to allow this process to advance to the point where it made sense for the president to take the baton. Now's that time," said senior advisor David Axelrod on July 19, "he's going to be very, very visible."[81]

We can see in table 2.2 what Axelrod meant. The president traveled, made public statements, gave interviews, held town meetings and a prime-time press conference, delivered a radio address, and released statements and reports on health care. In addition, the White House made heavy use of Internet video to broadcast the president's message beyond the reach of the traditional media.

For example, the administration sponsored a live video chat with Nancy-Ann DeParle, Obama's health policy czar, on Facebook and on the Web site, White-House.gov. Meanwhile, Organizing for America, the group run by the Democratic National Committee to rally support for Obama's agenda, declared this week "Health Care Reform Week of Action" and asked millions of supporters to sign up for events in their neighborhoods.

AUGUST RECALIBRATION   Nothing seemed to work, however. Democratic Party officials acknowledged that the growing intensity of the opposition to the president's health care plans had caught them off guard and forced them to begin an August counteroffensive.[82] The president and his proxies launched a blitz of town hall meetings, grassroots lobbying, and television advertising designed to rally public support for quick votes on health plans in the House and Senate following the August congressional recess. The president held town hall meetings in Portsmouth, New Hampshire, Bozeman, Montana, and Grand Junction, Colorado, and wrote an op-ed in the *New York Times*.

One aspect of the new strategy was geared toward reenergizing Web-savvy allies who backed Obama in the election. The president appeared in a six-minute video on the WhiteHouse.gov Web site, recounting some of the personal stories of average Americans. On August 20, he held a conference call with grassroots supporters hosted by Organizing for America during which an estimated 280,000 people dialed in.[83]

The effort by the president to create new momentum came as the Democratic National Committee and Organizing for America encouraged volunteers to fan out across the country to sway reluctant lawmakers to support the proposals moving through Congress. They also enlisted supporters to attend public events with members of Congress to counterbalance the sometimes angry outbursts from opponents.[84]

Reprising a strategy from the campaign, the White House began responding to attacks in the same medium in real time. Thus, on August 4, the White House reacted quickly with its own three-minute video in response to a Web video that officials said misrepresented the president's health care plan. The administration's video did not only appear on the White House Web site (http.whitehouse.gov) but was also promoted on Facebook and Twitter and sent to those on the e-mail list on www.healthreform.gov.

As part of the White House's rapid-response effort, on August 4, it launched an e-mail tip line where people could report "disinformation about health insurance reform." The effort quickly sparked concern among Republicans about the government collecting information on private citizens' political speech, however, and the administration shut it down after two weeks.

On August 10, the White House also launched a new online "Health Insurance Reform Reality Check" on its Web site, featuring administration officials rebutting questionable but potentially damaging charges that President

Obama's proposed overhaul of the nation's health care system would inevitably lead to "socialized medicine," "rationed care," and even forced euthanasia for the elderly.

As members of Congress left for their August recess, advertisements followed them. Groups saturated the airwaves with tens of millions of dollars in advertisements for and against health care reform. Much of the advertising was focused on wavering members of Congress and members from electorally competitive districts and states. Tellingly, the Campaign Media Analysis Group estimated that most of the advertising by early August had broadly favored overhauling the health care system.[85] Nevertheless, the public had become less supportive.

The Pharmaceutical Research and Manufacturers of America joined the nonprofit group Families USA to air an updated version of the iconic "Harry and Louise" ads, but this time the couple called for passage of reform. Conservative groups like the Club for Growth, Americans for Prosperity, the U.S. Chamber of Commerce, Conservatives for Patients' Rights, and, especially, the Republican National Committee ran ads against reform, while Americans United for Change, organized labor, including the American Federation of State, County and Municipal Employees (which represents health care workers), MoveOn.org, the Democratic Congressional Campaign Committee, Organizing for America, the powerful seniors lobby AARP, the American Nurses Association, and the American Medical Association sponsored advertisements in favor of reform.

By mid-August, health care reform was receiving the most attention in the news and was the story the public was following the most closely. This was not always an advantage for the president, however. Democrats had not anticipated Republicans and their allies hurling incendiary accusations that the Obama plan would empower "death panels," help illegal immigrants, and raid Medicare.

SEPTEMBER OFFENSIVE   Following the Labor Day holiday, Obama renewed his public relations offensive. Given the high stakes of passing health care reform and the downturn in public opinion about it, the president turned to what many considered the most powerful weapon in his arsenal—a nationally televised evening address before a joint session of Congress. As we have seen, Obama's speech was unusual. Presidents rarely focus such a nationally televised address on an issue before Congress.[86]

Obama had to reassure progressive activists that he had not lost his passion for reform, so his speech contained tough talk and denunciations of false or misleading claims that opponents had made about the legislation in Congress. The president knew, of course, that there was little possibility of moving Republicans from opposition to support. He had to reach the center of the electorate. It was this segment of the public that had become worried about the scope and

TABLE 2.3.
Going Public on Health Care: Mid-September 2009

Date	Location	Event
September 7	Cincinnati, OH	Speech to Cincinnati AFL-CIO Labor Day Picnic
September 8	Arlington, VA	ABC's *Good Morning America*
September 9	U.S. Capitol	Address to Joint Session of Congress
September 10	Washington, DC	Speech to American Nurses Association
September 12	Washington, DC	Weekly Radio Address
September 12	Minneapolis, MN	Speech at rally for health insurance reform
September 13	Washington, DC	Interview with CBS's *60 Minutes*
September 15	Lordstown, OH	Speech to General Motors employees
September 15	Pittsburgh, PA	Remarks at AFL-CIO Convention
Mid-September	White House	Interview with *Men's Health* magazine
September 17	College Park, MD	Speech at rally on health insurance reform
September 17	Washington, DC	Memorandum on medical liability reform
September 18	Washington, DC	Michelle Obama speech on health care reform
September 20	Washington, DC	ABC's *This Week*
	Washington, DC	NBC's *Meet the Press*
	Washington, DC	CBS's *Face the Nation*
	Washington, DC	CNN's *State of the Union*
	Washington, DC	Univision's *Al Punto*
September 21	New York City	*The Late Show with David Letterman*

nature of the president's proposal. Thus, much of his rhetoric provided reassurance and reflected an orientation toward compromise and bipartisanship.

Obama's audience was 32.1 million people, a large number to be sure, but only a small portion of the public and down from about 52 million for his February address to a joint session of Congress.[87] The Fox broadcast network chose not to televise the president's speech (although the Fox News channel did).

Obama followed up his speech with a series of speeches, interviews, and television appearances over the next two weeks, culminating in an unprecedented set of appearances on five Sunday interview shows on the same day (see table 2.3).

The president was so active in advocating health care reform in September that some commentators suggested he was in danger of overexposure. The White House disagreed. "The idea of overexposure is based on an old-world

TABLE 2.4.
Evaluations of Impact of Health Care Reform

Poll Dates	You and Your Family		Country as a Whole	
	% Better Off	% Worse Off	% Better Off	% Worse Off
February 3–13, 2009	38	11	59	12
April 2–8, 2009	43	14	56	15
June 1–8, 2009	39	16	57	16
July 7–14, 2009	39	21	51	23
August 4–11, 2009	36	31	45	34
September 11–18, 2009	42	23	53	26
October 8–15, 2009	41	27	53	28
November 5–12, 2009*	42	24	54	27
December 7–13, 2009	35	27	45	31
January 7–12, 2010	32	33	42	37
February 11–16, 2010	34	32	45	34
March 10–15, 2010	35	32	45	34

*Asked of partial sample (N=620)
Source: Kaiser Health Tracking Poll.
Question: "Do you think (INSERT AND ROTATE) would be (better off) or (worse off) if the president and Congress passed health care reform, or don't you think it would make much difference?"

view of the media," said Dan Pfeiffer, the White House's deputy communications director. Because the media are now so fragmented, "you would have to do all the Sunday shows, a lot of network news shows and late-night shows" to reach the number of viewers a president could address with one network interview twenty years ago.[88] According to an NBC/*Wall Street Journal* poll of September 17–20, 54 percent of the public said they were seeing and hearing Obama the right amount and only 34 percent (mostly Republicans) said they were seeing and hearing him too much. A majority of Independents, 52 percent, said Obama had the right amount of exposure.

By mid-October, the president lowered his profile on health care. The White House plan was for Obama to take a breather while Democrats resolved their internal conflicts. Then he was to come back strong with a fresh sales pitch when the legislation moved closer to floor votes.[89]

CONTINUED SLIPPAGE   The trends in evaluation of the overall effects of health care reform continued to worsen. Table 2.4 shows that the percentage of the public concluding that health care reform would make them and their families as well as the country as a whole worse off moved against the president. In the months leading up to the final votes on the health care reform in 2010, only about one-third of the people felt reform would benefit themselves and their families.[90] This low level of support added to the burdens of passing non-incremental change.

Perhaps most frustrating to the White House was the inability to clarify mistaken notions about its proposal that were damaging its case. In mid-September, 26 percent of respondents still believed that health care legislation would create organizations to decide when to stop providing medical care to the elderly—the so-called death panels—despite an all-out effort by Obama to debunk the false claim. Similarly, 30 percent said the bill would use taxpayer money to provide health care benefits to illegal immigrants despite the president specifically affirming that it would not.[91]

The president just could not break through. In early September, 67 percent of the respondents to a national poll said the issue was difficult to understand.[92] At the end of an interview with George Stephanopoulos on ABC's *This Week* on September 20, 2009, the president reflected on his leadership of the public regarding health care.

> There have been times where I have said I've got to step up my game in terms of talking to the American people about issues like health care. . . . I've said to myself, somehow I'm not breaking through. . . . this has been a sufficiently tough, complicated issue with so many moving parts that . . . no matter how much I've . . . tried to keep it digestible, . . . it's very hard for people to get their . . . whole arms around it. And that's been a case where I have been humbled.[93]

(In July 2010, 41 percent of the public still believed the law allowed a government panel to make decisions about end-of-life care for people on Medicare and an additional 16 percent said they did not know.)[94]

In January 2010, as the debate on health care reform was reaching its final stages, large segments of the public still were unaware of major elements of the Democratic proposal (see table 2.5).[95] In addition, only 59 percent of the public understood that most people could keep their employer-provided insurance if health care reform passed.[96] Small businesses did not know about subsidies for them, seniors did not know the bill closed the "donut hole" on prescription drugs, and young adults did not know they could stay on their parents' health insurance policies until they were twenty-six.[97] Unaware of the benefits of health care reform and concerned about losing the benefits they already had, it is little wonder that many in the public opposed the president.

More than a year after the bill passed, the Kaiser Foundation found in June 2011 that most Americans were unaware that the health care reform law would close the Medicare "doughnut hole" on prescription drugs, eliminate co-pays and deductibles for many preventative services under Medicare, and develop ways to improve health care delivery. On the other hand, 31 percent of the public incorrectly believed the law allowed a government panel to make decisions about end-of-life care for people on Medicare—and another 20 percent were

TABLE 2.5.
Awareness of Health Care Proposals

Reform Proposal*	% Aware
1. Prohibit insurance companies from denying coverage or charging higher premiums because of a person's medical history or health condition	61
2. Place a limit on the amount that insurance companies can charge older people compared to younger people	44
3. Provide tax credits to small businesses that want to offer coverage to their employees	52
4. Penalize all but the smallest employers if they don't offer health insurance to their workers	58
5. Increase income taxes for the highest income Americans as a way to help pay for health reform	68
6. Require drug makers, medical device manufacturers, and health insurance companies to pay a tax based on how much business they have, to help pay for health reform	49
7. Prohibit use of federal money for abortions, except as allowed by current law, which is in cases of rape, incest, or if the woman's life is in danger	56
8. Specify the amount of money that insurance companies must spend on paying for health care compared with the amount they spend on administrative costs and their own profits	43
9. Limit future increases in Medicare payments to health care providers as a way to help pay for health reform	47
10. Expand the existing Medicaid program to cover more low-income uninsured Americans	62
11. Allow children to stay on their parents' insurance plans through age 25	48
12. Prohibit insurance companies from charging women higher premiums than men	37
13. Prohibit insurance companies from setting a limit on the total amount they will spend on a person's health care over their lifetime	42
14. Provide financial help to lower- and middle-income Americans who don't get insurance through their jobs to help them purchase coverage	72
15. Require nearly all Americans to have a minimum level of health insurance or else pay a fine	57
16. Help close the Medicare "doughnut hole" or "coverage gap" so seniors would no longer have a period where they are responsible for paying the full cost of their medicines	44
17. Increase the Medicare payroll tax for higher income Americans as a way to help pay for health reform	65
18. Impose a tax on insurers who offer the most expensive health plans, also called Cadillac plans, to help pay for health reform	51

Reform Proposal*	% Aware
19. Create a health insurance exchange or marketplace where small businesses and people who don't get coverage through their employers can shop for insurance and compare prices and benefits	58
20. Require insurance plans to offer a minimum package of health insurance benefits, to be defined by the federal government	63
21. Prevent illegal immigrants from receiving any federal money to purchase health insurance	40

*Items 1–11 and 12–21 asked of two partial samples (N=511 for each).
Source: Kaiser Health Tracking Poll, January 7–12, 2010.
Question: "I'm going to read you a list of specific reform proposals. For each, please tell me whether you think it is included in the health care reform legislation being discussed in Congress or not. First, to the best of your knowledge, would you say the legislation being debated does or does not (INSERT AND RANDOMIZE)?"

unsure. Forty-eight percent incorrectly felt the law would cut benefits that were previously provided to all people on Medicare, and another 17 percent were uncertain.[98]

Exploiting Technology

Although technological change has made it more difficult for the president to attract an audience on television, other changes may have increased the White House's prospects of reaching the public. Teddy Roosevelt gave prominence to the bully pulpit by exploiting the hunger of modern newspapers for national news. Franklin D. Roosevelt broadened the reach and immediacy of presidential communications with his use of radio. More recently, John F. Kennedy and Ronald Reagan mastered the use of television to speak directly to the American people. Now Barack Obama has positioned himself as the first Internet president.

On November 18, 2008, about 10 million of Barack Obama's supporters found an e-mail message from his campaign manager, David Plouffe. Labeled "Where we go from here," Plouffe asked backers to "help shape the future of this movement" by answering an online survey, which in turn asked them to rank four priorities in order of importance. First on the list was "Helping Barack's administration pass legislation through grassroots efforts."[99]

Plouffe's e-mail message revealed much about Barack Obama's initial approach to governing. The new administration was oriented to exploiting advances in technology to communicate more effectively than ever with the public. Bush State Department spokesman Sean McCormack started filing posts from far-flung regions during trips with his boss, Secretary of State Condoleezza Rice. On October 31, 2008, McCormack unveiled "Briefing 2.0" in the press briefing room of the State Department in which he took questions from the public rather than the press and then put the session on YouTube.[100]

In 2009, the new occupants of the White House were oriented to exploiting the emerging technology more systematically than their predecessors. Obama announced his intent to seek the presidency via Web video, revealed his vice presidential selection via text message, recruited about 13 million online supporters during the campaign, and used the electronic medium to sidestep mainstream media and speak directly with voters throughout the primaries and general-election campaign. This practice forged a firsthand connection and may have encouraged some supporters to feel they had a greater stake in the campaign's success. Some Obama videos have become YouTube phenomena: millions of people have viewed his speech on the Rev. Jeremiah A. Wright Jr. and race in America and his victory speech in Grant Park on November 4, 2008.

"It's really about reaching an extra person or a larger audience of people who wouldn't normally pay attention to policy," said Jen Psaki, a spokeswoman for Obama's transition team. "We have to think creatively about how we would do that in the White House, because promoting a speech in front of 100,000 people is certainly different than promoting energy legislation."[101]

Even before taking office, the president-elect began making Saturday radio addresses—but with a twist. In addition to beaming his addresses to radio stations nationwide, he recorded them for digital video and audio downloads from YouTube, iTunes, and the like. As a result, people could access it whenever and wherever they wanted. "Turning the weekly radio address from audio to video and making it on-demand has turned the radio address from a blip on the radar to something that can be a major newsmaking event any Saturday we choose," declared Dan Pfeiffer, the incoming White House deputy communications director. Videos are also easy to produce: a videographer can record Obama delivering the address in fewer than fifteen minutes.[102] After his inauguration, the White House put the president's Saturday videos on both the White House Web site and a White House channel on YouTube. However, between May 2009 and November 2010, no video had more than 100,000 views and most had close to 20,000.[103]

The Obama White House produces and distributes much more video than any past administration. To do so, it maintains a staff devoted to producing online videos for whitehouse.gov, Obama's YouTube channel, and other video depots. A search for "Barack Obama" is stacked with videos approved and uploaded by the campaign or the administration (which viewers may not realize). When filming a presidential speech, the production team tailors the video to the site, with titles, omissions, crowd cutaways, highlight footage, and a dozen other manipulations of sound and image that affect the impression they make, including applause that is difficult to edit out.[104] The president's YouTube channel had more than 650 video uploads in its first year. The administration also holds regular question-and-answer Webcasts with policy officials on White House.gov.[105]

In addition, the administration introduced *West Wing Week*, a video blog consisting of six- to seven-minute compilations that appear each week on the White House's Web site and on such video-sharing sites as YouTube. They offer what a narrator on each segment calls "your guide to everything that's happening at 1600 Pennsylvania Avenue."

The Obama White House wants to flood niche media markets via blogs, Twitter feeds, Facebook pages, and Flicker photo streams.[106] To exploit more fully developments in communications technology, the White House established an Office of New Media. It regularly alerts its 1.7 million Twitter followers of the president's policy stances.[107] When he nominated Sonia Sotomayor to the Supreme Court, Obama sent a video appealing for support for his candidate to the huge e-mail list accumulated during his campaign and the Democratic Party's own lists. The e-mail message included a directive from the president to share his views via Facebook, Twitter, and other Web connections.[108]

Politico.com is the most prominent face of the new media at the White House. It is a bulletin board of the stories on which the media is focused and what is happening in Washington on a given day. The White House starts communicating with Mike Allen, Politico's chief White House correspondent, at 5 a.m. to try to influence what others will view as important. It also uses Politico as a forum to rebut directly its adversaries in front of the rest of the news media.[109]

The Internet, which emerged in 2008 as a leading source for campaign news, has now surpassed all other media except television as a main source for national and international news. More people now say they rely mostly on the Internet for news rather than newspapers.[110] Young people are even more likely to report that they rely on the Internet as a main source of national and international news. Overall, 61 percent of Americans now use the Internet as a daily news source.[111]

Obama made the case for his economic agenda in a variety of forums, including the *Tonight Show*, *60 Minutes*, and a prime-time news conference. On March 26, 2009, he added a new arrow to his quiver. The president held an "Open for Questions" town hall meeting in the East Room of the White House. Bill Clinton and George W. Bush answered questions over the Internet, but Obama was the first to do so in a live video format, streamed directly onto the White House Web site.

For more than an hour, the president answered questions culled from 104,000 sent over the Internet. Online voters cast more than 3.5 million votes for their favorite questions, some of which were then posed to the president by an economic advisor who served as a moderator. The president took other queries from a live audience of about 100 nurses, teachers, businesspeople, and others assembled at the White House.

The questions covered topics such as health care, education, the economy, the auto industry, and housing. In most cases, Obama used his answers to advocate his policies. Although the questions from the audience in the East Room were mostly from campaign backers, the White House was not in complete control of the session. One of the questions that drew the most votes online was whether legalizing marijuana might stimulate the economy by allowing the government to regulate and tax the drug. (The White House listed the question on its Web site under the topics "green jobs and energy" and "budget." White House officials later indicated that interest groups drove up those numbers.)[112]

On February 1, 2010, the president sat for a first-of-its-kind group interview with YouTube viewers, who submitted thousands of questions and heard the president answer some in a live Webcast. YouTube viewers voted for their favorite questions, and Steve Grove, the head of news and politics at YouTube, selected the ones to ask in the half-hour session.

In April 2011, Obama sat down with Facebook founder Mark Zuckerberg and answered questions from Zuckerberg and Facebook users. The president next turned to Twitter. On July 6, 2011, he held the first Twitter town hall meeting, live from the East Room of the White House. The hour-long session involved the president answering questions submitted by Twitter users and selected in part by 10 Twitter users around the country picked by Twitter. Twitter's chief executive, Jack Dorsey, moderated the session.

Preaching to the Choir

When the Obama White House texts its supporters, it is preaching to the choir. There is nothing wrong with that. Perhaps the first rule in the politics of coalition building is solidifying the base. Yet, the base can only take you so far. Obama received about 53 percent of the national vote, and some of that support was certainly a negative response to George W. Bush in general and bad economic times in particular. It would be an exaggeration to conclude that Obama's base includes even half the public. Moreover, once Obama took office, Bush was gone and the public began reacting to the new president.

Moreover, widespread home broadband and mobile access to the Internet has created the potential for people to communicate easily with each other as well as to receive communications from leaders. Conservatives can exploit this technology to reinforce their opposition to the new administration. Equally important, however, is the potential for liberals to use the new technologies to oppose the president's evident pragmatism and tendencies toward moderation.

Communications technology users glory in the freedom to dissent that is at the heart of blogging. Even during the transition, there were hints of conflict within the base. Candidate Obama allowed his supporters to wage an online revolt—on his own MyBarackObama.com Web site—over his vote in favor of legislation granting legal immunity to telecommunications firms that participated in the Bush administration's domestic wiretapping program. President-elect Obama, however, did not provide a forum for comments on his YouTube radio address, prompting grumbling among some in the netroots crowd that YouTube without comments was no different from radio.[113]

Internet users are creative, however. The day after Obama announced that the Rev. Rick Warren would deliver the opening prayer at his inauguration, a discussion forum focused on community service instead filled with pages of comments from people opposing the choice. In early January, visitors to Change.gov, the transition Web site, voted a question about whether Obama would appoint a special prosecutor to investigate possible Bush administration war crimes to the top of the questions submitted to the new administration. Progressive Web sites blasted the new administration's efforts to dodge the issue. Within a day, MSNBC's Keith Olbermann picked up the story. A day later, Obama was compelled to answer the question in an interview with ABC's George Stephanopoulos, who quoted it and pressed Obama with two follow-ups. Obama's answer, which prioritized moving "forward" but did not rule out a special prosecutor, made the front page of the January 12 issue of the *New York Times*.

Dissent among liberals did not end with the transition. For example, Move On.org, one of Obama's staunchest supporters during the 2008 campaign, called on its members in April 2010 to telephone the White House and demand that Obama reinstate the ban on offshore oil drilling that he had ended.[114]

Mobilizing Supporters

Reaching people is useful for political leaders, but mobilizing them is better. Plouffe's emphasis on helping the Obama administration pass legislation through grassroots efforts indicates a desire to use public backing to move Congress to support the president's program. According to Andrew Rasiej, cofounder of the Personal Democracy Forum, a nonpartisan Web site focused on the intersection of politics and technology, Obama "created his own special interest group because the same people that made phone calls on behalf of him [in the campaign] are now going to be calling or e-mailing their congressman."[115] A Pew study during the transition found that among those who voted for Obama, 62 percent expected to ask others to support at least some of the new administration's policies.[116]

Plouffe did not take a formal role in the White House until 2011. He did, however, remain as an advisor and began overseeing the president's sprawling grass-roots political operation, which at the time boasted 13 million e-mail addresses, 4 million cell phone contacts, and 2 million active volunteers.[117] More than 500,000 people completed surveys following the election to express their vision for the administration, and more than 4,200 hosted house parties in their communities. On January 17, 2009, Obama sent a YouTube video to supporters to announce plans to establish Organizing for America (OFA), which was to enlist community organizers around the country to support local candidates, lobby for the president's agenda, and remain connected with his supporters from the campaign. There was speculation that the organization could have an annual budget of $75 million in privately raised funds and deploy hundreds of paid staff members. It was to operate from the Democratic National Committee headquarters but with an independent structure, budget, and priorities.[118] (By 2010, OFA had virtually supplanted the party structure. It sent about 300 paid organizers to the states, several times the number the national party hired for the 2006 midterms.)[119]

During the transition, the Obama team drew on high-tech organizational tools to lay the groundwork for an attempt to restructure the U.S. health care system. On December 3, 2008, former Democratic Senate majority leader Thomas Daschle, Obama's designee as secretary of Health and Human Resources and point person on health care, launched an effort to create political momentum when he held a conference call with one thousand invited supporters who had expressed interest in health issues, promising it would be the first of many opportunities for Americans to weigh in. In addition, there were online videos, blogs, and e-mail alerts as well as traditional public forums. Thousands of people posted comments on health on Change.gov, the Obama transition Web site, which encouraged bloggers to share their concerns and offer their solutions regarding health care policy.[120]

According to Rasiej, "It will be a lot easier to get the American public to adopt any new health-care system if they were a part of the process of crafting it." Simon Rosenberg, president of the center-left think tank NDN, was more expansive: "This is the beginning of the reinvention of what the presidency in the 21st century could be." "This will reinvent the relationship of the president to the American people in a way we probably haven't seen since FDR's use of radio in the 1930s."[121]

Democratic political consultant Joe Trippi took the argument a step further, observing, "Obama will be more directly connected to millions of Americans than any president who has come before him, and he will be able to communicate directly to people using the social networking and Web-based tools such as YouTube that his campaign mastered." "Obama's could become the most powerful presidency that we have ever seen," he declared.[122] Republican strategist and the head of White House political operations under Ronald Reagan, Ed Rollins, agreed. "No one's ever had these kinds of resources. This would be the greatest political organization ever put together, *if it works*" (italics added).[123]

Frustrations

Whether it would work was indeed the question. To begin, Obama's team found it difficult to adapt its technologically advanced presidential campaign to government. The official Web site, WhiteHouse.gov, was to be the primary vehicle for President Obama to communicate with the masses online. Yet the White House lacks the technology to send mass e-mail updates on presidential initiatives. The same is true for text messaging, another campaign staple. The White House must also navigate security and privacy rules regarding the collection of cell phone numbers.[124] In addition, there are time-consuming legal strictures such as a requirement in the Presidential Records Act to archive Web pages whenever they are modified, in order to preserve administration communications. Moreover, the White House cannot engage in overt politicking or fund-raising on a government Web site.

The Organizing for America team held several dry runs to test the efficacy of their volunteer apparatus, including a call for supporters to hold "economic recovery house meetings" in February to highlight challenges presented by the recession. The house parties were designed to coincide with the congressional debate over Obama's stimulus package and had mixed results. Although OFA touted the 30,000 responses the e-mail drew from the volunteer community and the more than 3,000 house parties thrown in support of the stimulus package, a report in McClatchy Newspapers indicated that many events were sparsely attended.[125]

The first major engagement of OFA in the legislative process began on March 16, 2009. An e-mail message was sent to volunteers, asking them to go door to door on March 21 to urge their neighbors to sign a pledge in support of Obama's budget plan. A follow-up message to the mailing list a few days later asked volunteers to call the Hill. A new online tool on the DNC/OFA Web site aided constituents in finding their congressional representatives' contact information so they could call the lawmakers' offices to voice approval of the proposal.

The OFA reported that its door-to-door canvass netted about 100,000 pledge signatures, while another 114,000 signatures came in through its e-mail network. Republicans scoffed at the effort, arguing that this proved that even the most die-hard Obama supporters were uncertain about the wisdom of the president's budget plan. Several GOP aides noted that the number of pledges gathered online amounted to fewer than 1 percent of the names on Obama's vaunted e-mail list. The *Washington Post* reported that interviews with congressional aides from both parties found the signatures swayed few, if any, members of Congress.[126]

By June, OFA was the Democratic National Committee's largest department, with paid staff members in thirty-one states and control of the heavily trafficked campaign Web site. Public discourse on health care reform was focusing on the high costs and uncertain results of various proposals. Remembering the "Harry and Louise" television ads that served as the public face of the successful challenge to Bill Clinton's health reform efforts, the White House knew it had to regain momentum. Thus, the president e-mailed millions of campaign supporters, asking for donations to help in the White House's largest-ever issues campaign and for "a coast-to-coast operation ready to knock on doors, deploy volunteers, get out the facts," and show Congress people wanted change. The DNC deployed dozens of staff members and hundreds of volunteers to thirty-one states to gather personal stories and build support.[127]

In late June, the DNC reported roughly 750,000 people had signed a pledge in support of the president's core principles of reducing cost, ensuring quality, and providing choice, including a public insurance option; 500,000 volunteered to help; and several hundred thousand provided their own story for the campaign's use. OFA posted thousands of personal stories online to humanize the debate and overcome criticism of the president's plan. It also trained hundreds of summer volunteers and released its first Internet advertisement—a Virginia man explaining that he lost his insurance when he lost his job.[128]

As the health care debate intensified in August, the president again turned to the OFA for support. Obama sent an e-mail to OFA members: "This is the moment our movement was built for," he wrote. He also spent an hour providing bullet points for the health care debate during an Internet video. OFA asked its volunteers to visit congressional offices and flood town hall meetings in a massive show of support.[129] There is no evidence that this show of strength ever materialized.

By August, Organizing for America reported paid political directors in forty-four states. Nevertheless, it had to moderate its strategy. In response to Democrat complaints to the White House about television commercials on health care, climate change, and other issues broadcast in an effort to pressure moderates to support the president's proposals, the group started running advertisements of appreciation. It also found that its events around the country were largely filled with party stalwarts rather than the army of volunteers mobilized by the 2008 campaign.[130]

Despite some success in generating letters, text messages, and phone calls on behalf of health care reform, OFA was not a prominent presence in 2009.[131] In response to the lack of action, in 2010 organizers held hundreds of sessions across the nation intended to re-engage the base from 2008.[132]

In a video to members of OFA in April 2010, Obama delivered an appeal saying that the Democratic majority in Congress—and his agenda—depended on their roles in that year's midterm elections. The recorded message was part of a new effort by the Democratic National Committee to impress upon Democrats—particularly those occasional voters who were likely to cast ballots only in presidential races—the importance of the midterm elections for the House and Senate.

At the end of 2010, OFA launched a public relations offensive to demonstrate support for repealing "don't ask, don't tell." The group ran online advertisements and staged events in the home states of moderate Republican senators inclined to support the repeal bill. OFA volunteers delivered petitions with tens of thousands of signatures to wavering senators in an effort to build momentum for repeal—and to try to show them that they were safe politically if they voted to overturn the ban.[133]

Overall, however, OFA had to be a disappointment to the White House. In the midterm elections, OFA tried to rally its network of millions of Obama supporters to help Democratic candidates across the country, but the group was not very successful. Aside from a handful of victories, such as Senate Majority Leader Harry Reid's reelection in Nevada, most OFA-backed candidates lost.[134]

The president also received help from an array of interest groups, such as Health Care for America Now, a progressive coalition that deployed 120 paid organizers to forty-three states, staged events, and launched ads in a number of states.[135] Nevertheless, as we will see in the next chapter, public opinion did not move in the president's direction.

Framing the Message

Presidents make a substantial effort to frame issues in ways that will favor their preferred policy options and to place their own performance in a favorable light. A *frame* is a central organizing idea for making sense of an issue or conflict and suggests what the controversy is about and what is at stake.[136] Structuring the choices about policy issues in ways that favor the president's programs may set the terms of the debate on his proposals and thus the premises on which the public evaluates them. As one leading advisor to Reagan put it, "I've always believed that 80 percent of any legislative or political matter is how you frame the debate."[137]

In most instances, the president does not have much impact on the values that people hold. Citizens develop these values over many years, starting in early childhood. By the time people focus on the president, their values are for the most part well established. However, people use cues from elites as to the ideological or partisan implications of messages[138] (the source of a message is itself an important cue).[139]

Because individuals typically have at least two, and often more, relevant values for evaluating issue positions, and because they are unlikely to canvass all their values in their evaluations, the president cannot leave to chance the identification of which values are most relevant to the issues he raises. Instead, the White House seeks to influence the values citizens employ in their evaluations.

Portraying policies in terms of criteria on which there is a consensus and playing down divisive issues is often at the core of efforts to structure choices.

By articulating widely held values and pointing out their applicability to policy issues, events, or his own performance, the president may increase the salience (and thus the accessibility) of those values to the public's evaluations of them. In the process, the president attempts to show the public that his position is consistent with their values.[140]

Instead of trying to persuade the public directly on the merits of a proposal, then, the White House often uses public statements and the press coverage they generate to articulate relatively simple themes. Public opinion research may have identified these themes as favoring the president's positions. For example, on the eve of the vote in the House on the climate change bill, President Obama shifted his argument for the bill to emphasize its potential economic benefits. "Make no mistake," he declared, "this is a jobs bill."[141] Climate change is a controversial topic, but everyone is for jobs, especially in a period of high unemployment.

Framing demands less of the public than directly persuading citizens on the merits of a policy proposal. The president does not have to persuade people to change their basic values and preferences. He does not have to convince citizens to develop expertise and acquire and process extensive information about the details of a policy proposal. In addition, framing—because it is relatively simple—is less susceptible to distortion by journalists and opponents than direct persuasion on the merits of a policy proposal.[142]

Attempts to frame issues are as old as the Republic.[143] Each side of a political contest usually attempts to frame the debate to its own advantage. Byron Shafer and William Claggett argue that public opinion is organized around two clusters of issues, both of which are favored by a majority of voters: social welfare, social insurance, and civil rights (associated with Democrats) and cultural values, civil liberties, and foreign relations (associated with Republicans). Each party's best strategy is to frame the choice for voters by focusing attention on the party's most successful cluster of issues.[144] John Petrocik has found that candidates tend to campaign on issues that favor them in order to prime the salience of these issues in voters' decision making.[145] Similarly, an important aspect of campaigning is activating the latent predispositions of partisans by priming party identification as a crucial consideration in deciding for whom to vote.[146]

Structuring choice is rarely easy. There is competition to set the terms of debate over issues.[147] We know very little about the terms in which the public thinks about policies. Studies that have shown powerful framing effects typically have carefully sequestered citizens and restricted them to hearing only one frame, usually in the context of a controlled experiment.[148] These frames tend to be confined to brief fragments of arguments, pale imitations of frames that often occur in the real world. Studies have found that conversations that include conflicting perspectives,[149] credible advice from other sources,[150] predispositions,[151] levels of education,[152] and relevant expertise[153] condition the impact of framing efforts.

Committed, well-organized, and well-funded opponents inhabit the president's world. Intense disagreement among elites generates conflicting messages. John Zaller argues that attitudes on major issues change in response to changes in relation to the intensity of competing streams of political communication. When there is elite consensus, and thus only one set of cues offered to the public, opinion change may be substantial. However, when elite discourse is divided, people respond to the issue according to their predispositions, especially their core partisan and ideological views.[154] Thus, when Paul Sniderman and Sean Theriault offered people competing frames, as in the real world, they adopted positions consistent with their preexisting values.[155]

Occasions in which elite commentary is one-sided are rare. Most issues that generate consensual elite discourse arise from external events such as surprise attacks on the United States—for example, the terrorist assaults on September 11, 2001—or its allies—for example, the invasion of Kuwait in 1990. Consensual issues also tend to be new, with few people having committed themselves to a view about them. In his examination of public opinion regarding the Gulf War, John Zaller argues that the president's greatest chance of influencing public opinion is in a crisis (which attracts the public's attention) in which elites articulate a unified message. At other times, most people are too inattentive or too committed to views to be strongly influenced by elite efforts at persuasion.[156]

In addition, for the president to frame issues for the public, people must perceive accurately the frame offered by the White House. There is reason to believe, however, that different people perceive the same message differently. The media is of little help, as it is unlikely to adopt uniformly or reliably the White House's framing of issues. Moreover, with all his personal, ideological, and partisan baggage, no president can assume that all citizens hear the same thing when he speaks. Partisanship is especially likely to bias processing perceptions, interpretations, and responses to the political world.[157]

Language

The new Obama administration was sensitive about the exact wording of its rhetoric. Even during the transition, congressional leaders and incoming officials actively tried to retire that term "stimulus" and use the more marketable "economic recovery program" as the descriptor for the multibillion-dollar economic initiative the president-elect was about to propose.[158]

Obama and his team also tried to scrub George W. Bush's national security lexicon. Although they sent 50,000 more troops to Afghanistan, much as George W. Bush did to Iraq, it was not a "surge." Although they still held people captured on the battlefield at the prison at Guantánamo Bay, Cuba, they no longer termed them "enemy combatants." Although they carried the fight to al Qaeda as their predecessors did, they were implementing "overseas contingency operations" instead of waging a "war on terror." Terrorist attacks became "man-caused disasters."[159]

In the battle over health care reform, the forces backing it had spent years polling and using focus groups to find the precise language that would win over voters. For example, when Obama told grassroots organizers in August 2009 that the mandatory purchase of health insurance would "be affordable, based on a sliding scale," the phrasing precisely mirrored language that had been poll-tested and put before batteries of focus groups by Democratic consultants over the past few years.[160]

In a presentation to House Republicans on May 6, 2009, consultant Frank Luntz, an expert on the language of politics, advised calling the Democratic plan a big government takeover that would deny care, interfere with the "doctor-patient relationship," cost too much, and restrict patients' choices. The next week, senior White House advisor David Axelrod and deputy White House chief of staff Jim Messina visited Senate Democrats and presented polling data on what Americans wanted from a health care plan; they also suggested empha-sizing that the Democrats' health care overhaul would bring down costs, give more people access to coverage, and allow people to keep their plan if they want.[161]

Congressional Democrats were so concerned about the public's lack of re-ceptivity to their proposals that their House and Senate leaders brought in Drew Westen, a psychologist and neuroscientist, to suggest the language they should use to sell their agenda. According to Westin, Democrats should not talk about "the environment," "the unemployed," or "the uninsured." Instead, they should replace those phrases with ones that have more appeal to voters, such as "the air we breathe and the water we drink," "people who've lost their jobs," and "people who used to have insurance." Westen argued that Democrats made a mistake by constantly try to sell policies to voters through reason and facts and ignoring research showing that people respond more to emotional appeals. "You speak to people's core values and concerns," he explained.[162]

Most presidents seek a strong, clear narrative to help them connect with the public and explain the essence of their administrations. Franklin D. Roosevelt's "New Deal" is perhaps the best known modern example. Although Obama came to office as the embodiment of hope and change, disappointments in the performance of the economy and the president's response to it, resistance to his major legislative proposals, and irritation at the continuity of some of his na-tional security policies undermined the utility of that narrative.

Barack Obama, like Bill Clinton, has an eclectic ideology. This complexity, along with his preference for complex explanations,[163] complicated the presi-dent's ability to articulate a clear, simple narrative to frame his presidency in his own terms. In his Inaugural Address, Obama introduced the phrase "new foun-dation" to encapsulate his ambitious program and then repeated it in a wide range of venues over the next few months.[164] The phrase has not yet caught on in the press or the public. Thus, in early 2010, the White House decided it needed to reinvigorate Obama's most successful message of the 2008 campaign: that he was an agent of change.[165]

The lack of a positive narrative, of course, invites opponents to craft a less flattering portrayal. In a question and answer session with the House Republicans in Baltimore on January 29, 2010, the president expressed his frustrations at the framing wars.

> That's why I say if we're going to frame these debates in ways that allow us to solve them, then we can't start off by figuring out A, who's to blame; B, how can we make the American people afraid of the other side? And unfortunately, that's how our politics works right now. And that's how a lot of our discussion works. That's how we start off—every time somebody speaks in Congress, the first thing they do, they stand up and all the talking points—I see Frank Luntz sitting in the front. He's already polled it, and he said . . . I've done a focus group and the way we're going to really box in Obama on this one or make Pelosi look bad on that one. . . . It's all tactics. It's not solving problems.
>
> So the question is, at what point can we have a serious conversation about Medicare and its long-term liability, or a serious . . . conversation about Social Security, or a serious conversation about budget and debt in which we're not simply trying to position ourselves politically? That's what I'm committed to doing. We won't agree all the time in getting it done, but I'm committed to doing it.[166]

Economic Stimulus Bill

In its first major proposal, the White House did not want to impose a bill on Republicans or to let them pick apart its own proposal. So it chose to let the House and Senate work their wills on the stimulus bill. One consequence of this strategy was a bill that Republicans and even some Democrats criticized for focusing too heavily on spending that would not provide an economic stimulus. Because the package was sold mostly as a short-term employment boost, the huge sums for long-term investments in health care, energy, education, and infrastructure were vulnerable to the charge that they did not immediately create many jobs.

Working with Congress behind closed doors to deal with the rising opposition, the president left a vacuum on 24-hour cable news that conservative critics eagerly exploited.[167] "We are definitely losing the framing of what this thing is," fretted one veteran Democratic operative.[168] Nothing sells news like confrontation with the president.

Over the first two weeks of the Obama presidency, the media's use of the unflattering term "pork" in association with the stimulus bill increased about 400 percent.[169] The White House was losing control of the debate as the Republicans framed discourse on the bill in terms of wasteful spending. Indeed, by the end of the first week in February, 49 percent of the public reported that what it had been hearing about the stimulus plan was "mostly negative," while only 29 percent replied that what they were hearing was "mostly positive."[170]

In response to the unfavorable portrayal of his priority policy, the president launched a media blitz. As the centerpiece of his campaign to reframe the debate on the stimulus proposal on his terms, the president held his first prime-time press conference—in the grand setting of the White House East Room—on February 9, where he adopted a sharper tone in making his case for the bill. Earlier in the day, Obama traveled to one of the most economically distressed corners of the nation, Elkhart, Indiana. The next day, he traveled to Fort Myers, Florida, and then moved on to East Peoria, Illinois.

The stimulus was simply too big and too complex to frame easily. If the administration had split the legislation into several bills, including a big tax increase, infrastructure spending, education, scientific and medical investment, and a clean energy bill, the president would probably have found framing easier.[171] The political necessity of bundling the components into one massive bill prohibited such an option, however.

Health Care

On health care, Obama's team won early, high marks for diverging from the Clinton approach by emphasizing the need to control costs and improve choices and coverage for those who were already insured instead of making the moral-duty argument about the need to cover the uninsured. He more often cited as potential beneficiaries the working and middle classes rather than the uninsured poor. Indeed, Obama never promised universal coverage except for children. Nevertheless, we have seen that many in the public were concerned about changes in the quality and cost of their health care.

Obama addressed the self-interest argument by emphasizing how rising health care costs affect people with insurance, not just the uninsured. Without an overhaul, he explained, health insurance premiums would eat up bigger chunks of middle-income paychecks and threaten even comfortable Americans with bankruptcy because of the uncovered costs of one major illness. When he spoke of covering the uninsured, Obama argued that doing so would also help the insured because hospitals, doctors, and insurers would no longer have to pass on unpaid expenses in higher premiums and prices to paying patients. Mindful that supporters would not agree on all details, Obama distilled his position to a frame involving three principles: reduce cost, ensure quality, and provide choice, including a public insurance option.[172]

Yet for all the president's efforts, the bill's sticker shock drew taxpayers' attention to the main expense, which was covering the uninsured. Democrats' plans would expand Medicaid for the poor and subsidize both low-income workers buying insurance and small businesses seeking coverage for employees. In addition, opponents aggressively portrayed his overhaul plan as a government takeover that could limit Americans' ability to choose their doctors and course of treatment while also bankrupting the country.

In response, Obama started talking more about health insurance reform instead of health care reform, a change calculated to appeal to the satisfied majority. He spoke often to people's personal stake in the health care system, assuring them that they would not have to switch doctors or plans if they liked what they had, that their costs would not increase, and bureaucrats would not be making health care decisions.

The president wanted the House and Senate to pass legislation before the August recess, but neither did so. Legislative wrangling, a well-coordinated Republican opposition, the sheer complexity of a policy dealing with a sector that consumes about 17 percent of the nation's economy, and the public's general concern that change would diminish the benefits most people were receiving took a toll on the president's bold ambitions. The White House's stress on abstract cost controls in order to address the cost of retooling the system also made it difficult to rally support. Obama initially seemed to conclude that because of the recession, he could sell health care reform as an economic fix.[173] If so, he was wrong. In addition, the administration was pinning its hopes on bills working their way through Congress that had become the objects of bitter partisan rancor.

With Republicans ridiculing the administration's effort, portraying it as big government meddling in personal health decisions and a risky experiment, the White House recalibrated its message. Although Obama's central goals remained expanding coverage to the estimated 47 million Americans who lacked it and controlling the costs of health care, including Medicare and Medicaid, the White House began emphasizing consumer-friendly aspects of health care reform. Guided by polls,[174] the administration framed the health care debate as a campaign against insurance companies—prohibiting practices that made buying coverage impossible or excessively expensive for many who are sick, older, or had a prior illness. Democrats, led by Obama, focused on communicating to people who had insurance that reform would bring a degree of security and stability that they lacked. The White House Web site listed eight "Health Insurance Consumer Protections" that would "bring you and your family peace of mind." Democrats also zeroed in on the health insurance industry's hefty profits.

In early February 2010, the White House got news from California on which the administration would seize. Anthem Blue Cross had notified policyholders that some would see an increase in premiums of up to 39 percent by March 1. The White House latched onto a story line that might sell their plan: why people with insurance should care about the health care bill and its cost controls.[175]

At about the same time, the president read a letter from Natoma Canfield aloud in a meeting with insurance executives. In seven poignant paragraphs, she wrote that sixteen years after being treated for cancer, she could no longer afford her health insurance and was terrified she would get sick and lose the house her parents built. Canfield's story allowed Obama to personalize the debate, reminding Americans that it was not just about numbers, but lives. The White House shared her letter with the news media. Within an hour, camera crews were at Canfield's door.[176]

Nevertheless, the challenge remained of on one hand stressing how people's existing relationships with doctors and health plans would not change if they were satisfied with them, and at the same time emphasizing that it was necessary to change the system to stop the trajectory in health spending. The increasingly harsh rhetoric against the health insurance industry was a departure for the White House, which began its reform campaign by trying to win over constituency groups—doctors, pharmaceutical companies, hospitals, and insurers among them—to neutralize historically powerful opponents of change. Moreover, insurers said they favored reform, just not a government-run insurance plan to compete against the private sector. The tough talk risked sending them from the negotiating table.

Post-Massachusetts

After Republican Scott Brown handily defeated Democrat Martha Coakley in the Massachusetts special election to fill Ted Kennedy's Senate seat, upending Obama's plans for a health bill by stripping Democrats of their 60-vote supermajority, the White House began to chart a new course in its public posture. The White House interpreted the results as a sign that Americans were angry and frustrated over the economy.

The president himself, in an interview with ABC, described a feeling of "remoteness and detachment" that many Americans had toward policymakers in Washington. Furthermore, the president told ABC anchor George Stephanopoulos,

> If there's one thing that I regret this year, is that we were so busy just getting stuff done and dealing with the immediate crises that were in front of us, that I think we lost some of that sense of speaking directly to the American people about what their core values are and why we have to make sure those institutions are matching up with those values. And that I do think is a mistake of mine.[177]

Thus, Obama began what his aides termed a "White House to Main Street Tour." This new public relations effort was designed to reframe the administration as one focused on the economy and reform of the financial services industry and thus to show that Obama was back in touch with ordinary Americans. The president traveled to the Cleveland suburb of Elyria to spread the message that his presidency was now all about jobs, jobs, jobs. He visited companies that made precision metal components, wind turbines, and sporting goods and then held a town hall meeting at Lorain Community College. Everywhere he promoted his economy recovery package.

At the White House and during his tour, the president struck a populist tone to combat perceptions of the administration as being too cozy with Wall Street. From this take, the enemy was big money, not big government. In announcing a plan to impose new restrictions on the nation's biggest banks, he promised that if Wall Street wanted to fight back, "it's a fight I'm ready to have." "Never again, he declared, "will the American taxpayer be held hostage by a bank that is 'too big to fail.'"[178] The president also proposed a tax on about fifty of the nation's biggest banks to recoup any losses from the bailout, and administration officials spread the word that Obama's proposal to create an independent consumer protection agency was "non-negotiable."

Health care reform was not to die, however, and after an intense effort on the part of the president and Speaker Nancy Pelosi (discussed in detail in chapter 5), it passed on a party line vote. Skepticism over the health care overhaul persisted, however, and the president and his allies began orchestrating an elaborate campaign to sell the public on the law. Convinced that his communications effort needed shoring up, Obama personally recruited Stephanie Cutter, an experienced Democratic communications strategist, to run the effort. The core goal was to reassure senior citizens, who were more likely to vote in the midterm elections and were the age cohort most skeptical of the bill.[179]

On June 8, the president traveled to Wheaton, Maryland, to conduct a nationally televised question-and-answer session with older citizens located in town hall meetings around the country to trumpet one of the law's most popular features: $250 rebate checks to help Medicare beneficiaries pay for prescription drugs. The timing of this event was no accident—the first checks were mailed two days later.

Supportive private organizations, including an ambitious initiative by Anita Dunn, Obama's former communications director, and Andrew Grossman, a top Democratic strategist, began orchestrating campaigns to echo the White House message. In addition, the AARP included an eight-page insert about the law in its newspaper, which reaches 40 million people. Health Care for America Now distributed leaflets at high school and college graduations, and Families USA put on "road shows" in cities around the country, where officials from the federal Department of Health and Human Services and the Centers for Medicare and Medicaid Services conducted presentations on important features of the legislation.[180]

Financial Regulation

After health care reform passed, financial regulation became the president's top legislative priority. Both parties jockeyed for position. Obama and his allies portrayed Republicans as handmaidens of Wall Street and themselves as defenders of average Americans. Republicans, on the other hand, accused Democrats of trying to strangle the market and institutionalize bailouts.

Despite the financial crisis, the president faced challenges in obtaining public support for a new regulatory regime. Americans did not readily translate their anxieties about the economy into concern for regulating big financial institutions.[181] Gallup found that the public, and especially Republicans, were considerably more likely to support regulating "Wall Street banks" than "regulating large banks and major financial institutions."[182] As we have seen, the public was also concerned about expanding government.

Obama seemed to recognize this public relations challenge and focused on clarifying the connection between personal financial concerns and regulating Wall Street. In the culmination of a month-long acceleration of his involvement with financial reform, he spoke in New York City on April 22, 2010. The president carefully framed the issue as one in which improving the economy required "addressing some of the underlying problems that led to this turmoil and devastation in the first place." Fixing these problems meant increased regulation of financial institutions because "What happens on Wall Street has real consequences across the country, across our economy."[183]

The president played another populist card when he pointed out that the financial industry had deployed squadrons of lobbyists to try to stop the financial reform bill. "I am sure that some of these lobbyists work for some of you," he told the Wall Street audience. "I want to urge you to join us, instead of fighting us."

The next week, Obama embarked on a new phase of his "Wall Street to Main Street" tour. However, in the week of May 3–9, the Times Square bomb plot accounted for 25 percent of the news hole, while the oil spill in the Gulf of Mexico filled another 20 percent. The economic crisis in general was only 13 percent, with a focus on the brief 1,000-point drop in the Dow Jones Industrial Average and the fiscal crisis in Greece.[184] Once again, the president encountered challenges to framing a key issue on his agenda.

Responding to Critics

One of the White House's biggest challenges in the Internet age is dealing with incendiary criticism that spreads through the population at the speed of light. Sarah Palin's claim on her Facebook page that the White House was trying to establish "death panels" for the elderly as part of health care reform, and assertions that the president was not born in the United States and thus not a legitimate president, received wide circulation. Worse, these vilifications found many ready to believe them, even in the face of clear evidence to the contrary. The insulation of the right in the media echo chamber makes it difficult to reach those predisposed to oppose the president, and the speed of circulation of provocative charges makes it difficult to get ahead of a story.

When critics lashed out at Obama for speaking to public school students at the beginning of the 2009 school year, accusing him of wanting to indoctrinate children to his politics, his aides reached out to progressive Web sites such as the Huffington Post, liberal bloggers, and Democratic pundits to make their case to a friendly audience. The controversy escalated, but by the time it was over, White House advisors thought they had emerged with the upper hand. The speech was the most-viewed live video on any government Web site in history, and they were pleased with the media coverage of the event.[185]

When Bloomberg News ran a headline suggesting that Obama was indifferent to the issue of bonuses for bankers, aides immediately posted a rebuttal on the White House blog. They e-mailed online news sites to change the headline and asked progressive bloggers to convey their interpretation of the president's remarks.[186]

White House officials wanted to anticipate conservative attacks and be ready to respond the moment they threatened to balloon into major stories. Yet they acknowledged having limited success. "In a world with Fox News and Rush Limbaugh and the Drudge Report and everything else that makes up the right-wing noise machine, nothing is clean and nothing is simple," a senior administration official said. "You don't stomp a story out. You ride the wave and try to steer it to safe water."[187]

One technique for steering the wave is to counter bad news with more news, or at least more information.[188] Yet information is not always readily available. In February 2010, Joe Sestak, a candidate for the Democratic senatorial nomination in Pennsylvania, told a local host in an oblique fashion that he had received a job offer from the White House as an incentive to drop his primary bid against Senator Arlen Specter. In a world in which party leaders and campaign operatives routinely try to dissuade potential candidates from running, it would seem like this would not be much of a story.

In highly polarized Washington, however, the opposition takes advantage of every possibility to make points. Reporters repeatedly asked White House press secretary Robert Gibbs in the intervening months about Sestak's allegation, but he deflected comment. As the story became more significant in the wake of Sestak's primary victory, the statements out of the White House grew increasingly opaque. Republicans happily cited the Sestak allegation to undermine the president's claim to be bringing greater transparency and accountability to Washington. Whether the White House was correct in waiting until it had all the facts to avoid a mistake or inconsistency in its statements, its extended silence on the matter created a public relations problem for a time.

On April 20, 2010, an explosion aboard the *Deepwater Horizon*, a drilling rig working for the oil company BP on a well one mile below the surface of the Gulf of Mexico, led to the largest oil spill in American history. The president, indeed, the federal government, was all but powerless to resolve the disaster, given the sheer technological challenge of plugging a leak. Nevertheless, Obama had to show that he was engaged and in command of the crisis.

On June 14 and 15, the president made a two-day tour of three Gulf States and then returned to Washington to deliver a 20-minute prime-time, nationally televised speech from the Oval Office. His first use of the solemn setting of the Oval Office escalated his personal engagement to a new level. Moreover, his meeting the next day with BP executives and his pressuring them to create an escrow account to compensate businesses and individuals for their losses from the oil spill in the Gulf of Mexico telegraphed a decisiveness of action. Famous for his "no drama" style, the president had to take pains to show that he was "furious" at BP and ready to compel it to act.

The White House also had to worry about protecting its credibility, its most precious resource in a time of crisis. For weeks, federal officials stood alongside BP executives at briefings, reinforcing doubts about who was really in charge and putting the government in the position of vouching, by its mere presence, for BP's veracity. After it became clear that there were gross underestimates of the amount of oil spilled into the Gulf, that BP had not followed industry standards in drilling the well, and that various efforts to cap the well had failed, the White House put an end to the joint appearances in early June.[189]

In general, it was difficult for the White House to win in such a situation. Some complained that the president was not engaged enough in the details of the response to the oil spill (as in professing not to know about the resignation of Elizabeth Birnbaum, head of the Minerals Management Service), while others criticized him for getting bogged down in them. Some argued that he should spend more time in the Gulf Coast making common cause with its residents, while others viewed his repeated trips there as mere publicity stunts.

Before Obama's trip to Asia in November 2010, the Drudge Report picked up an article from an unnamed Indian source claiming that the president's trip would cost the taxpayers $200 million a day, more than the war in Afghanistan. Republican Representative Michele Bachmann repeated this ridiculous figure on CNN, adding, "He's taking 2,000 people with him. He'll be renting over 870 rooms in India." The charge also quickly made its way into conservative talk radio, including shows hosted by Rush Limbaugh, Glenn Beck, and Michael Savage. The administration responded forcefully to the story, but not before millions of Americans heard the absurd charge delivered by authoritative sounding commentators who never checked the facts.

Conclusion

The Obama White House was aggressive in its efforts to lead the public. Nevertheless, it faced the frustrations all administrations experience in focusing the public's attention, reaching the public with its messages, framing issues to its advantage, and mobilizing its supporters.

It is difficult for the president to focus the public's attention. Despite the fact that rhetoric steadily flows from the White House, chief executives disperse their public remarks over a broad range of policies, and wide audiences hear only a small portion of them. The president faces strong competition for the public's attention from previous commitments of government, congressional initiatives, opposing elites, and the mass media. Equally important, presidents often compete with themselves as they address a range of issues.

Reaching the public is a continual and sizable challenge for the president. Most of the public is not attuned to listening to the White House, and it is now easier than ever to tune out the president. Many choose to do so. Many people do not accurately receive or perceive the president's messages. Technology has created new opportunities for reaching the public, and the administration has acted aggressively to exploit them. Nevertheless, most communications over the new media are received by supporters and are of little help in expanding the president's base.

Mobilizing these supporters has not been easy for President Obama. Technology may reinforce the converted, but it does not seem to ensure their political activity. The enthusiasm of the president's supporters in the 2008 campaign has not translated into sustained efforts to enact the president's proposals.

The president cannot depend on framing how the public views his policies and his performance. He faces committed, well-organized, and well-funded opponents who offer alternative frames, and many people do not perceive accurately the frames offered by the White House. In addition, it has been difficult for a president with a broad agenda and an eclectic ideology to create a clear narrative for his presidency.

Coupling the unfavorable context for leading the public we explored in chapter 1 with the difficulties of going public we have found in this chapter, we should not expect the president to have great success in obtaining the public's support. I examine the White House's level of success in public leadership in the next chapter.

CHAPTER 3

Evaluating Strategic Choices

LEADING THE PUBLIC

THE OBAMA WHITE HOUSE believes in the power of the presidential pulpit. More importantly, it believes that the president is an irresistible persuader. According to the president's top counselor, David Axelrod, "I don't think there's been a President since Kennedy whose ability to move issues and people through a speech has been comparable."[1] This faith in presidential persuasion underlies the administration's decision to try to move a large agenda simultaneously and explains its response to political problems.

It also underlies the president's views of party leadership. He wants to transcend partisan distinctions, rather than make them permanent. As one of his pollsters put it, "It gets back to being a transformational leader. A party leader isn't about transformation." The president typically declines to speak at the traditional Jefferson-Jackson dinners where state Democratic parties gather to raise money from the faithful. He prefers venues where he can reach voters who are not party regulars.[2] In other words, he has been more interested in persuasion than in mobilization of the already converted.

When times get tough, Obama goes public.[3] In the campaign season, he confronted the issue of Jeremiah Wright's incendiary comments with an extended address on race relations. When the White House encountered resistance to its stimulus program, the president held his first prime-time press conference. Rather than attempting to persuade individual members of Congress on his record-setting FY 2010 budget, he traveled outside Washington, appearing at town hall meetings, news conferences, and on late-night talk shows.[4] When support for health care reform was falling, the president delivered a prime-time televised address before a joint session of Congress. And when the president made his decision to send 30,000 additional American troops to Afghanistan, he delivered a prime-time televised address from West Point.

The history of the presidency clearly shows that expectations of transforming politics and creating opportunities for change through rhetoric and other public relations efforts are likely to be disappointed. Nevertheless, every president operates in a unique context and analysts must account for it. In chapter 1, I analyzed the climate of public opinion in the early Obama presidency and predicted that he was unlikely to enjoy substantial long-term success in moving the public in his direction, despite his impressive public relations skills. Issues that have ideological overtones should prove a tough sell, especially during periods of highly polarized politics. Polarization, of course, leads us to expect considerably more support from Democrats than Republicans on most issues, and more responsiveness as well.

In this chapter, I focus on some of the major policy initiatives of the Obama administration to determine whether the president was able to move the public in his direction to create opportunities for change. These policies include the bank bailout, stimulus plan, automobile company bailout, and limiting executive pay, as well as more general aspects of spending and economic policy. I also examine opinions on health care reform, climate change, increasing troop levels in Afghanistan, and closing the prison at Guantánamo Bay. Finally, because of the critical role of party support in the Obama presidency, I look at the changes in party identification and evaluations.

The Economy

The new president had little choice but to give priority to the economy. With both banks and mortgages failing at an alarming rate, unemployment rising rapidly, and automobile companies teetering on the verge of bankruptcy, Obama had to act and act fast. Programs designed to deal with unemployment are not inherently unpopular. Moreover, it seemed reasonable to conclude that in a time of severe economic crisis, when Americans were seeking reassurance from the White House, the public would defer to the president.

On the other hand, many of the economic policies of the early Obama administration dealt with fundamental questions regarding government intervention in the economy. The policies were also extraordinarily expensive, resulting in massive deficit spending. In light of our findings in chapter 1, we should expect that these policies would be polarizing, with many in the public finding them deeply troubling. Some of the proposals also seemed to reward those who had caused the financial crisis in the first place, irritating almost everyone.

The White House was under no illusion that "bailouts" would be popular. As Joel Benenson, Obama's lead pollster, put it,

> These were not matters of choice. . . . None of these reflect an agenda he campaigned on and, in fact, in doing a lot of them, he was very cognizant of the fact that they had big political downsides, that they weren't popular with the American people.[5]

Senior presidential advisor David Axelrod went further:

> Believe me, if we were charting this administration as a political exercise, the first thing we would have done would not have been a massive recovery act, stabilizing the banks and helping to keep the auto companies from collapsing. Those would not even be the first hundred things he [the president] would want to do.

But, he added, the president, confronted with "breathtaking challenges," did not have the luxury of moving more slowly or methodically.[6]

Bank Bailout and TARP Funds

The financial crisis had not abated by the time of the 2008–2009 presidential transition, and President Bush, accommodating a request from President-elect Obama, formally asked for the release of the remaining half of the Troubled Asset Relief Program (TARP) funds to help stabilize the financial sector. Congress had written the law so that it required releasing the funds fifteen days following a presidential request unless Congress passed a resolution blocking their release. A number of congressional leaders, including both Democrats and Republicans, threatened to do just that, citing concerns that the Obama administration needed to be much more explicit about what is going to be done with the second half of the appropriated TARP money. These concerns in part reflected criticism that spending of the first half of the TARP funds was badly mismanaged, and were also a response to a wave of populist anger that had been building since the Treasury Department first proposed Wall Street bailouts in September. Obama made a personal trip to Capitol Hill to lobby for release of the funds and to provide more details about how he intended to spend the money.

In general, the threat of blocking the release of the TARP funds appears to be one with which the average American was sympathetic. The president-elect met resistance, even in the midst of high approval for his performance during the transition. The public did not defer to Obama. Given three choices of what to do with the remaining funds, 62 percent, including majorities of Democrats as well as Republicans, said Congress should block the release unless Obama provided even more details about how he would spend the funds, and another 12 percent replied that Congress should block the funds entirely. Only 20 percent favored Congress' simply allowing the release of the funds.[7]

In February, with Obama in the White House, opinion was decidedly negative regarding the bank bailout. Only 39 percent favored "giving aid to U.S. banks and financial companies in danger of failing." Fifty-nine percent of the public were opposed.[8] By March, 41 percent of the public adopted the extreme option and were willing to allow the nation's largest banks to go out of business rather than give them any funds.[9]

By January 2010, the public overwhelmingly believed that the benefits of the unprecedented federal spending were accruing mostly to large banks, major corporations, and wealthy individuals, but not to average people (see table 3.1). In April, a plurality of the public felt the loans to troubled banks did not prevent a more severe crisis.[10] (The president knew it would be difficult to prove the counterfactual of what the economy would have been like with no bailouts.)[11] Throughout 2009 and 2010, the public thought the bank bailout was a bad idea.[12]

TABLE 3.1.
Beneficiaries of Economic Policies

Beneficiary	% Agreeing
Banks and investment companies	40
Major corporations	20
Wealthy individuals	16
Middle-class individuals	9
Low-income individuals	8
No one	2
Don't know/refused	5

Source: Allstate/*National Journal* Heartland Monitor poll, January 3–7, 2010.

Question: "Who do you think has benefitted most from the federal government's response to the financial crisis over the last 12 months?"

Financial Regulation

Subsidizing banks was one thing. Regulating them was something else. The same anger at financial institutions that underlay opposition to bailing them out supported restricting their activities. Throughout 2009 and 2010, the public supported the principle of stricter government regulations on major financial companies and institutions.[13] No White House efforts to influence public opinion were necessary to convince the public it did not want a repeat of the financial meltdown of 2008.

Perhaps because of its complexity, there was limited polling on the legislation regulating financial institutions that finally passed Congress in July 2010. Polls taken in the late spring and early summer found that majorities favored the bill.[14]

Nevertheless, a plurality thought the legislation did more to protect the financial industry than consumers.[15] Moreover, at the time the financial regulation reform bill passed Congress, only 44 percent of the public approved the way the president was handling regulation of the financial industry, while 50 percent disapproved. Majorities of Republicans (81 percent) and Independents (53 percent) gave Obama negative reviews.[16]

Stimulus Bill

The president's first major initiative once in office was a $787 billion economic stimulus package. Obama addressed the stimulus issue before a nationwide audience at his first prime-time news conference and conducted town hall meetings in Elkhart, Indiana, and Fort Myers, Florida, as part of his efforts to help sell the public on the urgency of passing a stimulus package. Unsurprisingly, conservative media personalities offered up blistering critiques.

TABLE 3.2.
Support for Stimulus Plan

Dates of Poll	% Approve/Good	% Disapprove/Bad	% No Opinion
January 6–7, 2009	53	36	11
January 27, 2009	52	37	11
February 4, 2009	52	38	10
February 10, 2009	59	33	8

Source: Gallup Poll.

Questions:

January 6–7, 2009: "Do you favor or oppose Congress passing a new $775 billion economic stimulus program as soon as possible after Barack Obama takes Office?"

January 27 and February 4, 2009: "As you may know, Congress is considering a new economic stimulus package of at least $800 billion. Do you favor or oppose Congress passing this legislation?"

February 10, 2009: "As you may know, Congress is considering a new stimulus package of at least $800 billion. Do you favor or oppose Congress passing this legislation?"

On January 27, 2009, the day before the House voted on his stimulus plan, in the midst of an historic economic crisis, after an extensive public relations effort by the White House, and in the glow of the presidential honeymoon, the Gallup Poll found that only 52 percent of the public favored Congress passing the bill. Although 73 percent of Democrats favored passage, less than half of the rest of the country agreed—only 46 percent of Independents and 29 percent of Republicans.[17] Moreover, public opinion on the stimulus bill was virtually identical to where it stood three weeks earlier[18] (see table 3.2). The public had not moved in the president's direction. A week later, the public still had not moved.[19]

At the end of January, Gallup asked whether people supported the president's stimulus plan as Obama proposed it, wanted "major changes," or wanted Congress to reject it altogether. Only 38 percent of the public supported passing Obama's stimulus plan as he proposed it, while 54 percent wanted it passed with "major changes" or rejected altogether. Support was tepid even among Democrats, of whom only 59 percent supported passage of the plan as Obama proposed it. Only 37 percent of Independents and 13 percent of Republicans joined them. Forty percent of Independents wanted major changes. Even worse, 62 percent of those following the issue "very closely" (31 percent of the public) favored major changes or rejection of the plan, while 50 percent of those "following somewhat closely" (26 percent of the public) held that view. The president's support was greatest among those who were not paying much attention.[20]

Near the end of Congress's consideration of the bill (it cleared Congress on February 13), Pew asked the public about "the economic stimulus plan being proposed by the President." It found that 51 percent of those who had heard about the plan said it was a good idea, while 34 percent said it was a bad idea. This support was *down* from 57 percent of those who had heard about the proposal viewing it positively, compared with just 22 percent who viewed it negatively, three weeks earlier. In February, support for the fiscal stimulus proposal was much lower than it was in January among those who have heard "a lot" about the economic stimulus (representing 46 percent of the public in February). Support among this group dropped from 63 to 49 percent, while opposition increased from 25 to 41 percent. Among those who had heard only a little about the plan (45 percent of the public in February), support decreased only 1 percentage point, from 53 to 52 percent, while opposition increased from 21 to 28 percent.[21] The CBS News/*New York Times* Poll also found that support for the stimulus bill dropped between mid-January and early February, where it stood at just 51 percent.[22]

There is one bit of evidence of presidential success in moving the public. In a poll on February 10, Gallup found that 59 percent of the public supported the stimulus bill (table 3.2). Whether this uptick in support was the result of the president's prime-time press conference the previous evening or was the product of the volatile nature of one-day polls is unclear. Gallup reported that most of the newfound support for the bill came from Democrats, who increased their support from 70 percent a week earlier to 82 percent.[23] Perhaps preaching to the choir paid off.[24]

Whatever the nature of the opinion in February, Americans soon had reservations about the economic stimulus plan. In August, 51 percent of the public, including most Republicans and Independents, said it would have been better for the government to have spent less money to stimulate the economy. In addition, a substantial proportion of the public (46 percent) said they were "very worried" that money from the economic stimulus plan was being wasted. Only 20 percent said they were not worried about wasteful stimulus spending. The public also harbored doubts about the effectiveness of the stimulus plan. Fifty-seven percent of the public thought the plan was having no effect or was making the economy worse. Whether or not the White House wanted to consider a second stimulus bill, the public served as a serious constraint, with 65 percent opposed, including 67 percent of Independents.[25]

The administration felt it was acting responsibly, but the country was not listening. The stimulus bill preserved jobs in state and local governments, but the preservation of jobs is inherently not particularly visible. The tax cuts did not arrive in notable single checks (which tend to be saved) but rather in small amounts in paychecks. The White House established a board to guard against waste and corruption, but this action had the consequence of slowing down the awarding of contracts, slowing the impact of the stimulus in the process.

Thus, the public was even less supportive as time went on. In January 2010, 56 percent of the public opposed the stimulus bill while only 42 percent favored it.[26] The following April, only 33 percent of the public felt the stimulus bill had helped the job situation.[27] By September 2010, 66 percent of the public thought the bill had made the recovery worse or had had no impact.[28] "There is real power there," White House senior advisor David Axelrod said of the president's public relations efforts. "But it's not a magic wand. The bully pulpit does not put people to work."[29]

Automobile Company Bailout

In December 2008, the federal government gave General Motors and Chrysler $17 billion in loans to keep them from going bankrupt. In February 2009, the automakers asked for more than $21 billion in additional loans as part of restructuring plans they submitted to the Treasury Department. In April, the Obama administration lent each automaker additional funds, and on June 1, the federal government announced that it was loaning General Motors $50 billion and would become the majority owner of the company.

The *New York Times* reported that Obama and his aides had "enormous faith in his capacity for communicating with the American people." When his advisors warned of a popular backlash against the auto bailout, he expressed confidence that he could explain it to the public.[30] It appears that the president was overly optimistic. Gallup reported that Americans were "remarkably well-informed" about the financial status of the Big Three U.S. automakers. And they did not like what they saw. At no point did a majority of Americans support loans for the automakers (see table 3.3). Moreover, support declined somewhat after Obama became president. At every point, majorities opposed the president. By June 2009, only 41 percent of the public approved of the way Obama was handling "the problems facing the auto industry."[31] In May 2010, 61 percent of the public persisted in the view that the government should not have helped the automakers.[32]

Deficit Spending

Polling organizations did not regularly ask questions about support for the president's stimulus plan once it passed, and they stopped questioning about the automobile company bailout in June 2009. They did continue to inquire about the public's views of the consequences of these policies, however. The extraordinary costs of the stimulus plan and the banking and auto-industry rescue packages dramatically increased the federal deficit, which was already mounting during the Bush administration. It is hardly surprising that Americans appeared to be suffering from sticker shock. Alarmed at the amount of government expenditures to boost the economy, by early summer a clear ma-

TABLE 3.3.
Support for Loans to Automakers

Date of Poll	% Favor/Right	% Oppose/Wrong	% No Opinion/Unsure
November 13–16, 2008	47	49	4
December 3–7, 2008	39	54	7
December 4–7, 2008	43	51	6
February 20–22, 2009A	25	72	3
February 20–22, 2009B	41	58	1
March 9–12, 2009	30	63	7
March 27–29, 2009	39	59	2
June 9–10, 2009	41	55	5
June 10–14, 2009	36	58	6
June 12–15, 2009	39	53	8

Sources and Questions:

Gallup polls, November 13–16, and December 4–7, 2008: "Would you favor or oppose the federal government giving major financial assistance to the Big Three U.S. automotive companies if they are close to going broke or declaring bankruptcy?"

Pew Research Center poll, December 3–7, 2008: "Do you think it is the right thing or the wrong thing for the government to spend billions of dollars in loans to General Motors, Ford, and Chrysler to keep them in business?"

Gallup poll, February 20–22, 2009A: ". . . Earlier this week, General Motors and Chrysler asked the government for $21 billion in additional loans as part of restructuring plans they submitted to the Treasury Department. Do you think Congress should or should not approve these additional loans?"

Gallup poll, February 20–22, 2009B: ". . . Please tell me whether, in general, you favor or oppose the government giving aid to U.S. automakers who are in danger of going bankrupt."

Pew Research Center poll, March 9–12, 2009: "Do you think it is the right thing or the wrong thing for the government to spend billions of dollars in loans to General Motors and Chrysler to keep them in business?"

Gallup poll, March 27–29, 2009: "Do you approve or disapprove of the federal loans given to General Motors and Chrysler last year to help them avoid bankruptcy?"

Gallup poll, June 9–10, 2009: "As you may know, the U.S. government is investing $50 billion in General Motors and will own 60% of that company when General Motors emerges from bankruptcy. All in all, do you approve or disapprove of these government actions?"

Pew Research Center poll, June 10–14, 2009: "Do you approve or disapprove of the government spending billions of dollars in an effort to keep General Motors and Chrysler in business?"

Wall Street Journal/NBC News poll, June 12–15, 2009: "Do you approve or disapprove of the federal government providing loans and financial assistance to Chrysler and GM?"

jority of the public felt the government should focus more on reducing the deficit than on stimulating the economy.[33]

It is logical to expect that the public would not only be wary of the president's spending policies, but that they would disapprove of his handling of the deficit as well. By July 2009, a clear plurality, followed soon by a majority, of the

TABLE 3.4.
Obama Handling of the Deficit

Date of Poll	% Approve	% Disapprove	% No Opinion
March 26–29, 2009	52	43	5
April 21–24, 2009	51	43	6
June 18–21, 2009	48	48	5
July 15–18, 2009	43	49	8
August 13–17, 2009	41	53	5
September 10–12, 2009	39	55	6
October 15–18, 2009	45	51	4
November 12–15, 2009	42	53	5
December 10–13, 2009	37	56	6
January 12–15, 2010	38	56	6
February 4–8, 2010	40	56	4
March 23–26, 2010	43	52	5
April 22–25, 2010	40	55	5
June 3–6, 2010	39	56	6
July 7–11, 2010	40	56	4
August 30–September 2, 2010	39	58	4
December 9–12, 2010	38	55	7
January 13–16, 2011	43	44	6
March 10–13, 2011	39	55	6
April 14–17, 2011	39	58	3
June 2–5, 2011	33	61	6
July 14–17, 2011	38	60	2

Source: ABC News/*Washington Post* Poll.
Question: "Do you approve of the way Barack Obama is handling the federal budget deficit?"
Asked of half the sample except March 2011.

public disapproved of Obama's handling of the deficit issue (table 3.4). This lack of support was not a momentary blip in opinion. The president has suffered majority disapproval ever since.

Limiting Executive Pay

There was one Obama policy related to the economy that the public clearly supported. There had been considerable public anger over executives who received large paydays while their companies teetered on the brink of collapse and required government money to survive. The most prominent example of taxpayers subsidizing wealthy executives occurred when many top executives at the insurance company AIG, the recipient of the largest amount of government bailout money, received substantial bonuses. In conjunction with the economic stimulus legislation, the Treasury Department put limits on the pay of executives at companies receiving federal bailout money. A federal "pay czar" had to approve their pay plans, and their bonuses could be no greater than one-third of their total compensation. Most Americans (59 percent) endorsed government action to limit executive pay at major companies.[34]

Handling the Economy

Overall, the president maintained general support for his handling of the economy for seven months, despite a severe recession. He was helped, of course, by the fact that most people blamed George W. Bush and Wall Street for the economic downturn.[35] By November 2009, however, he was below 50 percent approval (see table 3.5), sinking below 40 percent approval in October 2010 and the first half of 2011.

Health Care Reform

The biggest legislative battle of the early Obama administration was health care reform. Substantially changing any policy that dealt with 17 percent of the nation's GDP was going to be difficult. Doing so in a context of highly polarized partisan politics, enormous budget deficits, and broad skepticism about government activism only made matters worse for the White House. Nevertheless, the president forged ahead. He faced stiff opposition from the beginning. Republicans had found their voice in opposing his stimulus bill and budget and did not hesitate to mobilize against the Democrats' health care proposals.

Despite the president's efforts to address the public's misgivings in speeches, news conferences, town hall-style meetings, and interviews, the public did not respond. Instead, it displayed a lack of support for Obama and what the public perceived as his health care plan. It is true that he did not endorse a specific health care plan from among the many bills working their way through House and Senate committees during the spring and summer of 2009. It is possible that some well-informed Americans might have trouble answering a question about "Obama's plan." Nevertheless, we have seen that he was actively advocating health care reform in this period. Table 3.6 gives us a general sense of Americans' impressions of whatever they believed his plan to be.

The NBC/*Wall Street Journal* poll question is especially appropriate for our use because it offered "no opinion" as an option. Opinions were likely to be soft early in the summer because few Americans were closely following the debate

TABLE 3.5.
Obama Handling of the Economy

Poll Dates	% Approve	% Disapprove	% Unsure
February 2–4, 2009	55	24	21
February 18–22, 2009	57	32	11
March 21–16, 2009	56	33	11
March 20–22, 2009	61	29	10
April 1–5, 2009	56	34	10
April 22–26, 2009	61	29	10
May 6–12, 2009	56	33	11
June 12–16, 2009	57	35	8
July 9–12, 2009	48	44	8
July 24–28, 2009	51	41	8
August 27–31, 2009	53	41	6
September 19–23, 2009	50	40	10
October 5–8, 2009	54	38	8
November 13–16, 2009	49	43	8
December 4–8, 2009	47	43	10
January 6–10, 2010	41	47	12
February 5–10, 2010	42	52	6
March 18–21, 2010	45	45	10
April 5–12, 2010	43	46	11
April 28–May 2, 2010	48	47	6
May 20–24, 2010	43	48	9
June 16–20, 2010	45	48	7
July 9–12, 2010	40	54	6
August 20–24, 2010	44	48	8
September 10–14, 2010	41	51	8
October 1–5, 2010	38	50	12
October 22–26, 2010	42	40	8
November 7–10, 2010	40	53	7
November 29–December 2, 2010	43	50	7
January 15–19, 2011	41	52	7
February 11–14, 2011	42	50	8
March 18–21, 2011	39	53	8
April 15–20, 2011	38	57	5
June 3–7, 2011	37	56	7
June 24–8, 2011	39	52	9

Source: CBS News/New York Times Poll and CBS News Poll.
Question: "Do you approve or disapprove of the way Barack Obama is handling the economy?"

TABLE 3.6.
Support for Health Care Plan

Date of Poll	% Good Idea	% Bad Idea	% No Opinion/ Not Sure
April 23–26, 2009	33	26	41
June 12–15, 2009	33	32	35
July 24–27, 2009	36	42	22
August 15–17, 2009	36	42	22
September 17–20, 2009	39	41	20
October 22–25, 2009	38	42	20
December 11–14, 2009	32	47	21
January 10–14, 2010	33	46	21
January 23–25, 2010	31	46	23
March 11, 13–14, 2010	36	48	16
May 6–10, 2010	38	44	18
June 17–21, 2010	40	44	16
January 13–17, 2011	39	39	22

Source: NBC News/Wall Street Journal Poll.

Question: "From what you have heard about Barack Obama's health care plan, do you think his plan is a good idea or a bad idea? If you do not have an opinion either way, please say so."

For May and June 2010: "From what you have heard about Barack Obama's health care plan that was recently passed by Congress and signed into law by the president, do you think his plan is a good idea or a bad idea? If you do not have an opinion either way, please just say so."

For January 2011: "From what you have heard about Barack Obama's health care plan that was passed by Congress and signed into law by the president last year, do you think his plan is a good idea or a bad idea? If you do not have an opinion either way, please just say so."

on health care until July. June's CBS/New York Times Poll, for example, found only 22 percent of Americans saying they have heard or read "a lot" about the health care reform proposals.[36] By late July, the public had become more attentive to the issue. Pew found that health care reform had become the story named most often (31 percent) as the news story Americans said they were following most closely, with 44 percent of the respondents saying they were following it "very closely."[37] In a separate survey, it found that stories about health care filled 25 percent of the news hole.[38]

Two significant trends emerge from the data in table 3.6. First, there was a substantial decrease (19 percentage points) in the percentage of the public with no opinion on the issue between April and July. Second, although support held steady over the period, there was a substantial increase (16 percentage points) in opposition to what people perceived to be Obama's plan. Although we do not have a panel study, it appears that those who formed opinions over the three months from April to July, when debate heated up on health care reform, moved overwhelmingly to opposition.

TABLE 3.7.
Support for Health Care Plan

Date of Poll	% Favor	% Oppose	% Don't Know
July 22–26, 2009	38	44	18
August 20–27, 2009	39	46	15
September 10–15, 2009	42	44	14
September 30–October 4, 2009	34	47	19
October 28–November 8, 2009	38	47	15
November 12–15, 2009	42	39	19
December 9–13, 2009	35	48	17
January 6–10, 2010	39	48	13
February 3–9, 2010	38	50	12
March 10–14, 2010	38	48	13
April 1–5, 2010	40	44	16
July 8–11, 2010	35	47	17
September 9–12, 2010	38	45	17

Source: Pew Research Center for the People and the Press Poll.

Question: "As of right now, do you generally favor or generally oppose the health care proposals being discussed in Congress?"

April 2010: "Do you approve or disapprove of the health care legislation passed by Barack Obama and Congress last month?"

July and September 2010: "Do you approve or disapprove of the health care legislation passed by Barack Obama and Congress in March?"

Table 3.7 displays the results of the Pew Research Center for the People & the Press Poll regarding support for the health care proposals in Congress. The results are similar to those in table 3.6. Disaggregating the results (table 3.8) shows that support for the health care reform bills under consideration in Congress was highly polarized, with few Republicans and Republican leaners in support. Other major polls had similar findings of plurality opposition to the bills and majority support only among Democrats.[39] Worse for the president, a third of Democrats and more than 40 percent of Democratic-leaning Independents did not support the bills. Only a third of Independents supported the bills, although a solid majority had supported the principle of health care reform in late 2008.[40]

Despite the lack of support for reform in general, the public did favor a number of the provisions advocated by the administration. The option of a public plan (run by the government) that would compete with private plans, expanding government plans to cover low-income Americans, and requiring insurance companies to cover everyone regardless of preexisting conditions, found majority support. The public also agreed with a number of different ways of paying for health care reform, including raising taxes on those mak-

TABLE 3.8.
Partisan Support for Health Care Plan

	% Favor				
Month	Republican	Democrat	Independent	Republican Leaning	Democratic Leaning
July 2009	12	61	34	15	59
August 2009	13	64	37	14	63
September 2009	17	68	37	15	62
October 2009	14	59	26	15	42
November 2009	15	61	33	18	58
December 2009	11	59	32	9	56
January 2010	12	63	34	17	55
February 2010	14	65	33	12	56
March 2010	11	64	32	10	57

Source: Pew Research Center for the People and the Press Poll.

Question: "As of right now, do you generally favor or generally oppose the health care proposals being discussed in Congress?"

ing over $280,000 a year, requiring employers to pay a fee if they did not provide health insurance, and offering tax credits to help some people pay for health insurance. The public did not support taxing costly private insurance plans or reducing payments to Medicare providers such as doctors and hospitals.[41]

The public's evaluations of the president's handling of health care mirrored the erosion of support for his proposals. As table 3.9 shows, at least by June 2009 Obama received less than majority approval—and he never recovered. The decrease in his rating on health care was particularly notable among Independents. By August, a plurality of the public disapproved of the president's handling of health care, and majorities have continued to disapprove. Using an almost identical question, Gallup found similar ratings to the CBS News/New York Times Poll.[42]

The ultimate goal of the White House's effort to obtain public support was to use it to move Congress. Table 3.10 shows that the president was not successful. With the exception of the early October poll, there was always a slight plurality of the public who wanted their member of Congress to vote against health care reform.[43] The table also shows that there was no change in the advice the public would offer their member of Congress regarding voting for a reform bill following the president's national address on the subject. Thirty-eight percent said they would advise their member of Congress to vote for a bill, 40 percent would advise a "no" vote, and 22 percent did not have an opinion. For seniors, the figures were worse for the president, with 32 percent advising support and 42

TABLE 3.9.
Approval of Obama's Handling Health Care

Date of Poll	% Approve	% Disapprove	% No Opinion
June 12–16, 2009	44	34	22
July 9–12, 2009	49	37	14
July 24–28, 2009	46	38	16
August 27–31, 2009	40	47	13
September 19–23, 2009	47	45	8
October 5–8, 2009	47	42	11
November 13–16, 2009	44	48	8
December 4–8, 2009	42	50	8
January 6–10, 2010	36	54	10
February 5–10, 2010	35	55	10
March 18–21, 2010	41	51	8
April 5–12, 2010	41	51	8
May 20–24, 2010	42	52	6
August 5–8, 2010*	40	57	3
February 2–5, 2011*	40	56	3
March 25–27, 2011*	40	56	4

Source: CBS News/New York Times Poll; Gallup Poll (*).

Question: "Do you approve or disapprove of the way Barack Obama is handling health care?"

Gallup: "Do you approve or disapprove of the way Barack Obama is handling health care policy?"

percent opposition.[44] The inability to reassure seniors was perhaps the greatest setback in the entire health care debate for the White House.

The role of the context in which consideration of health care reform occurred is clear. The results in tables 3.6–3.10 reflect considerable stability in opinion, especially after the debate on health care reform heated up in the summer. Partisanship is part of the answer. It appears that Republicans and Democrats reached decisions early in the process and stuck to them. In ad-dition, Americans seemed to focus more on the ideological underpinnings of health care reform than on the details of proposals. Gallup found that supporters generally favored a new law because they wanted to expand coverage to the uninsured. Opponents were most likely to say they were against a new law because of worries about increased government involvement in health care.[45]

The Speech

We saw in chapter 2 that to try to stem the tide of opposition to health care reform, the president gave a nationally televised evening address before a joint

TABLE 3.10.
Advice to Member of Congress on Health Care Bill

Date of Poll	%		
	Vote For	Vote Against	No Opinion
August 6–9, 2009	35	36	29
August 31–September 2, 2009	37	39	25
September 11–13, 2009	38	40	22
October 1–4, 2009	40	36	25
November 5–8, 2009	29	38	33
November 20–22, 2009	35	42	22
December 11–13, 2009	36	43	21
January 8–10, 2010	37	41	23
March 4–7, 2010	45	48	7

Source: Gallup Poll.

Questions:

August 6–9 and August 31–September 2, 2009: "Would you advise your member of Congress to vote for or against a healthcare reform bill when they return to Washington in September, or do you not have an opinion?"

September 11–13 and October 1–4, 2009: "As of today, would you say you lean more toward advising your member of Congress to vote for or against a health care bill this year, or do you not have an opinion?"

November 5–8 and 20–22 and December 11–13, 2009, and January 8–10, 2010 polls: "Would you advise your member of Congress to vote for or against a health care bill this year, or do you not have an opinion?"

March 4–7, 2010: "Would you advise your representative in Congress to vote for or against a health care reform bill similar to the one proposed by President Obama?"

session of Congress on September 9, 2009.[46] Because it was so central to the White House's efforts to obtain public support for its initiative, the impact of the speech bears closer scrutiny.

A small poll with a large margin of error on the evening of the speech found that about one in seven people *who watched the speech* changed their minds about Obama's health care plan. Going into the speech, a bare majority of his audience—53 percent—favored his proposals. Immediately after the speech, the percentage in favor rose to 67 percent, with only 29 percent opposed. (Bill Clinton got similar numbers after his 1993 address to Congress, but five months later a majority of the country no longer supported his plan.) It is important to note that 45 percent of the viewers of the speech were Democrats and only 18 percent were Republicans, substantially over-representing the former and under-representing the latter.[47] The day after the president's speech, the CBS News Poll re-sampled 678 persons first questioned in a poll conducted August 27–31, 2009, and found a 12-point increase in approval for Obama's handling of health care after his speech, moving from 40 percent to 52 percent approval. These findings were the good news.

Gallup found no change in the approval of the president's handling of health care but an increase to majority disapproval (52 percent).[48] The *Washington Post*-ABC News Poll found only a 2 percentage point change in views of the president's handling of health care (see table 3.5) and just a one-point improvement in support for the president's plan over that found in a poll conducted in mid-August (although those "strongly opposed" decreased by 4 percentage points, and those with "strongly support" increased by 3 percentage points). Opposition still exceeded support by 48 to 46 percent.[49] Similarly, Pew found support for the health care proposals being discussed in Congress rose 3 percentage points to 42 percent, but 44 percent still opposed them (table 3.6). This support fell 8 percentage points within the next three weeks.

The increase in Obama's health care numbers was principally the result of more Democrats rallying around his reform plan. Preaching to the choir is of some benefit. In August, 62 percent of Democrats thought Obama's plan was a good idea; in September, 69 percent believed that.[50] However, even choir members have lapses. Pew found that Democratic support dropped sharply by early October, as did the support of Democratic-leaning Independents (table 3.7).

Americans' views of how reform would alter their health care, the health care of others, their health insurance coverage and costs, and their ability to obtain health insurance were little changed after the president spoke (see table 3.11). Indeed, in most instances their views were slightly more *negative* after the speech, and pluralities were in the direction of "worse off" for all questions except ability to obtain health insurance.

Moreover, a majority of all adults still were not sure the president had clarified what reform would mean. Before the speech, just 33 percent said Obama had clearly explained his plans for reform. That number rose to 42 percent afterward, but 43 percent still said he had not clearly explained his plans. All of the improvement on this question came from those who watched the speech. Fifty-eight percent of those who watched the speech said the president had explained his plans, up from 40 percent before the speech. But among those who did not watch, only one in four said he had explained his plans—the same percentage as before the speech.[51] A poll ending two weeks later found that 55 percent of the respondents felt the president had not clearly explained his plans for reform.[52]

A 45 percent plurality said the reform plan would create too much government involvement in the system. Worse, 40 percent thought reform would weaken Medicare, a figure that rose to 56 percent among seniors, who remained solidly opposed to health care reform. Even worse yet, 54 percent of the respondents said the more they heard about Obama's health care plan, the less they liked it.[53]

Americans remained skeptical that the president's health care plan would be able to accomplish all he intended—to expand coverage to nearly all Americans without raising taxes on middle-class Americans or diminishing the quality of

TABLE 3.11.

Opinion of Health Care Proposal Before and After Obama's Health Care Address

Issue	Before/After Speech	Opinion on Effects of Reform (%)			
		Better	Worse	Same	No Opinion
Your health care	Before	19	33	47	2
	After	16	32	50	2
Health care for most people	Before	37	38	23	2
	After	35	38	24	2
Your health insurance coverage	Before	14	40	43	3
	After	11	37	49	2
Your ability to get health insurance	Before	56	10	30	4
	After	51	13	35	4
Your health insurance costs	Before	19	41	37	3
	After	20	40	38	3

Source: Washington Post-ABC News polls, August 13–17, 2009, and September 10–12, 2009.
Questions:
"Just your best guess, if the health care system is changed, do you think the quality of your health care/health care for most people will get (better), get (worse), or remain about the same?"

"And if the health care system is changed, do you think your insurance coverage [if insured]/your ability to get health insurance [if not insured]/your health insurance costs will get (better), get (worse), or remain about the same?"

care. Only 38 percent of the public, including 66 percent of Democrats, believed his plan would achieve all of these goals, while 60 percent, including 64 percent of Independents and 90 percent of Republicans, disagreed. The speech apparently failed to reassure a third of Democrats. Similarly, 56 percent of the public were not confident that Obama's plan could be paid for mostly through cost savings in Medicare and other parts of the health care system.[54]

On a more basic level, following Obama's speech Americans did not expect health care legislation to improve their personal health care or the overall U.S. health care system in a number of areas—including quality, coverage, cost, and insurance company requirements for procedures to be covered (see table 3.12). For seven of the eight questions in the table, more people predicted health care legislation would make the situation worse rather than better. Overall health care coverage was the only exception.[55] Moreover, opinion about the effects of health reform became more negative in October.

Dénouement

On January 19, 2010, the president's 365th day in office, the White House received what appeared to be a severe setback in its efforts to pass health care re-

TABLE 3.12.
Expectations of Health Care Bill, September and October 2009

| Issue | Month | Opinion on Effects of Reform (%) | | |
		Get Better	No Change	Get Worse
Health care coverage for you	September	22	41	33
and your family	October	20	40	37
Health care coverage	September	40	20	37
Costs you and your family pay	September	22	32	42
for health care	October	22	27	49
Overall costs of health care	September	34	23	40
Insurance company	September	22	35	38
requirements you have to	October	25	25	46
meet to get certain treatments				
covered				
Insurance company require-	September	31	25	42
ments to get certain treat-				
ments covered				
Quality of health care for you	September	18	48	33
and your family	October	19	40	39
Overall quality of health care	September	30	26	41

Source: USA Today/Gallup polls, September 11–13, 2009, and October 16–19, 2009.
Question: "Suppose a health care bill passes this year. Do you think – [RANDOM ORDER] – would get better, would not change, or would get worse than if no health care bill passes?"
Each question asked of half the sample in the September survey.

form. The president had traveled to Massachusetts the previous weekend to campaign for Martha Coakley, the Democratic candidate in the special election to fill Edward Kennedy's Senate seat. On Election Day, however, Republican Scott Brown won a decisive victory, leaving the Democrats one vote short of a filibuster proof majority in the Senate. The irony of Kennedy's replacement killing the chances of the Senate compromising with the House on major health care reform was coupled with the fact that the public in one of the most liberal and reliably Democratic states in the union had rejected the president's plea for support.

In a poll taken the next day, Gallup found that 55 percent of Americans, including 56 percent of Independents, favored Congress suspending work on the current bills and considering alternative bills that could receive more Republican support. Sixty-five percent felt health care reform should not be the top priority on the policy agenda.[56] The White House seemed to agree and began to reframe the administration by focusing on the economy and reform of the financial services industry.

The administration would not give up on health care reform, however, and kept looking for openings. The president held a televised summit that included congressional Republicans on February 25, 2010. The public did not expect the summit to lead to an agreement, and if one was not reached, by a 49 percent to 42 percent margin it opposed Congress passing a health care bill similar to the one proposed by President Obama and Democrats in the House and Senate. By a larger 52 percent to 39 percent margin, the public also opposed the Democrats in the Senate using a reconciliation procedure to avoid a possible Republican filibuster and pass a bill by a simple majority vote.[57]

Despite all his and his administration's efforts, the president never obtained majority—or even plurality—support for health care reform. He could not create an opportunity for change, especially in the context of a severe recession and his policies for dealing with it. Public opposition to those policies, an inherent skepticism of government programs, and a complex policy that was difficult to explain and easy to caricature all worked against the president. Despite these context-specific obstacles to leading the public, we should not forget the general principle that the president cannot depend on winning public support for his initiatives.

In the end, the president did achieve an historic victory on health care reform (which I discuss in chapter 5). One of the most notable aspects of the bill was that it was perhaps the least popular major domestic policy passed in the last century. A CBS News/*New York Times* poll taken right before the House voted to pass the Senate bill in the late evening of March 21, 2010, showed only 37 percent of the public (including 13 percent of Republicans and 30 percent of Independents) approved the bill while 48 percent of the public opposed it. A Gallup Poll taken on March 26–28, 2010, found that by a margin of 40 percent to 22 percent, Americans expected their own health care situation to be worse rather than better because of the bill, and by 45 to 42 percent, they expected the U.S. health care system to be worse off as well.

In the following months, opinion on the bill was stable—and lacking majority support.[58] In June, 50 percent of the public favored repealing all or much of the bill.[59] In July, only 36 percent of the public approved of the new health care law while 49 percent disapproved.[60] An August poll found 56 percent of the public opposing the president's signature legislative accomplishment.[61] In September, only 37 percent approved of the bill, while 49 percent disapproved.[62] Days before the new Republican House majority voted to repeal the entire bill in January 2011, Gallup found that 46 percent of the public wanted their representatives to vote for repeal while only 40 percent wished to preserve the law.[63] On the first anniversary of its passage, only 46 percent of the public thought the bill was a "good thing," and a plurality of 44 percent of the public thought it would worsen medical care in the United States.[64]

Unemployment Benefits

In July 2010, Obama engaged in a battle with Republicans over extending un-employment benefits. The GOP opposed the extension if paying for it would require increasing the deficit. Yet the public supported the president's position, even if it increased the deficit. One poll found 62 percent of the public, includ-ing 59 percent of Independents, favored extending benefits, versus only 36 percent who opposed it.[65] Another poll found the public in support by a smaller, but nevertheless clear, 52 to 39 percent margin, including half of Independents.[66]

Climate Change

Dealing with climate change has been a signature issue for Barack Obama. To combat global warming, the president and the Democratic congressional lead-ership proposed a "cap-and-trade" system. Such a system sets a limit on the nation's emissions of greenhouse gases, then issues or auctions emission allow-ances that can be bought or sold by individuals, funds, and companies. Over time, the government lowers the cap to reduce the nation's emissions. Making emitters pay for carbon dioxide, a by-product of burning fossil fuels, provides incentives for developing renewable energy sources and new technologies to limit emissions from coal plants.

Although legislation in support of environmental protection is generally popular with the public, and although there has been broad support for the principle of regulating greenhouse gases,[67] debate over the cap-and-trade ap-proach has focused on the cost to the average American of limiting greenhouse emissions. Republicans sharply criticized the proposal as a job killer. Moreover, many of them argued such a policy was unnecessary or at least premature be-cause it was not clear that human activity was the cause of global warming.

The cap-and-trade bill passed the House on a 219–212 vote on June 26, 2009. To succeed in the Senate, the president was going to have to convince the public that there was indeed global warming, that it was a serious problem, and that it was the result of human activity.

In 2009, at least, the president did not make his case (see table 3.13). Al-though a majority of the public agreed that the earth was warming, there was less support for viewing the problem as very serious or as due to human activ-ity. Moreover, the trends were moving *against* the president. Indeed, by the au-tumn, a plurality of 49 percent felt either that there was not global warming or that it was mostly the result of natural patterns in the earth's environment.[68] Gallup found in March 2010 that only 52 percent of the public understood that most scientists believed in global warming.[69]

Table 3.13.
Views on Global Warming

Poll Dates	% Very Serious Problem	% Evidence of Warming	% Due to Human Activity
April 28–May 12, 2009	47	NA	49
June 14–19, 2009	41	70	41
September 30–October 4, 2009	35	57	36
October 13–18, 2010	32	59	34

Source: Pew Research Center for the People and the Press Poll.
Questions:
"In your view, is global warming a very serious problem, somewhat serious, not too serious, or not a problem?"
"From what you've read and heard, is there solid evidence that the average temperature on earth has been getting warmer over the past few decades, or not?"
"Which of these three statements about the earth's temperature comes closest to your view? The earth is getting warmer mostly because of natural changes in the atmosphere. The earth is getting warmer mostly because of human activity such as burning fossil fuels. The earth is not getting warmer. Don't know/Refused/No answer."
October 2010 question for those answering "yes" that the earth is getting warmer: "Do you believe that the earth is getting warmer mostly because of human activity such as burning fossil fuels or mostly because of natural patterns in the earth's environment?"

Not unexpectedly, the public's thinking about global warming had a heavily partisan tinge. For example, in the autumn of 2009, only 35 percent of Republicans, in contrast to 75 percent of Democrats, agreed that the earth was warming. Only 18 percent of Republicans, in contrast to 50 percent of Democrats, felt the warming was the result of human activity. Interestingly, there were big changes in the views of Independents over the summer. In June, 71 percent of them thought the earth was warming, and 47 percent thought this was the result of human activity. By autumn, these figures had decreased to 53 and 33 percent, respectively.[70]

The cap-and-trade policy itself is quite complicated, and it is not clear how many people understood it.[71] The data we do have show that support had declined from the end of the Bush administration yet remained a bare but stable majority through 2009 (see table 3.14). We do know that support for the president's handling of the global warming issue declined substantially during the year (see table 3.15).

It is also significant that for the first time in the twenty-six years Gallup had been polling on the question, the public preferred economic growth to environmental protection in both 2009 and early 2010. Moreover, the preferences for economic growth strengthened during that period.[72] The oil spill in the Gulf of Mexico had the immediate impact of reversing that trend in May, with 50 percent of the public supporting environmental protection over economic growth

TABLE 3.14.
Support for "Cap-and-Trade" Greenhouse Emissions Regulation

Poll Dates	% Approve	% Disapprove	% No Opinion
July 23–28, 2008	59	34	7
June 18–31, 2009	52	42	7
August 13–17, 2009	52	43	6
November 12–15, 2009	53	42	5

Source: ABC News/Washington Post Poll.
Question: "There's a proposed system called 'cap and trade.' The government would issue permits limiting the amount of greenhouse gases companies can put out. Companies that did not use all their permits could sell them to other companies. The idea is that many companies would find ways to put out less greenhouse gases, because that would be cheaper than buying permits. Would you support or oppose this system?"

and 55 percent putting environmental protection ahead of obtaining energy supplies.[73] By March 2011, however, the public favored economic development again, and by the largest margin in the nearly three decades of Gallup's time series.[74]

Afghanistan

Even in the midst of economic crisis, the issue of Afghanistan loomed over the White House. Barack Obama had campaigned on reducing the U.S. presence in Iraq and increasing it in Afghanistan. True to his word, he decided to send an additional 17,000 troops to Afghanistan in February 2009. Sixty-five percent of the American public supported the new president's decision, including not only 65 percent of Democrats, but also 75 percent of Republicans and 57 percent of Independents. Fifty percent of the public said they would also approve if the

TABLE 3.15.
Obama's Handling of Global Warming

Poll Dates	% Approve	% Disapprove	% No Opinion
April 21–24, 2009	61	23	16
June 18–31, 2009	54	28	17
December 10–13, 2009	45	39	15

Source: ABC News/Washington Post Poll.
Question: "Do you approve or disapprove of the way Obama is handling global warming?" Asked of half the sample.

TABLE 3.16.
Support for Troop Increase in Afghanistan

Poll Dates	% Favor	% Oppose	% Unsure
September 22–23, 2009	41	50	9
Republicans	63	30	7
Democrats	30	62	8
Independents	38	54	8
October 6, 2009	48	45	7
Republicans	73	45	5
Democrats	36	59	5
Independents	41	50	9

Source: Gallup Poll.

Question: "Would you favor or oppose a decision by President Obama to send more U.S. troops to Afghanistan?"

president later decided to dispatch an additional 13,000 troops.[75] The next month, support for president's decision fell to 53 percent, while 38 percent disapproved of the troop buildup. Obama obtained the support of 63 percent of Republicans and 55 percent of Independents, but only a 49 percent plurality among Democrats.[76]

In mid-September, the public learned that General Stanley McChrystal, the commanding general in Afghanistan, had requested 40,000 additional U.S. troops, a recommendation that precipitated a lengthy evaluation by the White House. In the meantime, evidently in response to General McChrystal's request—the president had not made a decision and thus was not attempting to lead the public—opinion was moving toward sending more troops (see table 3.16). Republicans were particularly responsive, increasing their support for a troop increase 10 percentage points to 73 percent. Democrats lagged, with only 36 percent support in October.

As the country debated the general's request, less than 40 percent of the public supported complying with it fully, but near the end of November, 47 percent supported at least some increase in U.S. troops. At the same time, substantial segments of the public wanted to begin to *reduce* the number of American troops in Afghanistan (see table 3.17). Once again, Republicans were much more supportive of increasing the number of troops than were Democrats. In late November, 65 percent of Republicans favored increasing U.S. troop strength by 40,000 troops, but only 17 percent of Democrats shared this view. Support among Independents was only 36 percent.[77]

On December 1, 2009, President Obama announced in a nationally televised address that he was ordering an additional 30,000 U.S. troops to Afghani-

TABLE 3.17.
Support for Troop Increase in Afghanistan

Poll Dates	Increase by 40,000	Increase by < 40,000	Keep Same	Begin to Reduce Troops	Unsure
November 5–8, 2009	35	7	7	44	7
November 20–22, 2009	37	10	9	39	5

Source: Gallup Poll.

Question: "Which of the following would you like to see President Obama do? Increase the number of U.S. troops in Afghanistan by the roughly 40,000 the U.S. commanding general there has recommended. Increase the number of U.S. troops in Afghanistan but by a smaller amount than the 40,000 the U.S. commanding general there has recommended. Keep the number of U.S. troops in Afghanistan the same as now. OR, Begin to reduce the number of U.S. troops in Afghanistan." (Options rotated.)

stan to bolster the 68,000 already there. A Gallup Poll taken the following day found that 51 percent of the public favored the president's decisions, a slightly higher figure than the 47 percent who in November supported the basic concept of increasing troops in Afghanistan.[78] A CBS News/*New York Times* poll taken in the aftermath of the speech also found 51 percent in favor of the president's decision, but 55 percent opposed his decision to set a date for beginning troop withdrawals.[79]

This modest change in overall support for a troop increase masked significant changes in partisan sentiments, however. In response to a question asking specifically about Obama's strategy, including references to increasing troops *and* to the timetable, Democrats (58 percent) and Republicans (55 percent) showed similar levels of support. Independents were at 45 percent. In other words, Democrats rallied around the president while some Republicans moved away. Independent support changed only marginally.[80]

The wording of the poll probably distorted the responses, however. Both Democrats and Republicans had conflicting views about the troop increase and the timetable for withdrawing them. When Pew asked *only* about sending more troops to Afghanistan in a poll taken December 9–13, it found something quite different from Gallup. Although 51 percent of the public approved, this total was composed of 65 percent of Republicans but only 45 percent of Democrats and 49 percent of Independents.[81]

In the wake of the president's address explaining his decision to escalate U.S. troop levels, public approval of Obama's handling of the war in Afghanistan increased (table 3.18). The shift reflected a twist on the political polarization that had marked Obama's first year in office: on the question of overall handling of the situation in Afghanistan, Republicans and Independents rallied behind Obama, while Democrats remained cool to his stewardship of the war. In the

TABLE 3.18.
Obama's Handling of Afghanistan

Poll Dates	% Approve	% Disapprove	% Unsure
April 1–5, 2009	58	21	21
April 22–26, 2009	56	21	23
August 27–31, 2009	48	30	22
September 19–23, 2009	44	35	21
October 5–8, 2009	42	34	24
November 13–16, 2009	38	43	19
December 4–8, 2009	48	38	14
January 6–10, 2010	46	38	16
January 14–17, 2010	46	39	15
March 29–April 1, 2010	48	36	16
May 20–24, 2010	44	37	19
July 9–12, 2010	43	44	13
August 20–24, 2010	43	39	18
September 10–14, 2010	48	34	18
January 5–9, 2011	44	38	18
June 3–7, 2011	51	35	14
June 24–28, 2011	51	38	11

Source: CBS News/New York Times Poll.
Question: "Do you approve or disapprove of the way Barack Obama is handling the situation with Afghanistan?"

CBS News/New York Times Poll, for example, Republicans' approval increased from 23 to 42 percent while Independents increased from 30 to 45 percent. Democrats changed little, at only 42 percent.[82] The president maintained plurality approval throughout 2010 and rose to majority approval in June 2011 following the death of Osama bin Laden.

At the end of June 2010, Rolling Stone magazine published an article in which General McChrystal and some of his aides were critical of the president and other civilian foreign policy officials. The president immediately recalled the general to Washington and relieved him of command. A Gallup poll taken in the immediate aftermath of the event found that 53 percent of the public approved of the president's action.[83]

Nevertheless, the president was operating on thin ice. By September 2010, 54 percent of the public thought the United States should not be involved in Afghanistan. Similar percentages held that view throughout the first half of 2011.[84] By June 2011, 56 percent of the public, including a plurality of Republicans and majorities of Democrats and Independents, wanted to bring American troops home "as soon as possible."[85] It is not surprising, then, that a large majority of the public favored the president's plan to withdraw U.S. troops announced in a nationally televised address on June 22, 2011.[86]

Guantánamo Bay

On his first full day in office, President Obama signed an executive order that called for the closing of the prison holding terrorist suspects at the U.S. military installation at Guantánamo Bay, Cuba within a year. Days before, only 35 percent of the public supported such an action (see table 3.19). One-fifth of the public was undecided at that point.

Following the president's action, the public remained in opposition to the president's policy, although support increased shortly after his decision. In the following months, however, the public was even less supportive of closing the prison than it was before he took office. Indeed, it appears that those who were undecided in the first half of January eventually moved into opposition to the president's policy.[87]

Pew asked a question about closing the prison that did not include a reference to terrorists being held there. The results (see table 3.20) are a bit more supportive of the president than those found by Gallup in the previous table, but the trend is the same. By November 2009, a clear plurality of the public op-

TABLE 3.19.
Support for Closing Prison at Guantánamo Bay

Poll Dates	% Yes/Approve	% No/Disapprove	% No Opinion
January 16–17, 2009	35	45	20
January 30–February 1, 2009	44	50	5
May 29–31, 2009	32	65	3
November 20–22, 2009	30	64	5

Source: Gallup Poll.
Questions:
January 16–17: "Do you think the United States should—or should not—close the prison at the Guantánamo Bay military base in Cuba?"
January 30–February 1: "Thinking now about some of the specific actions Barack Obama has taken since he has been in office, would you say you approve or disapprove of each of the following. How about ordering that the Guantánamo Bay prison for terrorist suspects be closed within a year?"
May 29–31 and November 20–22:"As you may know, since 2001, the United States has held people from other countries who are suspected of being terrorists in a prison at Guantánamo Bay in Cuba. Do you think the United States should—or should not—close this prison and move some of the prisoners to U.S. prisons?"

TABLE 3.20.
Support for Closing Prison at Guantánamo Bay

Poll Dates	% Approve	% Disapprove	% No Opinion
February 4–8, 2009	46	39	15
April 14–21, 2009	51	38	11
June 10–14, 2009	45	46	8
October 28–November 8, 2009	39	49	12

Source: Pew Research Center for the People and the Press Poll.
Questions:
"Do you approve or disapprove of Obama's decision to close the U.S. military prison in Guantánamo Bay, Cuba within a year?"
October 28–November 8: "Do you approve or disapprove of Obama's decision to close the U.S. military prison in Guantánamo Bay, Cuba?"

posed the president's policy. Most of the loss of support came from Democrats and Independents.

The issue of closing the Guantánamo Bay prison was highly polarizing. In February, Pew found that 64 percent of Democrats supported the president's decision to close the prison, while 69 percent of Republicans opposed the decision. In November 2009, when overall support had diminished, 50 percent of Democrats but only 8 percent of Republicans supported the move (28 percent of Independents approved). We can also see that the president found it a challenge to attract support even among rank-and-file Democrats.[88]

Americans expressed even more widespread opposition to the idea of moving the prisoners to prisons in their own states if Guantánamo was closed. For example, at the end of May, only 23 percent of the public favored moving some of the prisoners to a prison in their state.[89] Thus, it is not surprising that on May 20, 2009, the Senate voted 90-6 to keep the prison at Guantánamo Bay open and forbid the transfer of any detainees to facilities in the United States. Similarly, both the House and Senate refused to finance the purchase or modification of prison facilities in the United States to house the Guantánamo prisoners. In the lame-duck session at the end of 2010, Congress voted to impose strict new limits on transferring detainees out of the Guantánamo Bay prison, dealing a major blow to president Obama's vows to shut down the center and give many of the prisoners federal court trials. One of the law's provisions banned the transfer into the United States of any Guantánamo detainee for the 2011 fiscal year—even for the purpose of prosecution. A second provision banned the purchase or construction of any facility inside the United States for housing detainees being held at Guantánamo. A third provision forbade the transfer of any detainee to another country unless Defense Secretary Robert M. Gates signed off on the safety of doing so.

Libya

In the spring of 2011, civil war broke out in Libya. The United States and NATO began military operations, mostly from the air, on behalf of those revolting against the government of Muammar Gaddafi. Although Americans did not play a central role in the fighting, there was substantial controversy regarding the appropriate level of U.S. effort. By late June, only 39 percent of the public approved of U.S. military action in Libya, while 46 percent disapproved.[90] Only 37 percent of the public approved of the president's handling of Libya, while 59 percent felt the United States should not be involved in the fighting there.[91]

A controversy also arose around the White House's claim that the War Powers Resolution did not apply to U.S. actions in Libya. Many liberal Democrats and conservative Republicans disagreed, and the public sided with them. Sixty-one percent felt Obama should have obtained congressional authorization for military action in Libya.[92]

Handling Foreign Policy

Evaluations of the president's handling of foreign policy followed the same downward trend as his overall job approval. Disapproval climbed steadily throughout 2009, and the president never achieved majority approval in 2010 or the first half of 2011 (see table 3.21).

Party Support

Presidents are party leaders who have strong impacts on the public's attitudes toward their parties,[93] and the success of the president's party is key to his success in Congress. Unfortunately for the Obama White House, in 2009 and 2010, Americans were moving away from the Democratic Party, not toward it. Disapproval of the president was central to the explanation.[94] In September 2010, Gallup found the lowest level of public favorability of the Democratic Party in the eighteen-year history of the measure.[95] For the year 2010, Gallup found that 31 percent of Americans identified as Democrats, down five percentage points from 2008 and tied for the lowest annual average Gallup had measured in the previous twenty-two years.[96] Gallup found that the number of solidly Democratic states declined from thirty in 2008 to fourteen in 2010.[97]

TABLE 3.21.
Obama Handling Foreign Policy

Poll Dates	% Approve	% Disapprove	% Unsure
February 2–4, 2009	50	15	35
February 18–22, 2009	57	17	26
April 1–5, 2009	59	19	22
April 22–26, 2009	59	23	18
June 12–16, 2009	59	23	18
July 9–12, 2009	53	30	17
July 24–28, 2009	54	24	22
October 5–8, 2009	48	28	24
November 13–16, 2009	50	36	14
February 5–10, 2010	47	34	19
April 28–May 2, 2010	48	38	14
July 9–12, 2010	44	41	15
November 7–10, 2010	46	37	17
November 29–December 2, 2010	40	45	15
January 15–19, 2011	46	32	22
February 11–14, 2011	46	33	21
March 18–21, 2011	47	36	17
April 15–20, 2011	39	46	15
June 3–7, 2011	47	37	16

Source: CBS News/*New York Times* Poll and CBS News Poll.
Question: "Do you approve or disapprove of the way Barack Obama is handling foreign policy?"

The Democratic Party was losing the public's confidence. In May 2010, 49 percent of the public said the party's views were "too liberal," while only 38 percent felt its views were "about right." In 2008, only 39 percent said the Democrats were too liberal. Most of the change came from Independents (Republicans always thought the Democrats were too liberal). The 49 percent figure was only one percentage point below the all-time high (since 1992) of the 50 percent Gallup found right after the 1994 elections. Equally disturbing for Democrats was the fact that only 40 percent of the public thought the Republican Party was "too conservative."[98]

The Ipsos/McClatchy Poll asked voters which party could do the best job of handling thirteen different issues. During the first year of the Obama administration, the Republicans gained substantial ground on all thirteen (see table 3.22). Indeed, Republicans moved into the lead on crucial policies such as taxes, deficit reduction, generating economic growth, and protecting against terrorism, and were in a virtual tie on the economy, encouraging morality, and foreign policy.

TABLE 3.22.
Which Party Will Do Better at Handling Issues

	Democratic Advantage/Disadvantage (percentage points)		
Issue	November 2008	December 2009	Percentage Point Change
Economy	+31	+1	-30
Generating economic growth	+30	-3	-33
Reducing federal deficit	+30	-7	-37
Taxes	+17	-2	-19
Health care	+39	+4	-35
Environment	+44	+25	-19
Education	+35	+15	-20
Morality	+20	+1	-19
Foreign policy	+20	+1	-19
Regaining international respect	+31	+8	-23
Iraq	+21	+5	-16
Protecting against terrorism	+9	-7	-16
Making America more competitive	+20	+3	-17

Source: Ipsos/McClatchy polls, November 20–23, 2008 and December 3–6, 2009.
Question: "Please tell me if you think the Democratic Party or the Republican Party could do a better job in each of the following areas. Which party could do a better job of [issue]?"

By August 2010, Republicans had large advantages on terrorism, immigration, federal spending, and the economy, and advantages on Afghanistan, jobs, and corruption in government. Democrats had a substantial advantage only on the environment. Only 44 percent of the public felt the Democrats represented their attitudes about government (compared to 52 percent for Republicans), and only 49 percent felt the Democrats represented their values (as opposed to 56 percent for Republicans).[99]

Republicans also enjoyed a substantial engagement advantage. Pew found that on many measures, the Republican engagement in 2010 surpassed historical records. Fully 70 percent of Republican likely voters had given a lot of thought to the election, the highest figure recorded among either Republicans or Democrats over the past five midterm election cycles, and the differential between Republicans and Democrats was larger than ever previously recorded.[100] Obama's opponents were much more eager than Democrats to participate in the election: on average, 63 percent of Republicans said they were more enthusiastic about voting than usual (the highest proportion of such voters recorded in midterm data going back to 1994), compared with 44 percent of Democrats.[101] The exit polls found that conservatives increased their percentage of the electorate for the House from 34 percent in 2008 to 42 percent in

2010, and 87 percent of them voted Republican, compared to 23 percent in 2008.[102]

Historically high percentages of Americans knew which party controlled Congress, and many voters wanted to punish the Democrats.[103] Although only 26 percent of Democratic likely voters said national issues were the primary factor in their votes at election time, 50 percent of Republicans and 45 percent of Independents reported that such issues were the primary factor in their votes. Nearly a third (32 percent) of likely voters supporting Republican candidates for Congress said their vote was mainly a vote *against* the Democratic candidate rather than for the Republican, and 38 percent viewed their vote as sending a message that they opposed Obama. Only 24 percent saw their vote as support for the president.[104]

Republicans owed much of their success to strong backing from Independents, who composed 28 percent of voters on Election Day. Fifty-six percent supported Republican House candidates, while only 37 percent voted for Democrats, a massive change from 2008. A comparable shift occurred in Senate elections.[105] Disapproval of the president's job performance, anger at the federal government, and opposition to the health care legislation were closely associated with support for Republican candidates. Moreover, Independents who expressed these views were also highly likely to vote.[106]

Lame-Duck Congress, 2010

There was an unusually active lame-duck session at the end of 2010, because Congress had failed to address a number of important issues during the regular session. As a result of the legislature's agenda, the president did not focus sustained commentary on these policies until after the midterm elections. Table 3.23 provides a convenient summary of public opinion on the policies at about the time one or both houses took up the legislation.

There was little controversy about food safety regulation, a policy that had lingered in Congress for years. Similarly, the public overwhelmingly supported the repeal of "don't ask, don't tell" and allowing gays and lesbians to serve openly in the military. Nearly half of Republicans, 47 percent, along with 70 percent of Independents and 81 percent of Democrats, supported repeal.[107] The public had favored allowing openly gay men and lesbians to serve in the U.S. military since 2005,[108] so there is little reason to think that the opinion held at the end of 2010 was a response to Obama's leadership.

Perhaps the biggest issue of the lame-duck Congress was extending Bush-era tax cuts. Obtaining the public's support for not raising their taxes is not a difficult task. The president, however, did not want to extend the lower tax rates for the wealthy and wanted to reinstate the estate tax at a level that would help reduce the deficit. He could not gain Republicans' agreement for these positions,

Table 3.23.
Public Support for Policies in the 111th Congress's Lame-Duck Session issue

	% For	% Against	% No Opinion
Increase government regulation of food safety	75	21	4
Allow gays and lesbians to serve openly in military	67	28	5
Extend income tax cuts for all Americans for 2 years	66	29	5
Extend unemployment benefits	66	30	4
Allow illegal immigrants brought to the U.S. as children to gain legal resident status if they join the military or go to college	54	42	4
Ratify the START treaty	51	30	19

Source: Gallup poll, December 3–6, 2010.

Question: "Suppose that on Election Day you could vote on key issues as well as candidates. Please tell me whether you would vote for or against a law that would do each of the following. First, would you vote for or against a law that would _____?"

but he did extract some concessions, including an extension of unemployment benefits and a reduction in Social Security taxes for 2011. The Republicans won a high exemption on inheritance taxes. Like tax cuts, winning public support for extending unemployment benefits during a period of economic sluggishness was not a challenge. In the end, the public clearly supported the compromise, although at least pluralities would have preferred not extending the tax cuts fully for the wealthy and the temporary reductions in Social Security taxes.[109]

Another major pending issue before the Senate was the New START treaty. Most Americans favored ratification, although a sizeable number had not heard much about it.[110] A final major issue was known as the DREAM act, which would provide a path for illegal immigrants brought to the United States as children to gain legal resident status if they joined the military or went to college. The public approved of this policy, although by narrower margins than the other policies listed in table 3.23. As we will see in chapter 6, the DREAM act fell to a Senate filibuster.

Conclusion

We saw in chapter 1 that the climate of public opinion in the early Obama presidency was not conducive to the president's obtaining public support for major liberal policies. That climate, along with the long-term obstacles to leading the public, provided the basis for predicting that the president was unlikely to enjoy substantial success in moving the public in his direction. The data presented in this chapter support this prediction.

With the exceptions of limits on executive pay, which was popular when George W. Bush occupied the White House, regulating the highly unpopular large financial institutions, food safety regulatory reform, which had always received public support, and repealing "don't ask, don't tell," which the public had backed for several years before Obama took office, there was no major Obama initiative that enjoyed widespread public support. Indeed, the president could not muster majority backing for his policies regarding the TARP program and bank bailouts, the automaker bailouts, his overall handling of the economy and of the deficit, and health care reform and his handling of it. The public supported the 2010 tax bill, but it is a stretch to call it an Obama initiative. From the White House's perspective, the bill was clearly a compromise position that contained a number of important elements that the president opposed. The public did back the compromise, however, largely because it adopted its standard pose of opposing an increase in taxes. A bare majority of the public supported ratification of the START treaty. Although a modest majority supported the cap-and-trade proposal, opinion on the underlying premises of climate change legislation moved clearly and rapidly against the White House, as did views of the president's handling of the global warming issue. The public also clearly opposed closing the prison at Guantánamo Bay and transferring prisoners from there to the United States, and it lost confidence in his handling of Afghanistan in particular and foreign policy in general. In addition, identification with the Democratic Party declined substantially, as did evaluations of the party's ability to handle issues relative to that of the Republicans. These party assessments provided the foundation for the Democratic losses in the 2010 midterm elections.

There is not much evidence that Barack Obama could depend on creating opportunities for change by obtaining public support and leveraging it to gain support for his proposals in Congress. There were glimmers of successful opinion leadership, such as the very end of the congressional debate on the economic stimulus program. The public remained deeply skeptical, however, even of a program designed to revive the stagnating economy, and opinion soon moved decisively to opposing it. The president also received a mixed public response on Afghanistan, where he adopted a relatively conservative policy. He could not maintain majority approval of his handling of the issue or of foreign policy over all.

In general, public opinion moved against the president over time. Andrew Kohut, president of the Pew Research Center, summarized these trends well when he declared at the end of 2009,

> What's really exceptional at this stage of Obama's presidency is the extent to which the public has moved in a conservative direction on a range of issues.

TABLE 3.24.
Approval of Major Legislation

Legislation	% Approve	% Disapprove	% No Opinion
Financial regulation	61	37	3
Economic stimulus	43	52	5
Automaker bailout	43	56	2
Health care reform	39	56	5
Bank bailout	37	61	2

Source: Gallup poll, August 27–30, 2010.
Question: "Now, thinking back on some of the major pieces of legislation Congress has passed in the last two years, would you say you approve or disapprove of _____?"

These trends have emanated as much from the middle of the electorate as from the highly energized conservative right.[111]

Shortly before the 2010 midterm elections, Gallup asked the public about its approval of some of the major legislation passed in the 111th Congress. As the results in table 3.24 show, the public approved only of financial regulation. Majorities disapproved of the other legislation about which Gallup inquired. Perhaps most troubling for the president, financial regulation was the only legislation that was receiving majority approval of Independents (table 3.25). No more than 40 percent of Independents approved of any of the other legislation.

Bill Clinton concluded that his health care reform failed because "I totally neglected how to get the public informed . . . I have to get more involved in crafting my message—in getting across my core concerns."[112] In other words, his strategy was not inappropriate, only his implementation of it. "I got caught up in the parliamentary aspect of the presidency and missed the leadership, bully pulpit function which is so critical."[113]

In a televised interview on the first anniversary of his inauguration and the day following the Democrats' stunning loss of Ted Kennedy's Senate seat in Massachusetts, Barack Obama also lamented that he had failed to communicate effectively with the public because he focused too heavily on policymaking.[114] Months later, he echoed these remarks: "I think anybody who's occupied this office has to remember that success is determined by an intersection in policy and politics and that you can't be neglecting of marketing and P.R. and public opinion."[115]

The president did not have a policy problem, he thought. Instead, he had a *communications* problem. Apparently the premise of the power of the presidential pulpit is so strong that each downturn in the president's efforts prompted new strategies for going public rather than a reconsideration of his policies. Obama's Democratic critics agreed. Former Clinton aide Paul Begala echoed

TABLE 3.25.
Partisan Approval of Major Legislation

Legislation	% Approve		
	Republicans	Independents	Democrats
Financial regulation	42	62	76
Economic stimulus	21	38	71
Automaker bailout	31	40	57
Health care reform	13	35	69
Bank bailout	27	32	51

Source: Gallup poll, August 27–30, 2010.

the sarcastic reaction of many of Obama's fellow Democrats who wanted him to fight against the Republican's insistence on extending tax cuts to the rich. "Imagine what he could have done to sell a position he wholeheartedly believed in," Begala proclaimed, adding that it "confirms my own belief that if President Obama had chosen to fight, he would have won."[116]

The premise of the potential of presidential public leadership seems to be nonfalsifiable. It should not be. Presidents would be much better off listening to the creator of the bully pulpit. Writing to Edward Thayer Mahan on March 12, 1901, Theodore Roosevelt explained why the United States could not at that time pursue a more militant foreign policy in China. "While something can be done by public men in leading the people, they cannot lead them further than public opinion has prepared the way."[117]

CHAPTER 4

Assessing Opportunities

CONGRESSIONAL SUPPORT

EVERY PRESIDENT NEEDS SUPPORT IN CONGRESS to pass his legislative proposals. Barack Obama began his presidency with what appeared to be a highly favorable strategic position in Congress. Democrats held 257 seats in the House, and after the resolution of the protracted recount in Minnesota, 60 seats in the Senate (including the two Independents who caucused with the Democrats). Recapturing the presidency in the historic election of 2008 was exhilarating for Democrats, and it is reasonable to infer that most of them felt they had a stake in their leader's success.

We saw in chapter 1 that it is natural for a new president, basking in the glow of an electoral victory, to focus on creating, rather than exploiting, opportunities for change. It may seem quite reasonable for a president who has just won the biggest prize in American politics by convincing voters and party leaders to support his candidacy to conclude that he should be able to convince members of Congress to support his policies. Thus, Obama lost no time to begin, as he put it in his inaugural address, "the work of remaking America."

As with leading the public, then, presidents may not focus on evaluating existing possibilities when they think they can create their own. Yet, assuming party support in Congress or success in reaching across the aisle to obtain bipartisan support is fraught with dangers. Not a single systematic study exists that demonstrates that presidents can reliably move members of Congress, especially members of the opposition party, to support them.

The best evidence is that presidential persuasion is at the margins of congressional decision making. Even presidents who appeared to dominate Congress were actually facilitators rather than directors of change. They understood their own limitations and quite explicitly took advantage of opportunities in their environments. Working at the margins, they successfully guided legislation through Congress. When these resources diminished, they reverted to the more typical stalemate that usually characterizes presidential-congressional relations.[1]

In his important work on pivotal politics, Keith Krehbiel examined votes to override presidential vetoes, focusing on those members of Congress who switched their votes from their original votes on the bill. He found that presidents attracted 10 percent of those who originally supported a bill but lost 11 percent of those who originally supported him by opposing the bill. Those closest in ideology to the president were most likely to switch to his side, which may indicate they voted their true views, rather than responding to other interests, when it really counted. Even among those most likely to agree with the White House, legislators within the cluster of pivotal or near-pivotal, the net swing was only 1 in 8. The majority of switchers were from the president's party, indicating that the desire to avoid a party embarrassment rather than presidential persuasiveness may have motivated their votes.[2]

It is certainly possible that there is selection bias in votes on veto overrides. Presidents do not veto the same number of bills, and some veto no bills at all. Moreover, presidents may often choose to veto bills on which they are likely to prevail. In addition, most override votes are not close, allowing members of Congress more flexibility in their voting. Whatever the case, Krehbiel's data do not provide a basis for inferring successful presidential persuasion.

There are several components of the opportunity for obtaining congressional support. First is the presence or absence of the perception of a mandate for change. Do members of Congress think the public has spoken clearly in favor of the president's proposals? The second component is the presence or absence of unified government. Is the president's party in control of the congressional agenda? A third aspect of the opportunity structure is the ideological division of members of Congress. Are they likely to agree with the president's initiatives? Are the parties unified or are there critical cross-pressures that threaten the president's support?

This chapter analyzes the prospects for support for the president's program in Congress. First, I examine the question of the perception of a mandate in the 2008 election. Next, I briefly discuss the impact of his party's majority control of Congress. Finally, and most importantly, I address the degree of ideological polarization in Congress and homogeneity or heterogeneity of each of the parties and its probable impact on the president's congressional support. By analyzing the opportunity for obtaining congressional support for Obama's initiatives, it is possible to understand and predict the challenges he faced in convincing members of Congress to support his proposals and the relative utility of this strategy for governing.

First, however, we need to consider the nature of the president's agenda. The more ambitious the agenda, the more likely it will meet with intense criticism and political pushback. A White House strategy built on the assumption of persuading members of Congress to support the president's programs can lead to an overly ambitious agenda that lacks the fundamental support it needs to weather the inevitable attacks from the opposition.

The Obama Agenda

In an article written days after the 2008 presidential election, Paul Light maintained that there was not room in government for the kind of breakthrough ideas that Obama had promised. Every Democratic president since Lyndon

Johnson had sent fewer major proposals to Congress, just as every Republican president since Richard Nixon had done as well. Thus, Light suggested that instead of presenting a massive agenda to Congress, the new president should start with a few tightly focused progressive initiatives that would whet the appetite for more. His best opportunity for a grand agenda was more likely to be in 2013 than in 2009.[3]

We saw in chapter 1 that Obama had a different view. He proposed an agenda that confronted the era's most intractable problems, from a tattered financial system that helped fuel a deep recession to health care, education, and energy policies that had long defied meaningful reform. He persuaded Congress to spend more than three quarters of a trillion dollars to try to jump-start the economy. On his own authority he altered federal rules in areas ranging from stem cell research to the treatment of terrorism suspects. He launched efforts to help strapped homeowners refinance their mortgages, sweep "toxic assets" off bank balance sheets, and shore up consumer credit markets. He also set a timetable for ending the occupation of Iraq, increased the U.S. presence in Afghanistan, and set about improving the American image in the world.

The president often declared that he did not have the luxury of addressing the financial crisis and issues such as health care, education, or the environment one at a time. "I'm not choosing to address these additional challenges just because I feel like it or because I'm a glutton for punishment," he told the Business Roundtable. "I'm doing so because they're fundamental to our economic growth and ensuring that we don't have more crises like this in the future."[4] He wanted a more sustained approach than patching the economy until the next bubble, like the technology bubble of the 1990s and the housing bubble of the 2000s.[5]

In Obama's view, it was impossible to deal with the economic crisis without fixing the banking system, because one cannot generate a recovery without liquid markets and access to capital. He insisted that the only way to build a strong economy that would truly last was to address underlying problems in American society like unaffordable health care, dependence on foreign oil, and underperforming schools. Reducing dependence on foreign oil required addressing climate change, which in turn required international cooperation and engaging the world with vigorous U.S. diplomacy. His appointment of five prominent White House "czars" with jurisdictions ranging across several departments reflected this syncretic outlook.

Moreover, the president had little patience for waiting to act. "There are those who say these plans are too ambitious, that we should be trying to do less, not more," he told a town hall meeting in Costa Mesa, California on March 18, 2009. "Well, I say our challenges are too large to ignore." The next day in Los Angeles he proclaimed, "It would be nice if I could just pick and choose what problems to face, when to face them. So I could say, well, no, I don't want to deal with the war in Afghanistan right now; I'd prefer not having to deal with climate change right now. And if you could just hold on, even though you don't have health care, just please wait, because I've got other things to do." Later, on *The Tonight Show With Jay Leno*, he repeated his standard response to critics who charged he was trying to do too much: "Listen, here's what I say. I say our challenges are too big to ignore."[6]

There was also an element of strategic pragmatism in the president's view. For example, Obama felt that health care was a once-in-a-lifetime struggle and a fight that could not wait. To have postponed it until 2010 would have meant trying to pass the bill in an election year. To have waited until 2011 would have risked taking on the battle with reduced majorities in the House and Senate.[7] Even when the administration began running into resistance to its health care plan in the summer of 2009, and Rahm Emanuel, Vice President Biden, David Axelrod, and others went to Obama and pushed for a pared-back approach that would focus on expanding coverage for lower-income children and families and on reforming the most objectionable practices of insurance companies, Obama persisted in his comprehensive approach.[8]

Obama and his top strategists, including Axelrod and Emanuel, repeatedly defended the administration's sweeping agenda by arguing that success breeds success, that each legislative victory would make the next one easier.[9] In other words, the White House believed success on one issue on the agenda would *create* further opportunities on additional policies. Victories would beget victories.

There were some efforts to set priorities, of course. The White House and congressional Democrats deferred fights over tax policy, despite the impending expiration of many of the George W. Bush tax cuts. The White House also opposed a high-profile commission to investigate Bush administration interrogation practices and declined to engage in hot-button debates over gays in the military (until 2010) or gun control.[10] The administration also did not make immigration and union card check legislation priorities.[11]

A Mandate for Change?

An electoral mandate—the perception that the voters strongly support the president's character and policies—can be a powerful symbol in American politics. It can accord added legitimacy and credibility to the newly elected president's proposals. That is why Obama declared that if he did not talk about health care reform during the 2008 campaign, he could not pass it in his first year in office.[12]

Concerns for representation and political survival encourage members of Congress to support the president if they feel the people have spoken.[13] And members of Congress are susceptible to such beliefs. According to David Mayhew, "Nothing is more important in Capitol Hill politics than the shared conviction that election returns have proven a point."[14] Members of Congress also need to believe that voters have not merely rejected the losers in elections but positively selected the victors and what they stand for.

More important, mandates change the premises of decisions. Following Franklin D. Roosevelt's decisive win in the 1932 election, the essential question became *how* government should act to fight the Depression rather than *whether* it should act. Similarly, following Lyndon Johnson's overwhelming win in the 1964 election, the dominant question in Congress was not whether to pass new social programs but how many social programs to pass and how much to increase spending. In 1981, the tables were turned; Ronald Reagan's victory placed a stigma on big government and exalted the unregulated marketplace and large defense efforts. Reagan had won a major victory even before the first congressional vote.

The winners in presidential elections usually claim to have been accorded a mandate,[15] but winning an election does not necessarily, or even usually, provide presidents with one. Every election produces a winner, but mandates are much less common. Even presidents who win elections by large margins often find that perceptions of support for their proposals do not accompany their victories. In the presidential elections held between 1952 and 2008, most of the impressive electoral victories (Richard Nixon's 61 percent in 1972, Ronald Reagan's 59 percent in 1984, and Dwight Eisenhower's 57 percent in 1956) did not elicit perceptions of mandates (Lyndon Johnson's 61 percent in 1964 is the exception).[16]

Candidates often appeal as broadly as possible in the interest of building a broad electoral coalition. Incumbents frequently avoid specifics on their second-term plans and attempt to increase their vote totals by asking voters to make retrospective judgments. Candidates who do not make their policy plans salient in the campaign undermine their ability effectively to claim policy mandates. Moreover, voters frequently also send mixed signals by electing majorities in Congress from the other party.

When asked about his mandate in 1960, John F. Kennedy reportedly replied, "Mandate, schmandate. The mandate is that I am here and you're not."[17] Bill Clinton could associate himself with popular initiatives in 1995–1996 to aid his reelection, but could not use this show of voter support as an indicator of public approval of initiatives he did not discuss in the campaign, especially since the public also elected a Republican Congress during his second term. In 2004, George W. Bush won with less than 51 percent of the vote, lacked substantial coattails, and did not emphasize specific policy proposals in his campaign. Thus, his claims of a mandate lacked credibility—as he soon discovered when the public and Congress were unresponsive to his proposals for reforming Social Security.

Certain conditions promote the perception of a mandate.[18] The first is a large margin of victory. Obama's 52.9 percent of the vote hardly qualifies as a landslide. Similarly, a surprisingly large victory accompanying a change in the party in the White House may have a powerful psychological impact, as it did in Ronald Reagan's victory over Jimmy Carter in 1980. Obama was the projected winner for weeks before Election Day, however, and he won by the margin that polls had predicted. The president can also benefit from hyperbole in media analyses of election results that exaggerate the one-sidedness of his victory. Although the press celebrated the election of an African American, it did not exaggerate the size of Obama's vote.

The impression of long coattails can also add to the perception of a mandate, and it is possible that some Democrats would view themselves as having benefitted from the president's coattails and thus give him the benefit of the doubt on tough votes. Ironically, more than half of the Democrats' net gain of 21 House seats in 2008 came in districts that Obama lost: 12 freshman Democrats won previously Republican-held seats in districts that John McCain carried. Overall, all but 35 of the 257 House Democrats won a higher percentage of the vote in their districts than Obama did. Furthermore, only 12 of the 33 first-term Democrats in the House ran behind the president. Six of the 12 won 52 percent or less of the vote in taking Republican-held seats and thus were likely to be heavily cross-pressured. Democrats who were able to establish their own political identity might not feel compelled always to vote hand-in-hand with the new administration, freeing them to vote independently if they saw some daylight between their constituents and the Obama administration.[19]

Most winning Democratic senatorial candidates ran ahead of Obama. Only in Colorado, Minnesota, New Hampshire, Oregon, and New Jersey did he run ahead of winning Democrats. Moreover, only in the first four of these was the winner's margin close enough that Obama's coattails could have made a difference in the outcome.

A campaign oriented around a major change in public policy coupled with the consistency of the new president's program with the prevailing tides of opinion in both the country and his party, and a sense that the public's views have shifted, may enhance the perception of a mandate. We have seen in chapter 1, however, that the public's views did not shift in 2008 and that Obama's program did not seem to be consistent with the prevailing tides of opinion in the country.

In sum, Obama won a clear victory but not one that encouraged perceptions of a mandate. Moreover, there was little he could do to influence these perceptions. To succeed in Congress, he would have to rely on other resources.

Unified Government

Attaining agenda status for a bill is a necessary prelude to its passage, and thus obtaining agenda space for his most important proposals is at the core of every president's legislative strategy. The burdens of leadership are considerably less at the agenda stage than at the floor stage, where the president must try to influence decisions regarding the political and substantive merits of a policy. At the agenda stage, in contrast, the president only has to convince members that his proposals are important enough to warrant attention. The White House generally succeeds in obtaining congressional attention to its legislative proposals,[20] and the Obama presidency was no exception.

Controlling the agenda also means setting the terms on which a chamber considers a proposal. In the House, the timing of a floor vote and the sequence, number, and substance of amendments on legislation are under the control of the majority party leadership. It was reasonable to expect the Democratic leadership to use this power to ease the path for the president's agenda.[21]

In the Senate, where power is more decentralized, we should expect that the president would face far greater difficulty in influencing the agenda. Moreover, Republicans were practiced at using the filibuster to prevent issues from coming to a vote. In addition, influence over the agenda offers the majority much less influence over the outcome of votes than it does in the House.

Despite David Mayhew's innovative study, which found that the likelihood of passing major laws was as great under divided government as when the White House enjoyed unified control,[22] other research has found that divided government reduces legislative productivity.[23] Party majorities and agenda control also largely free the president from having to deal with the opposition's legislation. The president does not need to invest his time, energy, and political capital in fighting veto battles, and he is much less likely to face the embarrassing situation in which he must veto popular legislation that he opposes.[24]

Unified government is not a panacea, however. Divided government is primarily a constraint on the passage of legislation the administration opposes, the congressional initiatives of the opposition party. The most significant proposals of presidents are no more likely to pass under unified government than under divided government.[25] There are other, powerful influences on congressional support for the president's programs. Among the most important of these are the partisan polarization and ideological diversity within Congress.

The Prospect of Republican Support

A primary obstacle to passing major changes in public policy is the challenge of obtaining support from the opposition party.[26] Such support can be critical in overcoming a Senate filibuster or effectively appealing to Independents in the public, who find bipartisanship reassuring. The *Washington Post* reported that the Obama legislative agenda was built around what some termed an "advancing tide" theory.

> Democrats would start with bills that targeted relatively narrow problems, such as expanding health care for low-income children, reforming Pentagon contracting practices and curbing abuses by credit-card companies. Republicans would

see the victories stack up and would want to take credit alongside a popular president. As momentum built, larger bipartisan coalitions would form to tackle more ambitious initiatives.[27]

Just how realistic was the prospect of obtaining Republican support?

Perhaps the most important fact about Congress in 2009 was that partisan polarization had been at an historic high. Important work on voting patterns in Congress has found that the 110th Congress had the highest level of party polarization since the end of Reconstruction.[28] Similarly, *Congressional Quarterly* found that George W. Bush presided over the most polarized period at the Capitol since it began quantifying partisanship in the House and Senate in 1953. There had been a high percentage of party unity votes—those that pitted a majority of Republicans against a majority of Democrats—and an increasing propensity of individual lawmakers to vote with their fellow partisans.[29]

There was no reason to expect partisan polarization to diminish in the Obama administration. Republican constituencies send stalwart Republicans to Congress, whose job it is to oppose a Democratic president. Most of these senators and representatives were unlikely to be responsive to core Obama supporters. They knew their constituencies, and they knew Obama was unlikely to have much support in them. Thus, few of the Republicans' electoral constituencies showed any enthusiasm for health care reform. As Gary Jacobson has shown, the partisan divisions that emerged in Congress on the health care issue were firmly rooted in district opinion and electoral politics.[30] Moreover, conservative Republicans were the group of political identifiers least likely to support compromising "to get things done."[31]

On the day before the House voted on the final version of the economic stimulus bill, the president took Aaron Schock, a freshman Republican member of Congress, aboard *Air Force One* to visit Illinois. Before an audience in Schock's district, Obama praised him as "a very talented young man" and expressed "great confidence in him to do the right thing for the people of Peoria." But when the representative stood on the House floor less than twenty-four hours later, his view of the right thing for the people of Peoria was to vote against the president. "They know that this bill is not stimulus," Schock said of his constituents. "They know that this bill will not do anything to create long-term, sustained economic growth."[32] Schock was typical of Republicans in early 2009, who viewed the stimulus debate as an opportunity to rededicate their divided, demoralized party around the ideas of big tax cuts and limited government spending.

In the 111th Congress (2009–2010), nearly half of the Republicans in both the House and Senate were elected from the eleven states of the Confederacy, plus Kentucky and Oklahoma. In each chamber, Southerners made up a larger share of the Republican caucus than ever before. At the same time, Republicans held a smaller share of non-Southern seats in the House and Senate than at any other point in its history except during the early days of the New Deal.[33] The party's increasing identification with staunch Southern economic and social conservatism made it much more difficult for Obama to reach across the aisle. Southern House Republicans, for instance, overwhelmingly opposed him, even on the handful of issues where he has made inroads among GOP legislators from other regions. Nearly one-third of House Republicans from outside of the South supported expanding the State Children's Health Insurance Program, but only one-tenth of Southern House Republicans did so. Likewise, just 5 percent of Southern House Republicans supported the bill expanding the national service program, compared with 22 percent of Republicans from other states.

The Republican Party's losses in swing areas since 2006 accelerated its homogenization. Few Republicans represented Democratic-leaning districts. As a result, far fewer congressional Republicans than Democrats had to worry about moderate public opinion. Fully thirty-one of the forty Republican senators serving in 2009 (thirty-one of forty-one in 2010), for example, were elected from the eighteen states that twice backed Bush and also voted for McCain. Five other senators represented states that voted for Bush twice and then supported Obama. Just six Republican senators were elected by states that voted Democratic in at least two of the past three presidential elections. One of these lawmakers, Arlen Specter of Pennsylvania, switched parties to become a Democrat.

Table 4.1 shows the impact of these constituency cross-pressures on voting of Republican senators in 2009 and 2010. Most Republican senators represented reliably Republican states, and these senators voted in a considerably more conservative direction than their party colleagues from states that were more likely to support Democratic presidential candidates. At the time of the vote to repeal "don't ask, don't tell," there were eleven Republican senators from states President Obama had won in 2008. Of these, seven voted for repeal, three voted against, and one did not vote. On the other hand, only one of the thirty-one senators from states John McCain carried in 2008 voted for repeal.[34]

In addition, Republican members of Congress faced strong pressure to oppose proposals of the other party. Senators Max Baucus and Charles Grassley, the leaders of the Senate Finance Committee's negotiations over health care reform, both confronted whispers that they might lose their leadership positions if they conceded too much to the other side. Iowa conservatives even threatened that Grassley could face a 2010 primary challenge if he backed Baucus. Obama had Grassley to the White House half a dozen times to talk about health care reform. Just before August 2009 summer recess, the president asked him, "If we give you everything you want—and agree to no public plan—can you guarantee you would support the bill?" "I can't guarantee I would," Grassley replied.[35] Before he switched to the Democratic Party, Arlen Specter reported that Republican Senate leader Mitch McConnell put heavy pressure on Republicans like himself, Olympia Snowe, Susan Collins, George Voinovich, Lisa Murkowski, and Mel Martinez not to cooperate with the White House.[36]

In a similar vein, the executive committee of the Charleston County, South

TABLE 4.1.
Senate Republican Conservatism by Partisanship of State, 2009–2010

Number of Times States Voted Republican in 2000–2008 Presidential Elections	2009		2010	
	Number of Senators	Average Conservative Score*	Number of Senators	Average Conservative Score*
0	3	60	3	63
1	2	69	2	71
2	5	73	5	71
3	31	82	30	83

Source: Ronald Brownstein, "Serving Behind Enemy Lines," *National Journal*, April 24, 2010; Ronald Brownstein, "Pulling Apart," *National Journal*, February 26, 2010.

*Calculated by *National Journal*, which ranks members along a conservative to liberal continuum.

Carolina, Republican Party censored Republican Senator Lindsey Graham because "U.S. Sen. Lindsey Graham in the name of bipartisanship continues to weaken the Republican brand and tarnish the ideals of freedom, rule of law, and fiscal conservatism."[37] Two months later the Lexington County Republican Party Executive Committee censored him for his stands on a range of policies, which it charged "debased" Republican beliefs.[38] When asked in 2010 if he would be as bipartisan if he were facing reelection that November, Graham replied, "The answer's probably no." Similarly, he understood that John McCain had to win his primary for renomination in Arizona and thus could not take bipartisan stances.[39]

In January 2010, 55 percent of Republicans and Republican leaners wanted Republican leaders in Congress, who were following a consistently conservative path, to move in a *more* conservative direction.[40] In perhaps the most extreme expression of this orientation, four months later the Utah Republican Party denied longtime conservative Senator Robert Bennett its nomination for reelection. The previous month, Republican Governor Charlie Crist had to leave his party and run for the Senate as an Independent in Florida because he was unlikely to win the Republican nomination against conservative Marco Rubio. In September, Senator Lisa Murkowski lost her renomination in Alaska to a largely unknown candidate on the far right of the political spectrum. The previous year, Republican Senator Arlen Specter of Pennsylvania switched parties, believing there was little chance he could win a Republican primary against conservative Pat Toomey.

Similarly, House Republicans with any moderate leanings were more concerned about the pressures from their right than about potential fallout from opposing a popular president. The conservative Republican Study Committee—

which included more than 100 of the 178 House Republicans—called for enforcing party unity on big issues and hinted at retribution against defectors. Conservatives also raised the prospect of primary challenges,[41] as they did in the 2009 race to fill the seat in New York State's 23rd congressional district. Led by Sarah Palin and Dick Armey, conservatives forced the Republican candidate to withdraw from the race shortly before Election Day.

Compounding the pressure has been the development of partisan communications networks—led by liberal blogs and conservative talk radio—that relentlessly incite each party's base against the other. These constant fusillades help explain why presidents now face lopsided disapproval from the opposition party's voters more quickly than ever—a trend that discourages that party's legislators from working with the White House.

These centrifugal forces affect most the Republican Party. The Right has more leverage to discipline legislators because, as we have seen, conservative voters constitute a larger share of the GOP coalition than do liberals of the Democratic Party. The Right's partisan communications network is also more ferocious than the Left's.

Given the broad influences of ideology and constituency, it is not surprising that Frances Lee has shown that presidential leadership itself demarcates and deepens cleavages in Congress. The differences between the parties and the cohesion within them on floor votes are typically greater when the president takes a stand on issues. When the president adopts a position, members of his party have a stake in his success, while opposition party members have a stake in the president losing. Moreover, both parties take cues from the president that help define their policy views, especially when the lines of party cleavage are not clearly at stake or already well established.[42] This dynamic of presidential leadership was likely to complicate further Obama's efforts to win Republican support.

According to Republican Representative Michael Castle of Delaware, the gulf between the parties had grown so wide that most Republicans simply refused to vote for any Democratic legislation. "We are just into a mode where there is a lot of Republican resistance to voting for anything the Democrats are for or the White House is for."[43]

The Prospect of Democratic Support

It was unlikely, then, that Obama would receive much support from Republicans. But what about the Democrats? Even before taking office, Obama endured a baptism by friendly fire. The expanded and emboldened congressional Democrats greeted his tax proposals with disdain, dragged him into a political squabble over his Senate successor, and chafed at key appointments to his administration. Obama called for bold action on a stimulus plan to rescue the sagging economy and saw his party's leaders respond by pushing the deadline for the package from Inauguration Day to mid-February.

Democrats described two forces as contributing to the less-than-full embrace of Obama out of the gates: a weariness of being taken for granted for eight years by the outgoing Bush administration, and a sense that the $700 billion Troubled Asset Relief Program was rushed through in the fall of 2008 in two weeks, a de facto abdication of Congress's responsibility. House Majority Leader Steny H. Hoyer dismissed a reporter's suggestion that Democrats would go easy on oversight of the administration, holding up a copy of the congressional newspaper *The Hill* with its headline quoting Senate Majority Leader Harry M. Reid's declaration that "I Don't Work for Obama."[44]

The new administration also faced a potential problem in trying to steer congressional leaders and committee chairs who might be reluctant to surrender too much of the power they regained from Republicans in 2006. "Many members of Congress have been there many years, and there are some people who just two years ago got back the gavel, who now have to cede some of their authority to the incoming administration," said Howard Paster, President Bill Clinton's first director of legislative affairs. "They are going to be supportive, but they are also not going to cede all of their authority. Human nature doesn't allow for that."[45]

Nevertheless, Democrats wanted the president to succeed and knew that their success was directly related to his. To succeed, however, the president would have to hold his party cohort together. Did Democrats represent a coherent coalition that would naturally support the president's initiatives? Did Democrats come from constituencies that were solidly behind Obama? To answer these questions, we need to explore the cross-pressures between party and constituency that have plagued Democratic coalitions since the New Deal as well as the diversity of ideological positions in the Democratic cohort.

Constituency Cross-Pressures

As each party's electoral coalition has grown more ideologically homogeneous since the 1960s, the country has witnessed an increase in straight party voting. The increasing sophistication of redistricting software, which has allowed state legislatures to draw districts that reliably lean toward one party, has reinforced the trend of House and presidential candidates of the same party winning a district. In 2004, there were only fifty-nine split districts, the lowest number in the post–World War II era. Bush carried forty-one Democratic House districts and John Kerry won in eighteen Republican ones.

The 2008 election represented an exception to the trend, however. The number of split districts increased to eighty-three. Forty-eight House Democrats represented districts that preferred Republican presidential nominee John Mc-

Cain to Obama in 2008. Most of these districts were in Southern and Border states or culturally conservative rural areas where Obama struggled. Twenty-three of these Democrats were serving their first or second terms in the 111th Congress. Nine won with less than 55 percent of the vote in 2008, and another ten obtained less than 60 percent.

In sum, the Democratic House majority depended entirely upon members whose constituents voted for John McCain. We should expect these cross-pressured members to find it more difficult to support liberal policies than other members of the caucus.

These members faced serious cross pressures when it came to voting on the president's most important initiatives. The opposition party views members representing split districts as tempting targets, especially when they are held by members who have yet to establish themselves or when the most recent presidential results seem to confirm longer-term changes in the district's demography and partisanship.

If we step back a bit further, we find even more Democrats would be cross-pressured. One-third (84) of the 257 Democratic House members elected in 2008 represented districts won by President Bush in 2004 or John McCain in 2008. Forty-eight of those Democrats—eight more than the size of their party' majority—were from districts that voted for both Bush in 2004 and McCain in 2008. That group composed nearly one-fifth of the Democratic House contingent. Thus, many of the gains of Democrats in 2006 and 2008 came from Republican-leaning districts.

By way of contrast, Obama won thirty-four districts that elected a Republican to the House. Only six of these representatives were not at least in their third term, however. It is true that nine of the remaining twenty-eight Republicans were reelected in 2008 with less than 55 percent of the vote, and another ten won reelection with less than 60 percent. One might think that legislators from such closely contested terrain would instinctively prefer compromise to confrontation and that such an orientation would benefit the new president. Yet we have seen that powerful forces pushed them toward confrontation rather than cooperation and thus offered little potential for Obama to obtain their support.

The Senate was no more favorable for the president. Although eight Republican senators represented states Obama won, twelve Democrats represented McCain states. Twenty-two of the sixty Democratic senators (37 percent) in 2009 represented states that had voted Republican in at least two of the previous three presidential elections. Table 4.2 shows the impact of these cross-pressures. Democrats from states that were more likely to support Republican presidential candidates were considerably less liberal than their Democratic colleagues from more reliably Democratic states. Moreover, a substantial number of Democratic senators represented Republican states.

There were constituency pressures in addition to partisanship, of course. Regarding climate change legislation, for example, ten moderate Senate Democrats from states dependent on coal and manufacturing sent a letter to Presi-

TABLE 4.2.
Senate Democratic Liberalism by Partisanship of State, 2009–2010

Number of Times States Voted Democratic in 2000–2008 Presidential Elections	2009		2010	
	Number of Senators	Average Liberalism Score*	Number of Senators	Average Liberalism Score*
0	13	59	12	60
1	9	64	8	64
2	4	78	4	76
3	33	76	30	76

Source: Ronald Brownstein, "Serving Behind Enemy Lines," *National Journal,* April 24, 2010; Ronald Brownstein, "Pulling Apart," *National Journal,* February 26, 2010.

*Calculated by *National Journal,* which ranks members along a conservative to liberal continuum.

dent Obama in August saying they would not support any climate change bill that did not protect American industries from competition from countries that did not impose similar restraints on climate-altering gases. Without their support, it was unlikely that the Senate could pass a major climate change bill.[46]

Ultimately, forty-four House Democrats opposed the bill. Many of them represented districts that relied heavily on coal for electricity and manufacturing for jobs. The president understood. "I think those forty-four Democrats are sensitive to the immediate political climate of uncertainty around this issue," Obama said. "They've got to run every two years, and I completely understand that."[47]

The Helping Families Save Their Homes Act lost its centerpiece: a change in bankruptcy law the president had once championed that would have given judges the power to lower the amount owed on a home loan. Twelve Democratic Senators joined thirty-nine Republicans to vote against the provision. Some Democrats, like Tim Johnson of South Dakota and Thomas R. Carper of Delaware, represented states that are the corporate home to major banks.[48]

Ideological Diversity

Constituency pressures are always important to members of Congress, but so are their policy views. Much of the growth of the Democratic contingents in the House and the Senate in the 2006 and 2008 elections was the result of success in areas characterized by ideological moderation. It is not surprising that such constituencies elected moderates to Congress. Coalescing these members with the large liberal core of the Democratic caucuses was likely to present a challenge to achieving party unity.

THE MODERATES   A substantial segment of Democrats were moderate on economic and fiscal matters. There were a number of centrist, pro-business Democratic groups, including the New Democrat Coalition (with sixty-nine members), the Democratic Leadership Council, the NDN (founded as the New Democrat Network), and the Third Way. Most visible were the fifty-four members of the House's Blue Dog Coalition of fiscally conservative Democrats.

Ideological differences represented more than fiscal or economic matters. The challenges presented by the diversity of views within the Democratic caucus were especially clear regarding the amendment to the health care reform bill offered by Representative Bart Stupak of Michigan. The amendment would prevent women who received federal insurance subsidies from buying abortion coverage (critics asserted it would make it difficult for women who bought their own insurance to obtain coverage). Stupak had the leverage to win a counterintuitive victory that forced a Democratic-controlled Congress to pass a measure that was hailed as an anti-abortion triumph. For his efforts, the *New York Times* reported, he endured more hatred than perhaps any other member of Congress, much of it from fellow Democrats.[49]

The *National Journal's* vote ratings for the 2009 session of Congress succinctly illustrate the diversity and the results of cross-pressures within the Democratic caucus. The seventy-seven House Democrats in the Progressive Coalition had an average liberalism score of 83 percent, while the average for the fifty-four Democrats in the Blue Dog Coalition was 53 percent. (The average for all House Democrats was 70 percent.)[50]

There were similar problems with the Senate. Charlie Cook calculated that the 111th Congress had twenty-three to twenty-six relatively centrist senators (mostly Democrats) and about forty-one true-blue liberals.[51] Therefore, even if fairly liberal legislation passed the House, which also had a substantial number of moderate Democrats, the odds were good that it would face difficulties in the Senate.

For example, a significant split developed between the two Democratic senators leading efforts to remake the nation's health care system. They disagreed over the contours of a public health insurance plan, the most explosive issue in the debate. Edward M. Kennedy of Massachusetts made it clear that he favored a robust public health care plan, a government-sponsored entity that would compete with private insurers. By contrast, Senator Max Baucus of Montana, chair of the Finance Committee, worked for months with the panel's senior Republican, Charles E. Grassley of Iowa, in the hope of forging a bipartisan bill which would not include the option of a public plan.[52]

Organized labor was a key element in Obama's electoral coalition, and it placed a high priority on the passage of the so-called card-check provision that would have required employers to recognize a union as soon as a majority of workers signed cards saying they wanted a union. Nevertheless, in an example of the power of moderate Democrats to constrain their party's more liberal legislative efforts, Democrats had to drop the provision.[53]

Often both ideological and constituency pressures overlapped. For example, thirty-three members of the Blue Dog Coalition represented districts won by McCain. It is not surprising that such members would be concerned about the midterm elections after domestic spending, the annual deficit, and the national debt all jumped by record amounts. Thus, the potential for clashes on major issues with a largely liberal Democratic majority was substantial. Moreover, it was just such members who became the targets of Republicans and their interest-group allies in major legislative battles.[54]

It is perhaps in recognition of the challenge of governing with his own party that the president planned to use the new Organizing for America network in part to pressure lawmakers—particularly wavering *Democrats*—to help him pass complex legislation on the economy, health care, and energy.[55]

Similarly, a group of liberal bloggers announced in February 2009 that it was teaming up with organized labor and MoveOn.org to form a political action committee, Accountability Now, that would seek to push the Democratic Party farther to the left. The bloggers said they were planning to recruit liberal candidates for challenges against more centrist Democrats currently in Congress. Their intention was to enable Obama to seek more liberal policies without fear of losing support from the more conservative members of his party serving in Congress. (They did not rule out occasional friction with Obama, as well.) The Service Employees International Union and *Daily Kos* also supported this effort.[56] The PAC's first candidate for the 2010 election was Arkansas Lt. Governor Bill Halter, who would challenge Democrat Blanche Lincoln for her Senate seat.

When the White House encountered resistance from moderate Democrats in the Senate on its budget, Americans United for Change, a group financed largely by organized labor, organized an ad campaign with the permission of Democratic strategists close to the White House. The new television advertisements urged centrist Democrats, many of whom had a streak of fiscal conservatism that made them leery of the increases proposed by the president, to support the budget. The spots were broadcast in eleven states and urged senators to support the administration's budget priorities as well. At the same time, Obama's former campaign team urged supporters to call their members of Congress.[57]

The Liberals   Governing from the left would be a challenge. Governing from the middle would be no picnic, either. One of Obama's biggest challenges was dealing with the left of his own party. Two weeks before his inauguration and just hours after he publicly called for speedy passage of a stimulus package to prevent the economic crisis from lasting for years, the president-elect's economic recovery plan ran into crossfire from congressional Democrats. They complained that major components of his plan were not bold enough and urged more focus on creating jobs and rebuilding the nation's energy infrastructure rather than cutting taxes. Further complicating the picture, Democratic senators said they would try to attach legislation to the package that would allow bankruptcy courts to modify home loans, a move Republicans opposed. While conservatives criticized the heavy spending, and moderate Democrats expressed concern about the swelling deficit, liberals pushed for even more money to be devoted to social programs, alternative-energy development, and road, bridge, and school construction.[58]

When Justice David Souter announced his resignation, President Obama's aides invited liberal activists to the White House to discuss his upcoming Supreme Court selection. They told the activists not to lobby for their favorites in the news media or talk down candidates they opposed.[59]

The president touched off a controversy with the left when he reversed his decision to release photographs showing prisoners being abused while in U.S. custody, arguing that public disclosure would threaten the safety of U.S. military personnel abroad and could inflame the rest of the world as he was trying to win new respect for the United States. This action was followed by the decision to resume, with some modifications, the military tribunals used by the Bush administration since the attacks of September 11, 2001. Although administration officials insisted that prisoners would be given more rights than they had under Bush, human rights and civil liberties groups condemned the decision.

The war in Afghanistan was likely to prove an especially difficult sell among Democrats. As we have seen, as early as March 2009, only 49 percent of Democrats in the public approved of Obama's decision to send 17,000 more troops to Afghanistan.[60] By October 2009, only 36 percent of Democrats supported sending even more troops in response to General Stanley McChrystal's request for 40,000 additional soldiers. Indeed, 50 percent of Democrats wanted to begin *withdrawing* troops.[61]

In a year-end briefing on the legislative session, House Speaker Nancy Pelosi made it clear that the president would have to argue his own case to House Democrats as he sought support for a planned surge of 30,000 troops into Afghanistan. She added that she was finished asking her colleagues to back wars that they did not support. "The president's going to have to make his case," Pelosi told reporters. In June, she had urged her colleagues to support a more than $100 billion supplemental funding bill for the wars in Iraq and Afghanistan, arguing that they needed to give the new president time to come up with a plan. But she also promised never to ask them to vote for war spending again.[62]

As Obama's and the Democrats' approval ratings fell and the president attempted to reposition himself to appeal to the middle of the electorate, some on the left excoriated him. When word leaked that in his first State of the Union message, he would propose freezing a portion of the domestic budget for three years, Rachel Maddow of MSNBC likened the plan to "stupid Hooverism." Many liberals remained angry that the president had not pushed harder for the "public option" on health care.

Perhaps the biggest collision with the left occurred over the extension of the Bush-era tax cuts during the lame-duck session of the 111th Congress. Many prominent liberals attacked the president for abandoning his principles in agreeing to extend the tax cuts for the wealthy and to a high threshold for the estate tax. House Democrats passed a resolution opposing the compromise plan the White House worked out with Republican leaders. The Progressive Change Campaign Committee, a liberal group that had repeatedly attacked Obama on the left, aired two television commercials demanding that the president not agree to any compromise with the GOP that would extend tax cuts for household incomes above $250,000 a year. At the same time, Moveon.Org released its own new ad that included a video montage from Americans all over the country urging the president not to compromise.[63] Sam Graham-Felsen, who described himself as Obama's chief blogger during the 2008 campaign, wrote an op-ed in the *Washington Post* complaining that the president had not activated his grassroots supporters in major legislative battles and needed to do so on taxes.[64]

This opposition frustrated the president. In an unscheduled visit to the White House briefing room, Obama displayed uncharacteristic emotion when he suggested that liberals were unrealistic about what they could achieve in Washington.

> This is the public option debate all over again. So I pass a signature piece of legislation, where we finally get health care for all Americans, something that Democrats have been fighting for for a hundred years, but because there was a provision in there that they didn't get, that would have affected maybe a couple of million people, even though we got health insurance for 30 million people and the potential for lower premiums for 100 million people, that somehow that was a sign of weakness and compromise.[65]

In addition, liberals should not keep complaining every time they do not get everything they want:

> Now, if that's the standard by which we are measuring success or core principles, then, let's face it, we will never get anything done. People will have the satisfaction of having a purist position and no victories for the American people. And we will be able to feel good about ourselves and sanctimonious about how pure our intentions are and how tough we are, and in the meantime, the American people are still seeing themselves not able to get health insurance because of a preexisting condition, or not being able to pay their bills because their unemployment insurance ran out.[66]

Conclusion

Despite large Democratic majorities in both houses of Congress, Barack Obama was unlikely to find it easy to pass the most significant components of his legislative program. To begin, he did not enjoy a widespread perception that his election signaled a mandate for substantial changes in public policy. His margin of victory was not especially large and his coattails were short. Moreover, the public had not shifted its views in a more liberal direction. Unified government was certainly an advantage in influencing the congressional agenda, but it did not guarantee presidential dominance of the legislature.

The White House anticipated that it could attract bipartisan support from Republicans. The foundations of this expectation were weak, however. Partisan polarization was at an historic high, and the Republican Party's locus in the economic and social conservatism of the South reinforced the disinclination of Republicans to offer support across the aisle. Indeed, the more homogeneous conservative ideology of Republican activists and the Right's strident and ever-expanding communications network meant that Obama would face a vigorous partisan opposition with strong incentives not to cooperate with the White House.

Democrats were more ideologically diverse than Republicans, posing yet another challenge for Obama. Many Democratic members of Congress represented Republican-leaning districts, and many were more moderate than the president. Democratic majorities in both chambers of Congress depended entirely upon members whose constituents voted for John McCain.

These cross-pressured and ideologically divergent members were much less likely to support Obama's initiatives than the rest of the Democratic caucus. At the same time, liberals were likely to be frustrated at efforts to placate their more moderate colleagues.

The analysis of Barack Obama's opportunities for obtaining congressional support leads us to predict that obtaining the legislature's backing for his most significant initiatives would pose challenges. It seems especially clear that he would attract few Republican votes for these policies and, thus, that bipartisanship would not be a successful strategy for governing. Instead, he would have to rely on party leadership. In chapter 5, I examine the president's leadership of Congress, and in chapter 6, I test the prediction by examining the congressional support the president actually received.

CHAPTER 5

Creating Opportunities?

LEADING CONGRESS

Barack Obama came to office with a large agenda. His most important proposals required congressional approval, and the White House moved aggressively to obtain it. In this chapter, I examine the Obama White House's efforts to lead Congress, focusing especially on its efforts to obtain bipartisan support and the president's leadership of his own party.

These two approaches represent different strategies for governing. We saw in chapter 4 that the prospects for Republican support were quite limited. Nevertheless, the president pursued bipartisanship in an energetic effort to create opportunities for major changes in public policy by persuading some in the opposition to support his proposals.

We also saw in chapter 4 that keeping the large Democratic majorities in both houses of Congress unified enough to pass significant legislation was likely to pose a challenge for the White House. Leading his party and exploiting the opportunities these majorities offered the White House would be a core activity of Obama's presidency.

Emphasis on Legislation

Befitting a presidency seeking to pass a huge agenda, the Obama administration placed a high priority on recruiting personnel with congressional experience. The president was the first chief executive elected directly from Congress since John F. Kennedy took office nearly a half century earlier. Vice President Biden had served in the Senate since 1972. White House Chief of Staff Rahm Emanuel was a rising star in the House. Four Cabinet secretaries and the head of the CIA also were former members of Congress.

Obama chose as his legislative director Phil Schiliro. President Bill Clinton's first director of legislative affairs Howard Paster noted that Schiliro's appointment as the chief liaison to Congress was announced within a week of the election, while his own appointment to that job did not occur until January 1993.[1]

Schiliro was for twenty-five years Henry Waxman's closest aide. Waxman, the chair of the House Energy and Commerce Committee, was a central figure in drafting health care and climate change legislation. Lisa Konwinski, Schiliro's deputy, spent nearly a decade working for Kent Conrad, the chair of the Senate Budget Committee.[2] Melody Barnes, the domestic policy director, had been a trusted aide to Ted Kennedy. Emanuel hired Jim Messina, who was Senate Finance Committee chair Max Baucus's chief of staff, as a deputy chief of staff at the White House.

Peter Orszag, the former director of the Congressional Budget Office, became head of the Office of Management and Budget (OMB). Rob Nabors, former majority staff director of the House Appropriations Committee, served in the number two position at OMB until he moved to the White House as a deputy chief of staff. Senior advisor Peter Rouse had worked for Obama in the Senate, and, equally important, had been Democratic leader Tom Daschle's chief of staff. Many other former congressional aides served in departmental and agency legislative liaison posts.

Emanuel was well aware that many new appointees had pivotal friendships on the Hill that Obama could exploit, and he encouraged them to be constantly in touch with their old bosses and colleagues in Congress, advancing the president's program and gathering intelligence from the halls of the Capitol. "That was a strategy," he said. "We had a deep bench of people with a lot of relationships that run into both the House and Senate extensively. And so we wanted to use that to our maximum advantage."[3]

From the first, Emanuel hosted a daily meeting in his White House office to review congressional business. Attendees included Schiliro and his congressional team, along with representatives of the policy, political, and press offices. Emanuel also maintained contact with committee chairs and ranking members to catch up on business before their panels. The president attended at least part of those sessions. Emanuel also met with all the major groups of Democrats, including the Blue Dog budget hawks, the moderate New Democrats, and the House freshman class. He spoke to House and Senate leadership aides multiple times every day, and consulted with House Speaker Nancy Pelosi and Senate Majority Leader Harry Reid several times a week. Even GOP lawmakers praised the White House attention. "He always takes my calls," said Senator Olympia Snowe, a moderate Republican who was often the object of White House efforts at persuasion.[4]

In addition, the administration was ready to move rapidly with its legislative agenda. We don't intend to stumble into the next administration," Obama declared during the transition. "We are going to hit the ground running. We're going to have clear plans of action." To that end, emissaries of the president-elect met with every congressional committee chair. Obama worked the phones and sent Emanuel to the Hill. When Henry Waxman won a bitter contest to become the next chair of the House Energy and Commerce Committee, Obama called to congratulate him.[5] The White House's goal was to have economic, health (the Children's Health Insurance Program), and spending legislation on the new president's desk soon after he took office.[6]

The administration was similarly prepared for the retirement of Supreme Court Justice David Souter. Emanuel had commissioned a strategy memorandum intended to dictate the process, declaring, "The day we get a vacancy, we want to have a short list of people ready." The White House had full dossiers on nearly all the major candidates within days of Souter's announcement.[7]

Bipartisanship

From the beginning, Barack Obama tried to strike a bipartisan pose. On the night of his election, he implored Democrats and Republicans alike to "resist the temptation to fall back on the same partisanship and pettiness and immaturity that has poisoned our politics for so long." In his press conference on November 25, 2008, the president-elect declared, "it's important . . . that we enter into the new administration with a sense of humility and a recognition that wisdom is not the monopoly of any one party. In order for us to be effective . . . Republicans and Democrats are going to have to work together."[8]

Moreover, the president and his aides believed that a fair number of Republican lawmakers would rally behind the nation's first African American president at a time of crisis.[9] They saw his liberal programs drawing on Americans' desire for action and also counted on Obama's moderate, even conservative, temperament, to hurdle the ideological obstacles that had paralyzed Washington.[10]

Democratic activists agreed. "It is quite possible to see him as liberal and having an activist agenda, but being a type of leader who does not polarize partisans and finds ways of bringing people together to work on the things where they can find common ground," said Stanley B. Greenberg, a pollster in Bill Clinton's White House. "With this type of leader, the pent-up demand for action on the economy, health care and energy allows us to reach a series of big moments where many Republicans join the process and perhaps proposals pass with overwhelming majorities."[11]

The Anti-Bush

Any move toward bipartisanship would have been a major change from the orientation of George W. Bush. Early in his first term, Bush concluded that it would not be possible to obtain Democratic support, as he had as governor of Texas, so he made few efforts at bipartisanship. He rejected the approach of obtaining the support of a broad majority of Congress through consultation, collaboration, and compromise. Instead, he centered his legislative strategy on maximizing unity among Republicans. As one of his senior political advisors declared, "This is not designed to be a 55 percent presidency. This is designed to be a presidency that moves as much as possible of what we believe into law while holding fifty [percent] plus one of the country and the Congress."[12] The White House's emphasis was to find the "right" solution and ram it through the legislature. During Bush's first term, despite narrow Republican majorities on Capitol Hill, he enacted several of his key priorities, such as tax cuts and prescription drug coverage under Medicare, into law.

In the 2004 presidential election, Republican strategists concluded that there was little pliability in the electorate. As a result, they felt they could not substantially broaden their electoral coalition. Instead, they focused most of their efforts in 2004 on energizing their partisan base and encouraging turnout rather than on changing the preferences of the electorate.[13] As Republican political strategist Matthew Dowd put it, the presidential election was "about *motivation* rather than *persuasion*."[14]

Bush's partisan strategy incited impassioned resistance, making it difficult to advance legislative proposals such as reforming Social Security and immigration policy that required bipartisan support. Moreover, his unbending approach proved self-defeating because it provoked a backlash that helped deliver the government to his Democratic critics. Obama hoped to avoid the hostility that characterized the Bush presidency.

Going the Extra Mile

As president-elect, Barack Obama did not adopt a partisan posture during the transition or the early days of his presidency. "We don't have Republican or Democratic problems. We have got American problems," Obama said after meeting with congressional leaders from both parties in an effort to obtain support for his economic stimulus package. He listened as Republicans raised concerns about waste and transparency and agreed with a suggestion by House Republican Whip Eric Cantor that the White House put the entire contents of the legislation online in a user-friendly way so others could see how the money was being spent. Senate Minority Leader Republican Mitch McConnell later reported, "I thought the atmosphere for bipartisan cooperation was sincere on all sides."[15]

Obama resisted inserting himself in the unresolved Senate contests in Georgia and Minnesota. Although he recorded a radio advertisement for the Democratic candidate in Georgia, he did not visit there to avoid appearing to be too political. The president-elect also won praise from conservatives for retaining Robert Gates as defense secretary, for naming General James L. Jones as his national security advisor, and for selecting the moderate Timothy F. Geithner, who helped draw up the Bush administration's Wall Street bailout plan, as his Treasury secretary. He named three Republicans, including Gates, to his cabinet.

Shortly after being named White House chief of staff, Rahm Emanuel signaled to Republicans that the president-elect wanted to work alongside them. He met with Senate Republican leaders, gave them his cell phone number and personal e-mail address, and promised to return any communication within twenty-four hours. He told them to call at any hour if they needed to reach him, and he asked them to submit their ideas for the economic recovery plan and other issues of potential agreement.[16]

On ABC's *This Week* on January 11, Obama hinted at an inclusive and interactive approach when he spoke of a "collaborative . . . process" that produces a great compromise in which "everybody is going to have to give" to confront gaping federal deficits. Rahm Emanuel declared that Obama was committed to "coupling" the public investment prized by liberals with "deadly serious spending reform" in areas from military procurement to entitlements that could appeal to conservatives.[17]

A few days before his inauguration, the president-elect was the guest of honor at a dinner at conservative columnist George Will's Chevy Chase home. Others attending were some of the right's most prominent commentators, including syndicated columnist Charles Krauthammer, CNBC television host and commentator Lawrence Kudlow, *Weekly Standard* editor William Kristol, *New York Times* columnist David Brooks, *Wall Street Journal* editorial page editor Paul Gigot, *Wall Street Journal* columnist Peggy Noonan, and Fox News commentator Michael Barone.[18] "Obama's a man who has demonstrated he is interested in hearing other views," said Krauthammer.

In yet another gesture of goodwill, Obama frequently sought John McCain's advice on national security matters, including potential nominees, and kept him fully briefed on his thinking. Obama also made McCain the guest of honor at a dinner on the night before the inauguration.[19]

Rahm Emanuel and Lawrence H. Summers, Obama's economic advisor, met privately with Senate Republicans the day before the Senate voted on freeing the remaining $350 billion in TARP funds. Even Republicans who were not persuaded by the consultation said they were impressed by the candor of the two men. "I think they have been pretty impressive," said Senator Mitch McConnell of Kentucky, the Republican leader. "They are saying all the right things, and I think they did themselves some good in the briefing." The president-elect also telephoned some senators, including Republican Olympia J. Snowe, urging them to release the money.[20]

Once he took the oath of office, Obama dispatched a top official to brief congressional Republicans before he issued executive orders on terrorism detainees. He also met with the leaders of both parties in Congress, in keeping with his campaign promise of bipartisanship. Yet in a polite but pointed exchange with House Republican Whip Eric Cantor, the president noted the parties' fundamental differences on tax policy toward low-wage workers, and insisted that his view would prevail. "We just have a difference here, and I'm president," Obama told Cantor. Obama was being lighthearted, and lawmakers of both parties laughed.[21]

The president went further on the stimulus bill. He made Republican-favored tax cuts a key component of his stimulus plan, at the cost of complaints from his fellow Democrats. At Obama's urging, Democrats also stripped from the bill provisions such as aid for family planning services and restoration for the National Mall that Republicans had ridiculed as wasteful spending and unrelated to economic stimulus. The president met with congressional leaders of both parties at the White House. Most impressively, the day before the House voted on the bill, Obama traveled to Capitol Hill and spent three hours speaking, separately, to the House and Senate Republican caucuses. GOP members emerged saying nice things about him. White House chief of staff Rahm Emanuel also met with eleven of the more moderate Republicans at the White House that evening.[22]

The day's debate contrasted with the president's conciliatory gestures, as did the lack of Republican support for the president. Nevertheless, Obama followed the House vote with a cocktail party at the White House for the House and Senate leaders of both parties.[23] The president also met individually with Republican senators Susan Collins and Olympia Snowe,[24] and he invited some members from both parties to the White House to watch the Super Bowl on the eve of the Senate debate.

In addition, congressional Democrats allowed Republicans to offer amendments on the floor during debate, and the House Appropriations Committee held a formal mark-up session to deal with amendments to the economic stimulus bill. Democrats even convened a conference committee on the bill. Although it was largely irrelevant to the final agreement because its members met after Senate Democrats and three Republicans had already cut a deal on the plan, Republicans had yet another venue for expressing their dissent.[25]

The president also reached out to Republicans and conservative interests outside of Congress. He obtained the support of both the National Association of Manufacturers and the United States Chamber of Commerce for the stimulus bill. In addition, four Republican governors—California's Arnold Schwarzenegger, Connecticut's Jodi Rell, Florida's Charlie Crist, and Vermont's Jim Douglas—signed a letter calling for its enactment. Obama later felt he had failed to exploit properly the support he received on the stimulus from Republican governors and that he was courting the wrong Republicans (those in Congress).[26]

Frustration

As I discuss in more detail in chapter 6, seeking bipartisan support did not prove to be a useful strategy for the president. By the second week in February, he had apparently given up on winning many Republican votes. Frustrated that debate over the stimulus bill was being dominated by Republicans' criticism, and that his overtures had yielded little in the way of support from across the aisle, the president switched to publicly pressuring them, and rallying fellow Democrats, with a hard-line message about his unwillingness to compromise his priorities. Democrats began a radio advertising campaign in the districts of twenty-eight House Republicans, calling them "out of step."

The president held his first prime-time press conference on February 9, three weeks into his tenure. Acknowledging that his effort to change the political climate in Washington had yielded little, he made it clear that he had all but given up hope of securing a bipartisan consensus behind his economic recovery package. The sharp tone at the news conference and at a rally in Indiana earlier in the day signaled a shift by the White House in the fractious debate over his stimulus package. With no Republicans in the House voting for the economic plan and just three in the Senate, Obama began a week of barnstorming stops that would also take him to Florida and Illinois to create momentum behind his program. Gone were the soothing notes of the previous three weeks. The president offered a barbed detailed critique of the Republican argument that his plan would just create more government jobs and authorize billions in wasteful spending.[27]

White House Chief of Staff Rahm Emanuel conducted a post-mortem analysis of the battle over the economic stimulus bill in which the president's senior advisors concluded that a bipartisan approach to governing was unlikely to succeed; consequently, Obama began scaling back his appeals to congressional Republicans.[28] Of necessity, the president would have to focus on managing and maintaining the support of members of Congress already inclined to support him.

The White House stopped hosting bipartisan "cocktail parties," and the only Republican invited to the 2010 Super Bowl party was Representative Ahn Cao, the sole Republican in either chamber to support the health care bill. Republican leaders and the president spent little time together, and White House and congressional aides who witnessed the interactions described the encounters as "strained" and "scripted."[29] In March 2010, House Republican Whip Eric Cantor recalled, "When they first came into office, I could have a meeting or two with Rahm and talk with him about the stimulus bill. But the conversations have been few and far between over the last six months."[30]

A Second Wind

Nevertheless, the president wanted the legitimacy of bipartisan support—and the votes of Republicans—for his comprehensive health care reform plan. The White House focused on persuading moderate Republican Senators Susan Collins and Olympia Snowe and lavished attention on the latter.[31]

In April 2009, the president renewed his call for bipartisan cooperation during a White House meeting with congressional leaders of both parties. However, Senate Minority Leader Mitch McConnell said the session did little to change the equation for Republicans. "We discussed bipartisanship and—of course—that will depend entirely on what the substance looks like," he said.[32] Yet the changes the Republicans demanded were not ones the president could make. His bipartisanship was more about collegiality and civility than it was about compromise on core issues.

Still, the president made efforts. Before he made his selection of Sonia Sotomayor to replace Justice David Souter, he called every member of the Senate Judiciary Committee. "He asked if I had any suggestions for nominees," said Republican Senator Charles Grassley. "This is the first time I've ever been called by a president on a Supreme Court nomination, be it a Republican or a Democrat."[33] He also called all the members of the committee in preparation for his second nomination to the Court.[34]

In October, former Senate Republican leader Bill Frist, George W. Bush health and human services secretary Tommy G. Thompson, Medicare chief Mark McClellan, California Republican Governor Arnold Schwarzenegger, and New York Mayor Michael R. Bloomberg (a Republican turned independent) spoke favorably of overhauling the nation's health care system (although they couched their comments with plenty of caveats regarding the details). Most of the endorsements came at the prompting of the White House, which immediately circulated and promoted the statements in e-mails and telephone calls.[35]

After Scott Brown won the special election in Massachusetts to replace Ted Kennedy in the Senate in January 2010, the Democrats lost their ability to defeat a filibuster and the president tried once again for bipartisan support. Obama made bipartisanship a key element of his State of the Union address eight days later. In a high-profile televised question-and-answer session at a Republican policy forum, the president sparred with House Republicans, earning praise for his agility during a gathering that was meant to put the spotlight on the minority party and force its leaders to provide alternative solutions rather than simply object to the president's plans. Neither side gave much in terms of policy, even as they professed interest in moving past the bitterness of the past year and working together. Obama promised to invite Republican leaders to the White House once a month in 2010 to talk through issues with him and Democratic leaders.

Most significantly, the president hosted a bipartisan summit on health care at the Blair House, across the street from the White House. Obama felt that such an event could be an antidote to the cynicism about Washington expressed by voters and perhaps provide an opportunity to woo a few Republicans. Some White House allies said the session proved critical in putting health care back on the national agenda. The event enabled Obama to claim the high ground on bipartisanship; after Brown's victory, he needed to be seen as reaching out to the other side. He also wanted to force Republicans to put their ideas on the table, so that the public would see the debate as a choice between two ways to attack a pressing problem, not just a referendum on what Republicans derisively called "ObamaCare."[36]

On February 25, 2010, Obama and twenty-eight lawmakers squeezed around a square of tables in the Garden Room of Blair House. After more than seven hours of discussion, the president lingered behind, shaking hands, making one last pitch for his stalled initiative. "There were some good things that came out of that," he told advisors in the Oval Office afterward. He said he wanted the final legislation to incorporate a handful of ideas Republicans raised during the session. A few aides protested, asking if the White House should not extract a few votes in return. Yet Obama still held out hope for a couple of converts. "We're going to accept some of these," he replied.[37]

The president sent a letter to congressional leaders of both parties on March 2, 2010, offering to address some of the concerns expressed by Republicans in the health care debate. Obama said that he was open to four specific ideas raised by Republicans at the daylong health care forum the previous week, including encouraging the use of tax-advantaged medical savings accounts and increasing payments to doctors who treat Medicaid patients.[38]

Administration officials made overtures to several Republicans. They spoke to Peter Roskam. They conferred with John Shadegg about ways to sell insurance across state lines and with Tom Coburn regarding his idea to hire undercover Medicare fraud investigators. The president spent hours courting Olympia Snowe. Even so, Republicans denounced the summit as an 11th-hour publicity stunt and declared that they would not help pass Obama's health care bill, even if it did include some of their proposals.[39] To maintain the integrity of his proposal, the president could not accept key suggestions of even moderate Republicans like Susan Collins.[40]

On March 20, 2010, the day before the final House vote on health care reform, Obama told House Democrats that the bill was a compromise measure including many Republican ideas, even though congressional Republicans were all opposing it. "This bill tracks the recommendations not just of Democrat Tom Daschle, but also Republicans Bob Dole and Howard Baker," the president declared.[41]

After the passage of health care reform, the White House focused on financial regulation. Once again, he met with Republican leaders and sought their support. Once again, however, they rejected his overtures. For example, during a meeting with leaders of Congress from both parties at the White House, Republicans, and notably their leader in the Senate, Mitch McConnell, declined to support the measure offered by Senate Democrats, arguing that it would only make bailouts of gigantic, risk-laden institutions more likely.[42]

On May 25, 2010, the president had a private 75-minute session with Senate Republicans at their weekly luncheon. Obama and the senators engaged in spirited and at times confrontational exchanges over immigration, spending, White House tactics, and other issues.[43] Nevertheless, Republicans aggressively opposed the president's jobs creation measures, plan for regulation of financial institutions, and what was to be a bipartisan deficit-reduction commission.

The president had more success with Republicans on two important issues during the lame-duck session of the 111th Congress. First, he was able to negotiate a deal on the extension of Bush-era tax cuts, largely by agreeing to the extension, which is what the Republicans wanted the most. To obtain ratification of the New START treaty, Obama mounted an intensive five-week campaign that included a war room on Capitol Hill and an active role for Vice President Biden, who had at least fifty meetings or phone calls with senators. The White House sent reassuring letters to senators concerned about missile defense and the modernization of the nation's nuclear stockpile. The president met with many senators and activated luminaries ranging from Henry Kissinger to Angela Merkel.[44] In the end, thirteen Republicans voted for ratification.

Short Term Gain versus Bipartisanship

In addition to the centrifugal forces of ideology and polarized partisanship, the natural tension between gaining political advantage and obtaining Republican votes made it difficult to cultivate bipartisan cooperation. For months, Republican Senator Lindsey Graham worked with Democratic Senator John Kerry and independent Joseph Lieberman to craft climate change legislation by reconciling the needs of the business and environmental communities. Graham had also visited the White House nineteen times since Obama took office.[45] The senators sounded out key legislators, business groups, advocacy organizations, and others interested in the issue. In an effort to convince wavering senators to embrace the package, the senators focused on lining up support among business interests the bill would impact, holding dozens of closed-door meetings with groups ranging from the American Gas Association to the National Mining Association and the Portland Cement Association.

They planned to announce their bill with considerable fanfare on the morning of April 26, 2010. On April 24, however, Graham sent a sharply worded letter to his two colleagues announcing that he would no longer participate in negotiations on the energy bill. Graham's participation was essential because his support was needed to try to obtain support from other Republicans. As a result, the announcement was canceled.

Graham was troubled by reports that the Senate Democratic leader Harry Reid and the White House were planning to take up an immigration measure before the energy bill. (Graham had worked with Democrats in the past on immigration matters and was expected to be an important bridge to Republicans on that issue as well.) Graham argued that any Senate debate on the highly charged subject of illegal immigration would make it impossible to deal with the difficult issues involved in national energy and global warming policy. He said in his letter that energy must come first and that Democrats appeared to be rushing to take up immigration because of rising anti-immigrant sentiment, including a harsh new measure signed into law in Arizona a few days before.

Graham had taken a substantial risk to be the lone Republican actively working on climate change legislation. He was infuriated that it looked like the Democrats were going to leave him hanging. "I've got some political courage, but I'm not stupid," Graham declared in an interview. "The only reason I went forward is, I thought we had a shot if we got the business and environmental community behind our proposal, and everybody was focused on it. What's happened is that firm, strong commitment disappeared."[46] Graham also feared being labeled as supporting a gas tax. "I won't introduce a bill and have the majority leader . . . say, 'I can't support that gas tax.' I will not let this get blamed on me. It would be the worst thing in the world to take the one Republican working with you and make him own the one thing you don't like."[47]

Unlike an immigration bill, a climate change bill had passed the House in 2009. However, Harry Reid was running for reelection in a state with a large Hispanic population. In addition, Republicans in Arizona gave Democrats a gift when they passed what many viewed as an extreme anti-immigration bill that received national attention. Some Democratic strategists saw the chance to cement relations with Hispanics. Nevertheless, after fellow Democrats voiced skepticism, Reid backed off from his pledge to fast-track an overhaul of the nation's immigration laws on April 27.

The president tried to revive the bipartisan effort. On June 29, he invited twenty-three senators, of both parties, to the White House to try to find some way out of the impasse on climate change legislation. He repeated his call for putting a price on climate-altering pollution through a cap-and-trade system or some other sort of emissions tax. A White House account of the meeting noted, "Not all of the senators agreed with this approach, and the president welcomed other approaches and ideas."[48] There was no reconciling the differences, however, and the bill never came to a floor vote. The well of bipartisanship had been poisoned.

Graham had also been working closely with the White House on legislation that would close the military detention center at Guantánamo Bay, move some of the war-on-terror prisoners there to the U.S. mainland, and create a system to detain al Qaeda members captured later. Graham thought they were close to a deal. Indeed, he later said the meetings were better than he had ever had with the Bush administration. Nevertheless, in early May, and shortly after the ruckus over climate change legislation, the line of communication, in Graham's words, "went completely dead."[49]

Party Leadership

No matter what other resources presidents may have at their disposal, they remain highly dependent on their party to move their legislative programs. Representatives and senators of the president's party usually form the nucleus of coalitions supporting presidential proposals and provide considerably more support than do members of the opposition party. Thus, every president must provide party leadership in Congress, countering the natural tendency toward conflict between the executive and legislative branches that is inherent in the government's system of checks and balances.[50]

The Personal Touch

Rahm Emanuel concluded that previous White House teams tended to focus almost entirely on the handful of leaders of each caucus rather than on building relationships with individual members. "If I think of one thing that we did that was a mistake under President Clinton," he said, "it was that early on it was just too driven through a couple of committee chairmen."[51]

Obama adopted a different approach, holding countless one-on-one meetings with lawmakers. His calls to the Senate Judiciary Committee on Supreme Court nominations took the "advise" part of "advise and consent" to a new level.[52] On the economic stimulus bill, he met with lawmakers in the Capitol, made dozens of phone calls, and held several private meetings with Republicans and Democrats in the Oval Office, the residence of the White House, and aboard *Air Force One*.[53] With regard to his budget, the president, Vice President Biden, and a cadre of advisors arrived on Capitol Hill to talk to a group of sixteen centrist Democrats who wanted to pare the spending proposals.[54] Later, he emphasized health care reform in his personal meetings, sometimes meeting alone and at other times including aides such as Chief of Staff Rahm Emanuel, health czar Nancy-Ann DeParle, or Legislative Affairs Director Phil Schiliro.[55] The president called or met with dozens of Senate and House Democrats regarding the extension of the Bush-era tax cuts in late 2010.[56]

Like most presidents, Obama did not use high-pressure tactics or engage in arm twisting when he met with members of Congress. He made his positions clear but did not force the issue. Instead, he engaged in a discussion, sometimes in detail, of policy, and spent as much time probing their views and reasoning as in expressing his own. He often seemed to be looking for ways to address a member's concerns without compromising his own views.[57]

He did, however, show himself willing to exercise his presidential muscle when he thought it was necessary. In April 2009, Senator Kent Conrad, the

Budget Committee chair, balked at the idea of having the Senate consider health legislation under the fast-track process known as reconciliation, which could avoid a Republican filibuster. At a private meeting, Obama pressed him on it. "I want to keep it on the table as an option," he told the senator. Not long after that, Emanuel visited Conrad on Capitol Hill. Conrad was not convinced, but decided not to stand in the way. "The Budget Committee chairman does not top the president of the United States," he said.[58]

In the final push for health care reform in March 2010, Obama engaged in a round-the-clock effort in which he delved into arcane policy discussions, promised favors, and mapped out election strategy. He met with or called dozens of lawmakers,[59] including ninety-two in the week before the final House vote in March 2010.[60] As one Washington reporter put it, "Some fence-sitters nearly drowned in presidential attention."[61]

When members of Congress visited the White House to talk to Rahm Emanuel, the chief of staff often choreographed "spontaneous" presidential drop-bys so Obama could say hello personally.[62] One of Emanuel's targets in the run-up to the 2009 budget vote was Representative Marion Berry, an Arkansas Democrat who opposed Obama's proposal to save nearly $10 billion over ten years by cutting federal payments to large farms. Berry still seemed agitated after a brief session in Emanuel's office, so the chief of staff played his trump card. "I walked him down to the Oval" and introduced Berry to Obama, Emanuel recalled. The two traded farm jokes and agreed to talk later in the year about a comprehensive review of federal agriculture policy. Berry, a longtime Clinton ally, said he "really did appreciate" the attention and was relieved that Obama appeared willing to back off the cuts, at least for now. When the House voted, he was a yes.[63]

Obama worked hard for the climate change bill, as did senior White House officials, including Emanuel and energy and environment policy coordinator Carol Browner. They focused their efforts on persuading undecided Democrats. A few were taken in to speak to the president. Obama also hosted a Hawaiian-style luau for lawmakers on the south lawn of the White House, providing an opportunity to cajole lingering undecideds over spit-roasted pork and pineapple.[64]

The president doused a brush fire with organized labor over changes to a new excise tax that unions did not like. In a chance encounter in an aide's office that was actually well planned out, Obama pulled AFL-CIO President Richard Trumka into the Oval Office. "We're at the one-yard line. We've just got to get the ball in the end zone," the president said, imploring Trumka to hold his complaints for another day. "Rich, you've got to stay with me."[65]

At other times, the president made his appeals to larger groups of Democrats. In November, he traveled to the Capitol to urge wavering House Democrats to approve a health care overhaul as the House opened debate on legislation that would transform the nation's health insurance system. Obama's rare appearance on the Hill was part of an all-out Democratic effort to rally Democrats.[66]

On March 20, 2010, the day before the final vote on health care reform, the president again traveled to Capitol Hill to speak to House Democrats, making a forceful case for the legislation on both policy and political grounds. He told them they were on the verge of making history. Opening with a quote from Abraham Lincoln, "I am not bound to win but I am bound to be true," he exhorted them to approve the legislation and argued that it was the right thing to do even if it did not win Democrats political points.[67]

According to Emanuel, the Obama White House was well aware of special amenities that it could use to encourage or reward legislative support, and it tracked their use carefully. These amenities included the White House theater, where guests can watch movies and sporting events; formal state dinners; smaller gatherings in the first family's residence, which spouses can join; tickets to the Easter-egg roll for kids; and tickets to the White House tours that members like to give out to their constituents.[68] Almost all such amenities went to Democrats.[69]

There were plenty of complaints about the White House's treatment of party colleagues, however. State party leaders felt slighted and viewed the White House as a hapless and inattentive political operation. Some congressional Democrats and Democratic donors found Obama distant and did not forget Obama's lack of availability for pictures, handshakes, and the like at presidential events. On their own, each misstep or slight may have been trivial, but the cumulative effect did not help the president win the goodwill of many of the constituencies that is required to achieve success in Washington.[70]

More important than social amenities, of course, were concessions to Democrats for themselves or their constituencies. As the House and Senate debated the budget in 2009, Emanuel's West Wing office took on the feel of a legislative bazaar. Forty-six wavering Democrats filed in individually and in groups seeking audiences and expressing concerns. For some, the issue was farm payments; for others, veterans benefits. Fiscal conservatives balked at the $1.2 trillion deficit. One House member wanted to discuss a new federal building in his district. Another sought an appointment with the commerce secretary. On April 2, Emanuel's hospitality paid off. All but three of his visitors voted in the House or Senate for a $3.5 trillion blueprint that preserved Obama's ambitious domestic policy goals.[71]

Three months later, the House voted on the most ambitious energy and climate-change legislation in history. To win the votes of wavering lawmakers and the support of powerful industries required compromises and outright gifts. The biggest concessions went to utilities, which wanted assurances that they could continue to operate and build coal-burning power plants without shouldering new costs. They also won a weakening of the national mandate for renewable energy. A series of compromises was reached with rural and farm-state members that would funnel billions of dollars in payments to agriculture and forestry interests. Automakers, steel companies, natural gas drillers, refiners, universities, and real estate agents all got in on the action. The deal making continued right up until the final minutes, with the bill's co-author, Henry Waxman, doling out billions of dollars in promises on the House floor to secure the final votes needed for passage.[72]

On health care, moderate Senate Democrats such as Ben Nelson, Blanche Lincoln, and Mary Landrieu milked the issue for all it was worth.[73] Indeed, Nelson was so successful in obtaining funds for Nebraska that even Nebraskans viewed it as outrageous.

Making Common Cause

Early in Obama's presidency, the White House assumed it was possible to translate the presidency's strong approval numbers into legislative action. It hoped to provide what Rahm Emanuel called "air cover" for lawmakers to support the president's proposals. "Obviously," Emanuel said, "the president's adoption of something makes it easier to vote for, because he's—let's be honest—popular, and the public trusts him."[74]

When all else failed, Obama painted a grim portrait of what a weakened presidency would mean for Democrats and their lofty legislative ambitions. For example, during a closed-door meeting with Senate Democrats on March 25, 2010, Obama presented his basic political argument to the moderates, telling them that if voters viewed him as an effective president, then Democrats would likely do well in the 2010 elections. "If we don't get health care, and we don't do energy, and we don't take care of these priorities," Obama reportedly said, "I don't care how far you distance yourself from me. I don't care how many times you say I've gotten too liberal, it's just not going to do you any good. It's just not going to help you any."[75]

In 2009, the president met separately with House and Senate Democrats to urge support for his budget. He told them that their collective political standing and their ability to execute an aggressive agenda depended on remaining united. "We're all in this together," the president said.[76] As Emanuel put it at another point, voting for a health bill might be difficult politically, but doing nothing would be worse. "When a party fails to govern, it fails electorally," he declared.[77]

In his private sessions with lawmakers, the president drew the consequences for himself in the starkest terms. "If we fail at this," he told one congressman, "it's going to be harder for us to pull the line on this other stuff. It is going to weaken our presidency."[78]

On March 15, 2010, Obama rode in his private cabin on *Air Force One* with liberal Congressman Dennis Kucinich on a flight to a health care reform rally in Strongsville, Ohio. They cordially debated the substance of the bill but remained at loggerheads. Finally, the president recalled that it was Kucinich, during the Iowa caucuses, who directed his delegates to back Obama on a second ballot. "Dennis, you were the only candidate to do that," he said. Now, Obama said, his presidency was on the line. This was not about him, "but about our ability to get anything done."[79]

Obama gave his personal commitment to lawmakers who made tough votes for it that he would not abandon them at election time. David Axelrod said the president was eager to "campaign for folks who showed the courage to stand up," adding, "I think he'll do it with a special relish."[80] In a televised session with Senate Democrats on February 3, 2010, Obama delivered a message of solidarity, assuring the beleaguered lawmakers: "I'm there in the arena with you." The White House also signaled to lawmakers that assistance for midterm elections—for example, presidential visits and fund-raisers—would be prioritized for those who supported the bill.[81]

Nevertheless, by July 2010, House Democrats were lashing out at the White House, venting long-suppressed anger over what they saw as President Obama's lukewarm efforts to help them win reelection. The *Washington Post* reported that a widespread belief had taken hold among Democratic House members that they had dutifully gone along with the White House on politically risky issues—including the stimulus plan, the health care overhaul, and climate change—and were left to defend their votes on the campaign trail without much help from the White House. Moreover, the president did not push the climate change bill in the Senate. Many of them were angry that Obama had actively campaigned for Democratic Senate candidates but had done fewer events for House members. The boiling point came on July 13 during a closed-door meeting of House Democrats in the Capitol. Speaker Nancy Pelosi excoriated White House press secretary Robert Gibbs's public comments the previous weekend that the House majority was in doubt. Attempting to quell the uprising, Obama met privately with House Democratic leaders the next evening to reassure them of his support.[82]

Some congressional Democrats also complained that petty slights, dropped promises, poor communications, messaging mismanagement, the failure to inform Congress in advance of important policy or personnel decisions, and an occasional lack of White House engagement strained relationships between the president and Capitol Hill.[83]

Hands Off

"One of the mistakes of the past is that when presidents arrive on Capitol Hill with legislation chiseled into stone, it's not well received," reflected David Axelrod, one of Obama's most influential advisors. "You have to give people a sense of ownership."[84] Thus, the White House ceded Congress ample freedom. "The president set parameters or general principles of what he wants done," Axelrod said. "He's given them the latitude on how to achieve those ends."[85]

Although Obama's policy advisors had detailed plans for the economic stimulus package, it decided to offer only a vague outline to Congress, not wanting to appear to dictate to the legislative branch. The White House was surprised when aides to House Appropriations Committee chair David Obey soon complained that the Obama plan lacked enough detail. The suspicion in the House was that Obama was not really being sensitive to congressional prerogative when he punted on the details; instead, he was trying to dump the whole spending bill—and the potentially onerous responsibility for throwing around billions in taxpayer money—on lawmakers, so he would not have to own it. "There's a cognitive dissonance there," a senior administration official complained. "On one hand they want to feel like they're in charge, but then on the other they also want guidance and political cover." Ultimately, the White House understood that it could not simply depend on Congress to pass the legislation. "We realized we had to go out and sell it," declared deputy chief of staff Jim Messina.[86]

Obama defended his decision not to send a detailed blueprint to Congress, letting lawmakers figure out the specifics themselves. "Part of the reason that we did not simply design our own plan and try to jam it down the throats of Congress is we want them to see some of the contradictions in their own positions and, over time, you know, sort through some of those tensions, make some tough choices, working with us," he said.[87] White House aides also argued that if the new administration put a full plan on the table, both parties would inevitably have picked it apart. Moreover, Obama directed his staff members to set a respectful tone, keeping in mind that Republicans would be needed on future issues like energy and health care reform.[88]

Some members of Congress said Obama's team would have been better off taking a much stronger hand in writing the original House bill, keeping out provisions that Republicans would later use to portray it as stuffed with pork and programs that had little to do with the economy.[89]

When negotiators for the two chambers met to reconcile the differences in their bills and a bipartisan group of senators led by Ben Nelson and Susan Collins had secured enough votes to hold up final approval of the bill until it was scaled back to under $800 billion, the White House, led by Rahm Emanuel and budget director Peter Orszag, inserted itself as arbitrator and effectively took charge of the process. It repeated a similar routine in the battle over the president's budget and the omnibus spending bill. In each case, once the two chambers passed their versions of the bills, the White House stepped in to referee a compromise.[90]

The Helping Families Save Their Homes Act lost its centerpiece: a change in bankruptcy law the president had championed that would have given judges the power to lower the amount owed on a home loan. Twelve Democrats joined thirty-nine Republicans to vote against the measure. Administration officials barely participated in the negotiations, a factor that lobbyists said significantly strengthened their hand.[91]

Many Democrats drew lessons from President Clinton's health care reform effort,[92] which failed to receive a vote in either chamber of Congress—and which was followed by large Republican electoral gains in the 1994 midterm elections and the Democratic loss of both houses of Congress. The Clinton administration took nearly a year to prepare a plan behind closed doors while lobbyists marshaled their forces and then unveiled a 1,342-page proposal of comic complexity that befuddled even its allies. The detailed plan also stoked resentment among Congress's proud Democratic committee barons.

"The lesson we learned from 1994 is that it didn't work for the Clinton administration to come with a set plan," House Majority Leader Steny Hoyer said. "It's necessary to build this from the bottom up."[93] Thus, Obama provided just an outline of broad themes and fairly specific directives and invited lawmakers to fill in the details. "Had we put a plan out, the entire debate would have been changes to the plan," said Emanuel. "It would have been how the president is failing or succeeding."[94] The White House's vagueness also may have kept some key players from being angered early in the process and may have given members of Congress more sense of ownership of the bill.[95]

When Obama weighed in on questions of policy and strategy, the discussion pivoted mainly on broadly shared goals rather than the concrete means of achieving them.[96] Senate Finance Committee chair Max Baucus agreed with this approach, wanting the White House to back off and let the Senate worry about the details.[97] He spent months negotiating with Republicans Charles Grassley and Olympia Snowe.

There were costs to Obama's according Congress so much latitude to craft health care policy. The White House thought the congressional process would play out and then it would sell the bill to the public.[98] Yet the hands-off approach increased the chances for protracting the legislative process. The president opposed House Energy and Commerce Committee chair Henry Waxman's decision to move the climate change bill before dealing with health care, concluding that making representatives cast a tough vote for climate change legislation and then it not passing in the Senate would make it more difficult for them to support health care later. Moreover, because the Energy and Commerce Committee also had jurisdiction over health care, focusing first on climate change held up the health care bill.[99]

The president's critics suggested that he should have been more assertive to put his stamp on the process and the legislation.[100] More time considering the health care reform bill meant more stories focused on opposition to health care and also on the inability of Democrats to agree. A lengthy process also gave opponents more time to organize. The lack of guidance from the White House allowed the House, where vigorous liberals were in charge, to work its will and pass legislation that was too far to the left for the Senate and the country. This product increased criticism from the right and helped inspire Tea Party activists.

Critics, especially on health care, argued that Obama's approach gave Congress too much latitude to engage in backroom deal making and expedient trade-offs. Moreover, the months of delay, closed-door negotiations, and special deals—like the so-called Cornhusker kickback that would have given Nebraska extra money to pay for Medicaid—tarnished the effort and the president who won office by promising to change the way Washington operates. By the time of Scott Brown's election, the administration was coming to the conclusion that its fatal mistake had been giving up so much control to Congress.[101]

Obama and his top aides were more actively engaged in the Senate on health care[102] and immersed themselves in the Senate Finance Committee process. The president talked to committee chair Max Baucus several times a week and also had a few calls and meetings with the panel's ranking Republican, Charles Grassley. There were yet other White House meetings, and presidential advisors held long evening and weekend meetings with Finance Committee staff members.[103]

In early 2010, before the election of Scott Brown in Massachusetts, the White House became the center of negotiations between the House and Senate, with the president as chief mediator.[104] White House Deputy Chief of Staff Jim Messina guided a team of party strategists. Fed by information from lobbyists, Hill aides, and others, they tracked how every lawmaker intended to vote and prepared a television and radio campaign to counter the bill's opponents, who were spending lavishly.[105]

The administration was always heavily involved in developing legislation for financial regulation. Aides met weekly in the White House legislative affairs office to propose reforms and consider the best way to achieve them, and White House and Treasury officials were in congressional offices nearly every day following the president's inauguration, discussing how to shape regulatory legislation. The day after he signed the health care legislation into law, Obama brought Senate Banking Committee Chairman Christopher J. Dodd and his counterpart in the House, Rep. Barney Frank, to the Oval Office, signaling he was ready to begin the final push. Nevertheless, having learned its lesson, the White House spent little time trying to woo individual senators with sweetheart deals such as the ones that provoked controversy during the health care negotiations.[106]

Working with Party Leaders

From the beginning, the Obama team worked closely with Democratic Party leaders. Top congressional leadership communications aides coordinated daily with the White House communications director, and House Speaker Nancy

Pelosi's chief of staff spoke to Rahm Emanuel and legislative liaison chief Phil Schiliro regularly.[107]

Obama had the great advantage of working with an extraordinarily energetic and skilled Speaker of the House in Pelosi.[108] The president's sparse early involvement in health care reform added to Pelosi's legislative burden,[109] but she pulled it through. As Richard Cohen summed up the initial passage of the bill in the House,

> She was the player most responsible for guiding the complex measure to passage—not President Obama or White House Chief of Staff Rahm Emanuel, and not the committee chairmen. She engaged in constant deal making, in several dozen caucus meetings and perhaps thousands of phone calls and hallway conversations with Democratic members. Whether out of courtesy or desperation, she revisited some members who had made their opposition to the bill clear. "She is talking to everyone who is not a 'yes,' even if they have been 'no,'" a senior Pelosi aide said two days before the vote.[110]

One of her most difficult tasks was pushing through a controversial amendment related to abortion that brought moderate Democrats on board.

After Scott Brown's victory in Massachusetts, the Speaker was still determined to press ahead. "We're in the majority," Pelosi told the president. "We'll never have a better majority in your presidency in numbers than we've got right now. We can make this work." At a news conference on January 28, 2010, she declared, "We will go through the gate. If the gate is closed, we will go over the fence. If the fence is too high, we will pole vault in. If that doesn't work, we will parachute in. But we are going to get health care reform passed."[111]

The health care summit reassured some jittery Democrats that Obama was fully engaged in the fight and also gave the Democratic leadership time to consider their parliamentary options. In Pelosi's case, it gave her the opportunity to soothe her members' jangled nerves and to work on convincing recalcitrant members of her caucus that it would be politically disastrous for them simply to walk away.[112]

As the final vote drew near and dozens of House Democrats were still wavering, many concerned that a vote for the bill would cost them their jobs, House leadership aides brought Pelosi a list of sixty-eight lawmakers to lobby, turn, or bolster. The aides presumed the Democratic leadership would divvy up the names. "I'll take all sixty-eight," the Speaker declared.[113] It is no wonder that Vice President Biden later lauded her as "the single most persuasive, the single most strategic leader I have ever worked with" and referred to her as "the mother of health care."[114]

In addition, the Democratic leadership helped to coordinate the committees with jurisdiction over health care. Once Bill Clinton delivered his plan to Capitol Hill, three major House committees and two Senate panels began work. They moved in separate directions and with muddled outcomes, and these parochial efforts crippled the White House's proposal. Under Obama, congressional leaders made sure the committees set aside their jurisdictional rivalries to produce health care legislation that could obtain the caucuses' support.[115]

The Democratic leadership was not always an effective partner for the White House, however. During the lame-duck session of Congress following the substantial Democratic losses in the midterm elections, Obama concluded that the Democratic leadership lacked a viable plan to move forward regarding the expiring Bush-era tax cuts. Thus, in addition to negotiating with the leaders of his party, the president quietly sent Vice President Biden to pursue a parallel line of negotiations with Senate Republican leader Mitch McConnell.[116]

Cooperating with Organized Interests

Organized interests play a critical role in Washington. For example, more than 1,750 companies, trade groups, and other organizations spent about $1.2 billion and hired about 4,525 lobbyists to influence health care reform in 2009. There were about eight lobbyists for each member of Congress.[117]

The Obama administration conducted extensive outreach to business groups. Business executives formed a new coalition called Business Forward to support his proposals on energy, health care, financial regulation, and other hot-button issues. Initial members included AT&T, Facebook, Hilton, IBM, Microsoft, Pfizer, and Time Warner.[118]

In 1993–1994, the health care industry opposed Bill Clinton's reform bill, mounting an advertising blitz — including the infamous "Harry and Louise" television spots — to kill the effort. In contrast, the Obama White House rejected the Clintons' industry-bashing populism and gave the health care industry a hand in writing the bill. The president reached early deals with for-profit hospitals and the drug manufacturers. The administration also agreed with the American Association of Retired Persons (AARP) to eliminate the gap in Medicare coverage of prescription drugs. The White House even brought the insurance industry on board, offering millions of new customers in exchange for reforms in insurance coverage. The American Medical Association and nurses' groups also supported the president. On May 11, 2009, groups representing insurers, drug and device makers, doctors, and hospitals appeared with Obama to announce they would commit to helping reduce the growth of health care costs over the next decade.

In the final push for passage in March 2010, the coalition of about fifty groups, from the AARP to labor unions, held daily conference calls. They isolated three dozen lawmakers and had influential people in their communities—doctors, insurance agents, business owners—reach out to them.[119]

At the same time, many Democratic lobbyists complained that the president not only vilified their profession but also froze them out of discussions on key issues. This attitude may have cost the president valuable advice, political intelligence, and institutional backup. Business leaders reacted strongly negatively to what they saw as the White House's anti-corporate, confrontational rhetoric and its lack of effective diffuse outreach.[120]

Conclusion

Barack Obama actively sought Republican support for his legislative initiatives. He thought that by reaching across the aisle he could create opportunities for change by expanding his coalition. Republicans met his overtures with confrontation rather than cooperation, however, frustrating his strategy. Given the limited prospects for bipartisanship that we discussed in chapter 4, we should not expect the president to have had much success in obtaining Republican support for his major proposals.

To transform policy, it was likely that the president would have to rely almost exclusively on effectively exploiting the predispositions of the large Democratic majorities to support his initiatives. Thus, the White House invested heavily in party leadership. Devoting personal attention, making common cause with his party colleagues, letting Congress take ownership of issues, and working closely with party leaders characterized the Obama presidency. We should also expect that the diversity of constituencies and ideologies among Democrats would make Democratic resistance a prominent obstacle to fashioning winning coalitions.

The next chapter examines the White House's success in obtaining congressional support.

CHAPTER 6

Evaluating Strategic Choices

PASSING LEGISLATION

Barack Obama came to office with an ambitious agenda for policy change. Most of these changes required congressional approval. To obtain congressional support, he employed a variety of strategies for governing. One strategy centered on creating opportunities for change by taking his case to the public in an effort to leverage public support to win backing in Congress. We saw in chapter 3 that this effort did not succeed. The president found it difficult to move the public.

A second approach to creating opportunities for change is reaching across the congressional aisle and convincing the opposition party to lend support to the president's initiatives. After analyzing the opportunities for success in this endeavor in the Obama administration in chapter 4, I predicted there was little prospect of obtaining bipartisan support for the president's core initiatives. Nevertheless, we saw in chapter 5 that the White House made substantial efforts to win Republican votes.

Yet a third strategy for governing focuses on exploiting opportunities for change by managing and maintaining a supportive majority coalition of those predisposed to support the president. Barack Obama enjoyed comfortable majorities in both the House and the Senate as a result of the 2008 elections. I have predicted that if the president were to succeed, he would have to rely almost entirely on the support of his party.

In this chapter, I focus on the major policy initiatives during 2009–2010 to determine whether the president was able to create opportunities for change by convincing Republicans to provide bipartisan support for these proposals. I also examine the success of exploiting the support of the president's party, emphasizing both the White House's dependence on Democrats and the challenge of maintaining party unity.

Bipartisan Support

The president made concerted efforts to reach across the aisle and create opportunities for policy change. He wanted Republican votes both to pass legislation and to provide him political cover for controversial stands. Claiming bipartisan support, he felt, would lend legitimacy to the historic policy changes he was proposing. As we have seen, he and his top aides spent many hours meeting with Republicans in large groups and consulting with individual Republicans, especially senators, like Olympia Snowe, Susan Collins, and Charles Grassley. Despite consistent rebuffs, Obama kept trying.

From the beginning, Republicans offered stiff resistance to the president's overtures. When he went to Capitol Hill to meet with House Republicans on the stimulus bill shortly after his inauguration, Republican Party leaders told him even before negotiations began that their party would vote against the bill in a bloc. On health care reform, when the White House went a long way to meeting a Republican senator's wishes on health care reform, Obama asked the senator if he could now support the bill. The senator replied, "Unless I can get ten other Republicans to stand with me [an impossible task], I can't do it."[1] As the president's tenure unfolded, the divisions on Capitol Hill grew deeper, the rhetoric more hostile, and the cooperation across the aisle less frequent and meaningful. The day after the president upbraided Congress in his 2010 State of the Union address for excessive partisanship, Senate Republicans voted en masse against a plan to require that new spending not add to the deficit.

How successful were Obama's efforts at bipartisanship? How much Republican support did he obtain for his major initiatives? The discussion in chapter 4 leads us to predict that partisan predispositions would be difficult to change and that the president would obtain few Republican votes for his major initiatives. That is exactly what happened.

House

During the transition, President Bush accommodated a request from Obama and formally asked for the release of the remaining half of the TARP funds. Congress had the potential to pass a law blocking the increase, and a number of congressional leaders threatened to do just that, complaining that the Obama administration was not explicit enough about what it was going to do with the money. Obama made a personal trip to Capitol Hill, lobbying for release of the funds and providing more details about how the money would be spent. Nevertheless, all but four House Republicans voted to block release of the funds (table 6.1).

House Republicans were uniform in their opposition to the economic stimulus bill, the new president's highest priority. Minority Leader John Boehner told his caucus in a meeting before the president arrived that he was going to oppose the House package and that they should too. Similarly, the next day's debate contrasted with the president's conciliatory gestures. In the end, all but eleven Democrats voted for the plan, but not a single Republican supported it. Even after negotiations with the Senate that pared down the cost of the bill, no House Republicans voted for its final passage.

TABLE 6.1.
House Votes on Major Bills by Party, 111th Congress

Legislation	Democrats		Republicans	
	For	Against	For	Against
Economy				
Block release of TARP funds	99	151	171	4
Stimulus bill	244	11	0	177
Conference	246	6	0	177
Extension of unemployment benefits, homebuyer tax credit, business assistance, 2009	227	17	104	66
Conference report	247	0	156	12
Jobs creation measures, 2010	235	8	24	149
Conference	211	35	6	166
Extension of unemployment benefits, 2010	238	10	3	171
Conference	241	10	31	142
Aid to states and schools, 2010[a]	245	3	2	158
Vehicle trade-in program, second round	238	14	78	95
Small business aid, 2010	238	13	3	169
Conference	236	13	1	174
Financial Regulation				
Financial regulation reform	223	27	0	175
Conference	234	19	3	173
Health				
Expansion of Children's Health Insurance Program	249	2	40	137
Health care reform	219	39	1	176
Conference	219	34	0	178
Health care reconciliation[b]	220	32	0	175
Conference	233	17	0	176
FDA authority to regulate tobacco products	228	8	70	104
Conference	237	7	70	90
Food safety overhaul	229	20	54	122
Conference	205	8	10	136
Budget				
FY 20010 budget resolution	233	20	0	176
Conference	233	17	0	176
Increase debt limit, 2010	217	37	0	175
Taxes				
Extension of Bush-era tax cuts[+]	139	112	138	36

TABLE 6.1. *(continued)*

Legislation	Democrats		Republicans	
	For	*Against*	*For*	*Against*
Civil Rights				
Antidiscrimination on wages	244	4	3	167
Repeal "don't ask, don't tell"	235	15	15	160
Hate crimes expansion	231	17	8	158
Immigration				
Dream Act	208	38	8	160
Political Process				
Disclose Act (campaign finance)	217	36	2	170
Education				
Student loan overhaul	247	4	6	167
National Service				
Expand national service programs	250	1	71	104
Environment				
Designating wilderness areas	237	0	157	13
Conference[c]	247	4	38	136
Climate-change mitigation[+]	211	44	8	168
Consumer Protections/Aid				
Credit Cardholders' Bill of Rights[d]	251	1	106	69
Conference on credit cards	248	1	113	63
Conference on gun rights	105	145	174	2
Helping Families Save Their				
Homes Act	243	3	124	51
Mortgage loan modification	227	24	7	167
Administration				
Defense procurement reform	251	0	177	0
Conference	246	0	165	0

[+] Republican support necessary for presidential victory

[a] Conference report on air transportation bill to which aid to states and schools was added

[b] Health care reconciliation included overhaul of student loans that the House had passed separately

[c] Conference report got caught up in issue of gun rights issues in national parks

[d] Bill ultimately included right to carry loaded weapons in national parks

Supported by the likes of Rush Limbaugh (who declared that he hoped Obama's presidency failed) and Sean Hannity (who denounced the stimulus bill on Fox News as the European Socialist Act of 2009), Republicans found their voice in adamant opposition, just as they did with Bill Clinton in 1993 and 1994. Even in the glow of a presidential honeymoon, in the context of Obama's outreach efforts, and in the face of a national economic crisis, they chose to employ harsh language and loaded terms such as "socialism" to describe his policies. Rediscovering the shortcomings of budget deficits and pork barrel spending, Republicans ran radio advertisements in the districts of thirty Democrats, accusing them of "wasteful Washington spending."

The lack of bipartisan support on the stimulus bill took Obama by surprise. The White House was also naïve about the brazenness of the opposition. By early 2010, ninety-three Republican members of Congress had cut ribbons or put out press releases in their districts, taking credit for stimulus spending they had voted against.[2]

The president's next major battle was over the budget resolution for fiscal year 2010. It did not garner a single Republican vote in either chamber. The legislation to authorize the necessary increase in the debt limit received a similar level of Republican support.

In June 2009, the House passed the landmark American Clean Energy and Security Act, designed to curb U.S. greenhouse-gas emissions. It attracted the support of only eight Republican representatives. Reform of regulations for financial institutions, mortgage loan modification, job creation and small business aid in 2010, an overhaul of student loans, campaign finance (requiring greater disclosure of the role of corporations and other special interest groups in paying for campaign advertising), and civil rights issues regarding wages, hate crimes, and homosexuality in the military also received little or no Republican support. Nor did the DREAM Act proposal to allow illegal immigrants brought to the United States as children to gain legal resident status if they joined the military or went to college.

When the House voted on the health care reform bill on November 7, 2009, it received only one Republican vote. The sole supporter was Representative Anh Cao of Louisiana, a freshman from a New Orleans-based district that went 75 percent for Obama. His victory resulted from two unique factors. First, his opponent, incumbent Representative William J. Jefferson, was under indictment on federal corruption charges. Second, Hurricane Gustav pushed the congressional election in that district into December, when Democratic turnout was much lower than during the presidential election the previous month. Even Anh did not vote for the critical conference report the following March, and no Republicans supported the reconciliation bill on health care.

A few consensual issues brought bipartisan agreement. Protections for credit card holders (especially when it included an unrelated gun rights provision) were popular with the public. Congress was spurred into action by public outcry over such practices as sudden increases in interest rates even for those who paid their bills, hard-to-understand contract terms, and hidden fees. Not a single member of Congress voted against reforming procurement practices in the Department of Defense in committee or on the floor. A bill extending unemployment benefits, continuing a popular homebuyer tax credit, and expanding a tax credit for businesses in 2009 was also popular during an economic downturn, as was the Helping Families Save Their Homes Act.

A few other bills attracted considerable Republican support, including funding the popular "cash for clunkers" program (45 percent of voting Republicans),[3] expanding national service programs (41 percent), giving the FDA authority to regulate tobacco products (40 percent), and overhauling food safety law (31 percent). Expansion of the Children's Health Insurance Program won the support of 23 percent of the Republican representatives. Designating certain public lands as wilderness areas received Republican support in its initial passage, but only 22 percent of Republicans voted for the conference report after controversy arose over gun rights in national parks. All of these bills passed early in the administration and none of them were at the heart of the administration's legislative program. When the House cleared food safety legislation by agreeing to Senate amendments on December 21, 2010, only ten Republicans voted for the bill.

There were two issues that produced an unusual form of bipartisanship. One was in the area of foreign policy. Over the course of Obama's tenure, House Democrats became increasingly critical of the war in Afghanistan. Democratic opposition emerged early. The president defended his strategy for Afghanistan in a late-April 2009 meeting with the Congressional Progressive Caucus, a group of more than seventy liberal members. However, on May 14, 2009, when it came time to act on the president's request for more than $96 billion to fund the wars in Afghanistan and Iraq through the remainder of the fiscal year, fifty-one House Democrats opposed it.[4] The next month, with the inclusion of funds for the International Monetary Fund, the bill passed the House again, with thirty Democrats opposing it. We saw in chapter 4 that at the end of 2009, Speaker Nancy Pelosi vowed never again to ask her troops to vote for war spending.[5]

On March 10, 2010, the House of Representatives held a three-hour debate on a proposal to withdraw American troops by the end of the year. Although the House voted overwhelmingly to reject the withdrawal proposal, sixty Democrats joined with five Republicans in support of pulling out. By July 2010, 148 House Democrats and 160 Republicans backed an appropriations measure to fund the wars in Iraq and Afghanistan, but 102 Democrats joined 12 Republicans in opposing the bill. Among those voting against the bill was Representative David Obey, the Democratic chair of the Appropriations Committee, the panel responsible for the measure.[6]

A similar pattern of bipartisanship support occurred on the extension of the Bush-era tax cuts. Although the president was able to forge a compromise with Republicans that included an extension of unemployment insurance and a re-imposition of a tax on some estates, many Democrats were outraged at continuing tax cuts for the wealthy and exempting even substantial estates from inheritance taxes. As a result, many voted against the president. Republicans, on the other hand, were generally pleased to support the tax cuts and most supported the bill.

There was one foreign policy issue on which consensus developed *against* the president. On January 22, 2009, Obama issued an executive order to close the prison at Guantánamo Bay, Cuba, within a year. Immediately after the president acted, Republicans began warning against moving detainees to prisons on U.S. soil. To thwart the White House's plan, House Minority Leader John Boehner introduced the "Keep Terrorists Out of America Act." Lawmakers began tightening the purse strings against any attempt by the president to implement unilaterally a new policy, adding language to several appropriations bills that placed restrictions on moving the prisoners and on shutting down the detention center. Democrats held the line against preventing the administration from bringing prisoners to the United States for trial, but they did accede to a forty-five-day advance notification period and risk assessment for such actions.

In 2010, Congress imposed strict new limits on transferring detainees out of the Guantánamo Bay prison, banning the transfer into the United States of any Guantánamo detainee in fiscal year 2011—even for the purpose of prosecution, prohibiting the purchase or construction of any facility inside the United States for housing detainees being held at Guantánamo, and forbidding the transfer of any detainee to another country unless Defense Secretary Robert M. Gates signed off on the safety of doing so.

The pattern is clear. House Republicans overwhelmingly opposed the most significant legislation the president proposed in the 111th Congress. Whether the issue was the economy, regulating the financial industry, health care reform, the budget, civil rights, immigration, campaign finance reform, student loans, climate change, or mortgage loan modifications, Republicans uniformly opposed Democratic initiatives. Despite the president's efforts to reach across the aisle, he could not obtain bipartisan support for his major proposals. Even a modest bill on child nutrition championed by Michelle Obama garnered only seventeen Republican votes.

Of course, even a few Republicans could make a difference between winning and losing. On only two bills listed in table 6.1 did Republican support make a difference in the outcome, however. The eight Republican representatives who voted for the climate change mitigation bill made the difference in it passing, because forty-four Democrats voted against it. Whether the president could have won this much Republican support on a conference report if the Senate had also passed a version of the bill is an open question.

The opposition of many Democrats to the extension of the Bush-era tax cuts during the lame-duck session of Congress in 2010 necessitated obtaining Republican support for passage of the bill. Because Republicans were eager to continue the existing tax rates, this support was forthcoming.

Senate

Because of their large majorities, Democrats could generally prevail in the House in the face of uniform Republican opposition. The Senate was a different story, however. Given that the number of Democrats was sixty in 2009 and fifty-nine in 2010, and given the need to obtain sixty votes for closure on most measures, there was a premium on obtaining some Republican support as well as on maintaining Democratic unity. In the context of extreme partisan polarization, the president also wanted a patina of bipartisanship for his proposals.

The Senate approved the release of the TARP funds by a 52-42 margin, but only six Republicans voted for Obama's request (table 6.2). That, however, was a high point of support for the president's major initiatives. Despite his compromises, the president did little better with Republicans in the Senate than in the House on the stimulus bill. Only three GOP senators supported each version of the stimulus bill: Olympia Snowe and Susan Collins of Maine and Arlen Specter of Pennsylvania—the three most moderate Republican senators. (Soon after, Specter switched parties and became a Democrat.) Adding insult to injury, Republican Senator Judd Gregg of New Hampshire withdrew as nominee as secretary of Commerce, citing "irresolvable conflicts" with the president over his economic stimulus plan. "We are functioning," he added, "from a different set of views on many critical items of policy."[7]

Obama's efforts to negotiate with Charles Grassley, Olympia Snowe, and Susan Collins on health care reform came to naught. Indeed, Democrats were startled by the speed of the Republican's rejection of health care proposals they had supported in previous years.[8] No Republican senators supported health care reform or the follow-up reconciliation bill.

Similarly, no Republican senator voted for the FY 2010 budget resolution or the authorization for increasing the national debt. None voted for mortgage loan modification, and only two supported aid to states and schools and the conference agreement on the extension of unemployment benefits in 2010. Five or fewer Republican senators supported financial regulation reform, hate crimes expansion, protection against wage discrimination, small business aid in 2010, and the confirmation of Elena Kagan as a Supreme Court justice. Only seven Republican senators voted for the second round of the cash for clunkers program, and only nine supported expansion of the Children's Health Insur-

Table 6.2.
Senate Votes on Major Bills by Party, 111th Congress

Legislation	Democrats*		Republicans	
	For	Against	For	Against
Economy				
Block release of TARP funds[+]	9	46	33	6
Stimulus bill	58	0	3	37
Conference	60	0	2	38
Extension of unemployment benefits, homebuyer tax credit, business assistance, 2009	58	0	40	0
Jobs creation measures, 2010	57	2	14	26
Conference	57	1	11	28
Extension of unemployment benefits, 2010	56	1	6	35
Conference	57	1	2	38
Aid to states and schools, 2010[a]	59	0	2	39
Vehicle trade-in program, second round	53	4	7	33
Small business aid, 2010	59	0	2	38
Financial Regulation				
Financial regulation reform	55	2	4	37
Conference	57	1	3	38
Health				
Expansion of Children's Health Insurance Program	57	0	9	32
Health care reform	60	0	0	39
Health care reconciliation[b]	55	2	0	41
Conference	53	3	0	40
FDA authority to regulate tobacco	54	1	23	16
Food safety overhaul	56	0	15	25
Budget				
FY 2010 budget resolution	55	2	0	41
Conference	53	3	0	40
Increase debt limit, 2010	60	0	0	39
Taxes				
Extension of Bush-era tax cuts[+]	44	14	37	5
Civil Rights				
Antidiscrimination on wages	56	0	5	36
Repeal "don't ask, don't tell"	57	0	8	31
Hate crimes expansion	58	0	5	28

TABLE 6.2. *(continued)*

Legislation	Democrats*		Republicans	
	For	*Against*	*For*	*Against*
National Security				
Ratification of New START Treaty[+]	58	0	13	26
Supreme Court Nominations				
Sonia Sotomayor	59	0	9	31
Elena Kagan	58	1	5	36
National Service				
Expand national service programs	58	0	21	19
Environment				
Designating wilderness areas	57	0	20	20
Consumer Protections/Aid				
Credit Cardholders' Bill of Rights[c]	55	1	35	4
Helping Families Save Their				
Homes Act	54	0	35	5
Mortgage loan modification	45	12	0	39
Administration				
Defense procurement reform	54	0	39	0
Conference	56	0	39	0

* Includes Senate Independents who caucus with Democrats

[+] Republican support necessary for presidential victory

[a] Conference report on air transportation bill to which aid to states and schools was added

[b] Health care reconciliation included overhaul of student loans

[c] Included right to carry loaded weapons in national parks

ance Program and the confirmation of Sonia Sotomayor as a Supreme Court justice. Eight Republicans voted to repeal "don't ask, don't tell," while fourteen supported jobs creation measures in 2009 (eleven in conference).

Not only did the Republicans overwhelmingly oppose Democratic, and especially White House, initiatives when they came to a vote, but they also did their best to prevent final votes altogether. Their frequent resort to the filibuster succeeded in preventing action on climate change, immigration, and campaign finance.

As in the House, there were a few policies that were widely popular and achieved bipartisan agreement. Protections for credit card holders (with its unrelated gun rights provision), the Helping Families Save Their Homes Act, reforming procurement practices in the Department of Defense, and a catch-all bill extending unemployment benefits, a homebuyer tax credit, and business assistance were consensual issues. Granting the FDA authority to regulate to-bacco products won 59 percent of voting Republican senators, expanding national service programs won 53 percent of that group, 50 percent of Republicans voted for designating certain public lands as wilderness areas, and 38 percent supported overhauling food safety regulation. A third of Republicans voted to ratify the New START treaty.

The president's compromise proposal to extend the Bush-era tax cuts irritated a number of Democratic senators, just as it did Democratic members of the House. A third of these senators voted against the president, but Republicans overwhelmingly supported the bill, as tax cuts remained a top priority for them.

Also similar to the House, there was consensus against the president on the question of the disposition of detainees held at Guantánamo Bay. At one point, the Senate voted 90-6 in favor of an amendment prohibiting funding for transferring, releasing, or incarcerating detainees at Guantánamo Bay to or within the United States. The Senate also joined the house in imposing strict restrictions on the president's movement of prisoners in fiscal year 2011.

Republican support was not crucial to the enactment of most of the president's program. There are only two bills in table 6.2 on which Republican support made the difference in the outcome. The first is the effort to block release of the TARP funds, which six Republicans opposed and occurred before Obama took office. The other bill is the compromise plan to extend the Bush-era tax cuts passed near the end of the lame-duck Congress in 2010. In addition, the president required Republican support to reach the two-thirds margin for ratifying the New START treaty and for breaking filibusters on issues such as the repeal of "don't ask, don't tell."

Elevated Partisanship

Rather than surmounting partisanship, Barack Obama was engulfed in it. *Congressional Quarterly* found extraordinarily high levels of party line voting, even in the first weeks of the Obama administration. An average of 50 percent of the roll call votes during the Bush years were party unity votes. In 2009, 51 percent of the votes in the House united the parties against each other. The big increase in partisanship was in the Senate, however. The average percentage of party unity votes in the upper chamber during the Bush presidency was 57 percent, including 60 percent in 2007 and 52 percent in 2008. In 2009, 72 percent of the roll call votes in the Senate were party unity votes, the highest percentage ever recorded. Party voting in the Senate was even higher in 2010, with 79 percent of the votes showing majorities of each party opposing each other. The figure for the House declined to 40 percent as it focused on less controversial issues while waiting for the Senate to act on the major issues.[9]

TABLE 6.3.
Presidential Support on Nonunanimous Votes

	% Support			
	House		Senate	
Year	Democrats	Republicans	Democrats	Republicans
2009	92	16	95	25
2010	85	19	95	12

Underlying the partisan conflict were the clear ideological differences between the parties. Indeed, the distance between the parties in both houses of Congress in 2009 and 2010 was the greatest since the end of Reconstruction.[10] Studies employing different methodologies found that there was no ideological overlap at all among Democrats and Republicans in the 111th Congress.[11] With a liberal Speaker and a supporting cast of liberal committee chairs running the legislative process in the House, legislation on issues such as the economy, health care, climate change, financial regulation, and civil rights was bound to favor the liberal worldview. Even the most moderate Republicans would have trouble with such policies. The need to obtain a filibuster-proof majority in the Senate gave Republicans more leverage for negotiating more moderate policies, but the number of Republicans interested in compromise was quite small. Thus, there was little potential for the president to obtain support from the opposition.

Table 6.3 shows the support of party groups in each chamber for votes on which *Congressional Quarterly* determined the White House had expressed a clear position. On these votes, the typical Republican representative supported the president only 16 percent of the time, while Republican senators supported the president on average just 25 percent of the time in 2009. In 2010, Republican members of the House supported the president on average 19 percent of the time, while Republican senators did so 12 percent of the time.

The power of a presidential phone call to Republicans, even moderate Republicans, had severe limits. For example, very early in his tenure Obama called Senator Richard Lugar of Indiana twice to appeal for support for the stimulus bill. One of the calls came just after the president returned from visiting a town in Indiana with one of the highest unemployment rates in the state. Nevertheless, Lugar told the president he was going to vote no.[12] Tellingly, Republican obstructionism was Obama's greatest surprise of his first year in office.

> [It wasn't that] I thought that my political outreach and charm would immediately end partisan politics. I just thought that there would be enough of a sense of urgency that at least for the first year there would be an interest in governing. And you just didn't see that.[13]

Costs of Bipartisanship

A strategy of bipartisanship not only failed to win Republican converts, but it also proved to be a costly effort. It blurred the president's message. Attempting to be bipartisan constrained the president's ability to clearly repudiate the policies of George W. Bush and keep past Republican policies and policy failures at the forefront of political discourse. It was not until the 2010 midterm elections that Obama freely invoked his predecessor's presidency in his rhetoric.

In addition, the White House's efforts to achieve bipartisan support hindered articulating the positive goals of its proposals. As White House Chief of Staff Rahm Emanuel told the *Washington Post*, "Rather than jobs being the message, [we had] bipartisanship being the message."[14] As the Democrats would soon learn, it was jobs, not bipartisanship, that concerned the public. In hindsight, White House officials largely agree they should not have let the health care process drag out while waiting for Republican support that would never come. As a top presidential advisor put it, "It lent itself to the perception that he [Obama] wasn't doing anything on the economy."[15]

The quest for bipartisanship also delayed the legislative process and gave the president's opponents additional opportunities to organize and criticize his proposals. For example, with Ted Kennedy ill, Max Baucus, chair of the Senate Finance Committee, became the lead Senate negotiator on health care and spent months trying to win the support of a few Republican senators, like Chuck Grassley of Iowa and Olympia Snowe of Maine. Few in the White House were pleased with Baucus as their point man, but they were pulled between two competing imperatives—speed and bipartisanship. Emanuel knew that the longer a big, complicated initiative like health care lingered in Congress, the more political freight it would take on. Yet he and Obama were determined to obtain Republican votes to give the effort more legitimacy, and that took patient negotiating.[16] In the end, of course, the negotiations failed, and the delays they caused gave opponents additional time to hammer "ObamaCare."

Finally, negotiating with Republicans risked alienating the enthusiastic supporters who helped Obama in the White House. Although it is not possible to know for certain, the lack of enthusiasm of Democrats about voting in the 2010 midterm elections may be traced in part to the president's willingness to negotiate, however futilely, with Republicans. Moreover, despite the supposed appeal of bipartisanship to Independents, they were the partisan grouping most likely to change their congressional voting from Democrat to Republican in 2010.[17]

Party Support

Receiving little or no support from Republicans, Obama had no choice but to rely on the votes of his fellow partisans. Fortunately for the president, Democrats had large majorities, including the decisive 60th Senate vote secured when Al Franken finally was declared the victor in the Minnesota Senate race and Arlen Specter switched parties. If the president and his Democratic allies were to succeed, they would have to exploit effectively the opportunity provided by the cohorts of Democrats predisposed toward activist government.

These robust majorities brought leadership challenges, however, because they represented a broad range on the ideological spectrum, stretching from the strongly liberal views of large blocs of Democrats in each chamber to the conservatism of Ben Nelson in the Senate and Bobby Bright in the House.

House

In the House, the leadership almost always prevailed, even in the face of legislation unpopular with the public such as health care reform. Only on climate change legislation did the Democrats need to rely on Republican votes to pass legislation. Democratic representatives supported the president on average 92 percent of the time on nonunanimous votes in 2009 and 85 percent of the time in 2010 (table 6.3). Democrats from the South averaged 89 percent support for the president in 2009 and 81 percent in 2010.

The core of Democratic support consisted of members elected from districts that Obama carried in 2008. For example, House Democrats who represented such districts voted 199-8 for final approval of the Senate health care bill, 201-1 for Obama's stimulus plan, 194-1 for federal tobacco regulation, 191-8 for financial reform, and 189-15 for climate-change legislation.[18]

As public support for the president and activist government eroded, Democratic support for the president's program declined. Most of the Democratic opposition was from cross-pressured members from more conservative constituencies than the typical member of the Democratic caucus. Twenty of the twenty-four Democrats who voted against the original passage of the Helping Families Save Their Homes Act were from McCain districts, as were fifteen of the twenty Democrats who opposed the FY 2010 budget resolution, and twenty-nine of the forty-four Democrats who opposed the climate-change bill.

Democrats were aware of dissatisfaction in their constituencies and acted strategically to try to preserve their seats while at the same time supporting the White House as much as they could. Two of the most controversial votes in the 111th Congress were on health care and climate-change legislation. Thirty-seven House Democrats did not support the leadership on just one of these issues, which allowed them to point in future ads to an instance in which they "bucked the leadership." Sixteen, almost all of them from GOP-leaning districts, who voted for the climate-change bill pivoted to vote against health care reform. Similarly, twenty-one House Democrats, many of them from Rust Belt blue-collar districts, who opposed climate change backed health care reform.

TABLE 6.4.

Support for Major Obama Initiatives and Success in Midterm Elections of House
Democrats Representing Districts Won by McCain in 2008

Policy	Voted For		Voted Against		% Reelected	
	N	%	N	%	Voting For	Voting Against
TARP	22	46	26	54	23	27
Stimulus	43	90	5	10	23	40
Health care reform	20	42	28	58	10	36
Climate Change	20	42	28	58	25	25
All four	5	10			20	
Three of four	15	31			13	
Two of four	15	31			20	
One of four	10	21			60	
None of four	3	6			0	

When the House passed the bill to increase the federal debt ceiling by $290
billion in December 2009, by a vote of 218-214, thirty-nine Democrats joined
all Republicans in opposition. Thirty-two of thirty-nine Democrats who voted
"no" were first- or second-term members who represented districts that they
wrested from Republican control. Of the twenty-six House Democrats who
captured Republican-held districts in the 2008 election, twenty bucked their
party leadership and voted with the Republicans on the debt limit bill. The
Democrats in opposition included Paul W. Hodes of New Hampshire and Ken-
drick B. Meek of Florida, who typically sided with their party but who were
running for open Senate seats in 2010.[19]

The Democrats elected in districts that preferred John McCain did not support Obama and the House leadership nearly as reliably as did those from more
Democratic districts. *National Journal* looked at eight key votes in the House in
2009 that were crucial to the Obama agenda: the economic stimulus package;
the budget resolution; climate-change legislation; student-loan reform; the
health care overhaul; financial regulation; the debt ceiling increase; and the jobs
bill. Democrats representing districts won by John McCain dissented from the
Democratic majority, on average, on three of the eight key votes.[20]

The second and third columns in table 6.4 show how Democrats representing House districts won by McCain voted on four key issues in the 111th Congress. Except for the stimulus bill, a majority of Democrats from these districts
opposed the key Obama proposals. Other Democrats, as we have seen, overwhelmingly backed the president.

By comparing the last two columns of the table, we can also see that it was appropriate for Democrats representing McCain districts to feel electorally insecure. They were likely to lose their seats no matter how they voted. Indeed, Democrats lost thirty-six of the forty-eight seats they held that McCain had carried in 2008. The greatest difference among the policies was with health care reform. Only 10 percent of this group who voted for the president's proposal won reelection, while 36 percent of those who opposed Obama won. With the stimulus bill, 23 percent of those voting for it won reelection, in contrast to a 40 percent rate for those opposing the bill.

Often constituency and ideological influences on the more moderate House Democrats reinforced each other. For example, twenty-three House Democrats voted against both health care reform and the cap-and-trade climate bill. Nineteen of these were right of the House's center, seventeen were from the South, and eighteen represented districts won by John McCain.

In 1994, the last time that a House Democratic majority was swept away, Democrats held 258 seats, just as they did after the 2008 elections. Ten Democrats from districts carried by President George H.W. Bush in 1992 voted against both the 1993 Clinton budget and the assault weapons ban in the 1994 crime bill. All ten won reelection. So did eleven of the nineteen Democrats from Bush districts who voted for only one of those measures. Conversely, only three of the ten Bush-district Democrats who voted for both measures survived the Republican wave.[21]

In the 111th Congress, Democratic leaders, including Speaker Nancy Pelosi and White House Chief of Staff Rahm Emanuel, understood that their House majority was built on a layer of conservative-leaning districts won under highly favorable conditions in 2006 and 2008. Having no wish to lose their majority in 2010, they actively discouraged members from some of those districts from voting in ways that would be construed as out of tune with their constituents.[22] On climate-change mitigation, health care reform, debt limit, and campaign finance legislation, the Democratic leaders managed to get the bill passed with just over the minimum votes necessary while giving maximum cover to their potentially vulnerable incumbents. Christopher Van Hollen, the chair of the Democratic Congressional Campaign Committee, signaled to members that they were free to vote their districts. "We can do both. . . . I am OK with members being independent-minded."[23]

Nevertheless, many vulnerable House Democrats took the risk to give the president the benefit of the doubt. This courage pleased Republicans. Speaking of Democrats' support for liberal legislation, Thomas Price, the chair of the Caucus of House Conservatives, happily declared, "Rarely do we see members of Congress vote against their own political survival in favor of their leadership so often." He called such votes an "absolutely unique-in-our-history activity on the part of representatives where they're not representing their districts over and over and over again."[24]

TABLE 6.5.

Support for Major Obama Initiatives and Success in Midterm Elections of House
Democrats Representing Districts Won from Republicans in 2006 and 2008*

	Voted For		Voted Against		% Reelected	
Policy	N	%	N	%	Voting For	Voting Against
TARP	10	33	20	67	50	35
Stimulus	30	100	0	0	43	—
Health care reform	27	90	3	10	32	33
Climate Change	25	83	5	17	44	33
All four	8	27		38		
Three of four	18	60		39		
Two of four	2	7		0		
One of four	2	7		50		
None of four	0	0		—		

*Omitted Democrats from districts in which Obama did not receive a majority of the vote

Table 6.5 shows how another set of cross-pressured Democrats, those representing districts won from Republicans in 2006 and 2008, voted on the four key
issues. I have omitted the Democrats who also represented districts that Obama
lost in 2008 to prevent overlap in the data. These Democratic representatives
offered the president much more support than those from the McCain districts
analyzed in table 6.4. Aside from TARP, they gave Obama high levels of support, ranging from 83 percent on climate change to 100 percent on the economic stimulus. These members were either more liberal than the members
from McCain districts (it is difficult to say, because many members in both
groups were new) or felt safer in taking a risk to support the president.

Apparently, these Democrats knew their districts, and their support for
Obama's initiatives pleased many of their constituents. Despite the fact that
they represented districts that had recently elected Republicans to the House,
43 percent won reelection. As the last columns of table 6.5 show, those supporting TARP and climate-change legislation were more likely to win reelection
than those who opposed them. Ninety percent supported health care reform,
and they won at the same rate as the three who opposed it.

Senate

The necessity of reaching the 60-vote threshold in the Senate put a premium on
party unity. Democratic leaders often had to muster every single member of

their caucus behind a vote. They continuously had to cajole recalcitrant members and alter legislation to suit senators most likely to defect.

The governing core was the thirty-seven Democratic senators elected from the states that had supported the party's presidential nominees in at least two of the previous three elections. These senators had almost perfect party unity scores in 2009 and 2010, as calculated by *Congressional Quarterly*. Around that axis, Democratic leaders assembled shifting coalitions of Democrats from states that were more closely divided.

Ultimately, they were remarkably successful. On the most historic votes, those on the stimulus plan and health care reform, every Senate Democrat backed Obama. Democratic senators supported the president on average 95 percent of the time on nonunanimous votes in both 2009 and 2010 (table 6.3). Only a few senators, Evan Byah, Claire McCaskill, and Russ Feingold, varied much around the mean. The seven Democrats from the South also averaged 95 percent support for the president, as did Joe Lieberman. In both 2009 and 2010, Senate Democrats voted with their caucus colleagues 91 percent of the time on party unity votes, eclipsing their record of 89 percent set a decade earlier.[25]

The high level of Democratic cohesion on votes dividing the parties obscures the considerable difficulty of achieving it. Figures on presidential support do not represent issues, such as legislation on immigration, climate change, "don't ask, don't tell," food safety, and campaign finance, that never came to a vote because the Democrats could not agree among themselves. Nor do they reflect the dilution of legislation to please a few holdouts on economic stimulus, health care, financial regulation, and other matters.

Fractures in the Coalition

Their impressive record of victories should not obscure the challenges the White House and Democratic leaders faced. A substantial number of House Democrats voted against the president on many of the most important bills. When the House passed Democrats' cap-and-trade energy legislation in June 2009, forty-four Democrats voted no. Thirty-seven voted against increasing the debt limit, thirty-six opposed campaign finance reform, thirty-five opposed jobs creation measures in 2010, twenty-seven voted against the initial version of financial regulation reform (nineteen opposed the final version), twenty-six opposed "don't ask, don't tell," and twenty voted against the FY 2010 budget resolution and the overhaul of food safety regulation. Given Republican unity in opposing Democratic initiatives, it is ironic that the bipartisan position was typically in *opposition* to the White House.

Health care reform illustrates the president's problem in holding his party coalition together. Democrats in both chambers engaged in protracted negotiations to try to reach agreement, repeatedly derailing the White House's schedule. They disagreed on a host of provisions, ranging from funding for abortions to a public option for health insurance.

At times, Democrats who favored remaking the health system attacked fellow Democrats who were undecided or opposed an overhaul. The Democratic National Committee, for example, ran ads intended to pressure Democratic senators like Kent Conrad, Evan Byah, Bill Nelson, Mary Landrieu, Blanche Lincoln, and Ben Nelson. Some ads were aimed at bolstering moderate and conservative House Democrats who needed ammunition to counter the intense campaign against revamping the system. Liberal groups like MoveOn. org, Health Care for America Now, Change Congress and its sister group Progressive Change Campaign Committee, and the Service Employees International Union sponsored more personal attacks against a few conservative House and Senate Democrats who voted against a Democratic health bill in committee or who were otherwise unsupportive.[26]

Liberal activists also ran television advertisements against moderate Democrats who were not supporting the public option. White House Chief of Staff Rahm Emanuel berated them as being counterproductive. Later, the Progressive Change Campaign Committee, a group formed in 2009 to advocate for liberal candidates and issues, ran ads in Emanuel's political base of Chicago (where he would eventually run for—and become—mayor). The ad featured a voter from Emanuel's old congressional district describing troubles with a health insurer. "A lot of us back home hope Rahm Emanuel is fighting for people like us as White House chief of staff," the man said into the camera. "But if he sides with the insurance companies and undermines the public option, well, he won't have many fans in Chicago."[27]

In the battle over health care, both sides targeted a few dozen moderate Democrats and a dozen anti-abortion Democrats.[28] The president had to make a personal visit to the House on the day of the first vote on the health care bill in November 2009 to bolster his troops. Nevertheless, the bill only passed on a 220-215 vote. Thirty-nine Democrats—more than 1 out of 7—voted against the White House and the Democratic leadership. Thirty-one of these members represented districts won by John McCain in 2008. Fourteen were freshmen and twelve were from districts that switched from Republican in 2008. Twenty-four were in the Blue Dog coalition of fiscally conservative Democrats. Dennis Kucinich of Ohio also opposed the bill—because he wanted a more liberal policy. Artur Davis of Alabama, who was running for governor in that conservative state, could not risk supporting the bill.

Following the election of Scott Brown in Massachusetts in January 2010, it became clear that the House would have to vote to accept the Senate health care bill, and it did so on March 21, 2010. Thirty-four Democrats voted "no," however, including five who had voted for the House version months earlier. Twenty-nine Democrats voted no on both versions of the bill. Only the switch of eight Democrats from "no" to "yes" saved the bill.

District competitiveness (and thus a representative's vulnerability) strongly influenced Democrats' votes on health care. None of the twelve Democratic representatives running in a constituency (their congressional district or the state if they were seeking statewide office in 2010) where Obama won less than 40 percent of the vote in 2008 supported the final version of health care reform. In addition, only thirteen of the thirty representatives running where the president won 40-49 percent of the vote supported the bill. On the other hand, all but seven of the 195 Democrats running in constituencies that Obama won voted for health care reform.[29]

Ideology mattered too. All but two of the 152 most liberal Democrats voted for the final version of the health care bill, as did forty-four of the next fifty-one most liberal. However, only twenty-five of the fifty most moderate or conservative Democrats supported passage.[30] Just over half of the conservative Blue Dogs coalition supported the bill.

Anti-abortion sentiment also made some difference in support for the bill. Twenty-four of the sixty-two Democrats who voted yes on the amendment to restrict funding for abortions voted against the final bill, while all but ten of the 191 Democrats voting no on the amendment supported the bill.

Impact of Party Leadership

Exploiting opportunities requires effective leadership. We saw in chapter 5 that the White House relied heavily on the very effective congressional party leaders to craft coalitions and then intervene at strategic points toward the end of the legislative process. It is difficult to determine the president's impact, but the fairest statement is probably that it was modest. We have seen, for example, that the most aggressive effort to persuade Congress during the Obama presidency was on the House's consideration of the Senate's health care reform bill in March 2010. The president was fully engaged, as was the House leadership. Nevertheless, the net gain among House Democrats over the initial approval of health care reform the previous November was three votes.

At the same time, these votes were critical at the margins of coalition building. Moreover, it is reasonable to argue that votes were much more difficult to obtain in March 2010 than in November 2009, especially after the victory of Scott Brown in the Massachusetts Senate election to fill Edward Kennedy's seat. Thus, the full court press may have held onto Democratic votes that might otherwise have slipped into opposition.

Not every Democrat responded to the president's pleas for support.[31] The president also called Democratic Representative Chet Edwards, the only member of the House on his public list of potential vice presidential candidates in 2008, asking for his vote on health care reform on the original House vote. Edwards declined "respectfully."[32]

At a party on March 17, 2010, to toast the enactment of a law imposing "pay as you go" budget restrictions, Obama put his arm around Representative Jason Altmire's shoulder, turned away from the others, and leaned in close to the congressman. "We have to do this," Obama said about the health care reform bill. "It is essential to bringing down the deficit." "I want to represent my district," Altmire replied. "As you know, it is politically split." As the president moved toward a lectern to address the entire room, Rahm Emanuel, who helped Altmire win his seat in Congress in 2006, cornered Altmire. "Your constituents like you; you've built up a reservoir of goodwill," Emanuel argued. "You have an opportunity before this vote to go back home and explain it to them."[33] The next day, Altmire was back at the White House for a meeting with centrists in the New Democrat Coalition.

Despite the high-level attention at the White House St. Patrick's Day party, a sit-down with Emanuel, a few more phone calls from the president, and three from Cabinet-level officials, Altmire e-mailed the chief of staff two days before the final vote to say that he planned to announce that he would vote no. "Don't do it," Emanuel punched back on his BlackBerry. Nevertheless, that afternoon Altmire released his statement. At 7:30, Obama called once more. "I want to give you something to think about before the vote," the president said gently into the phone. "Picture yourself on Monday morning. You wake up and look at the paper. It's the greatest thing Congress has done in fifty years. And you were on the wrong team." In the end, however, Altmire joined thirty-three other Democrats in voting against the president.

The White House had better luck with Representative Melissa Bean, employing a good cop/bad cop approach. After one group meeting, Obama asked her to stay behind. "Let me talk to my homegirl," he joked. They compared notes on their families—both have two daughters. Then Obama made a gentle plea: "These reforms are really important." A few days later, Emanuel was more direct, reminding Bean of the support he lent in her campaigns and why she came to Washington. "You ran because you care about the deficit," he said. "This is north of $1 trillion in deficit reduction." Bean wanted to see the final bill and a cost estimate. "The Senate bill is stronger than the House bill, and you voted for the House bill," Emanuel countered. "Melissa, name me once in the last six years you voted for a bill with more deficit reduction," he asked, and added that if she opposed the health care legislation, "don't ever send me another press release about deficit reduction." She voted yes.

Conclusion

Despite the Obama White House's efforts to reach across the aisle, bipartisanship was not a success. Critical features of the context of the Obama presidency, especially the high levels of partisan polarization in the public and

Congress that we discussed in chapters 1 and 4, made it unlikely that the president would obtain any significant Republican support for his core initiatives. Only if Obama would adopt Republican policies would he receive Republican support—and no one should have expected him to become a hard right conservative.

Lacking Republican support, the president had to rely on his party to change policy. Democrats gave the White House very high levels of support. The White House strategy of applying pressure quietly while letting congressional leaders find ways to build coalitions proved to be a wise one. Nevertheless, moderate Democrats representing conservative constituencies frequently voted with the Republicans in opposition to the White House.

The president was dependent on exploiting the opportunities presented by those disposed to support his initiatives. He could not create opportunities to expand his support in Congress. In this limitation, Obama was no different from other presidents. The impact of persuasion on the outcome of congressional votes is usually relatively modest. Conversion is likely to be at the margins of coalition building in Congress rather than at the core of policy change.

It should be no surprise that presidential legislative leadership is more useful in exploiting opportunities than in creating broad possibilities for policy change. Efforts at influencing members of Congress occur in an environment largely beyond the president's control and must compete with other, more stable factors that affect voting in Congress in addition to party. These influences include ideology, personal views and commitments on specific policies, and the interests of constituencies. By the time a president tries to exercise influence on a vote, most members of Congress have made up their minds on the basis of these other factors. As a result, a president's legislative leadership is likely to be critical only for those members of Congress who remain open to conversion after other influences have had their impact. Although the size and composition of this group varies from issue to issue, it will almost always be a small minority in each chamber.

CHAPTER 7

Persuasion and Opportunity in Presidential Leadership

MORE THAN A HALF CENTURY AGO, Richard Neustadt voiced what became the best-known maxim regarding the American presidency, that "presidential power is the power to persuade."[1] He was half right.

One of Neustadt's primary goals in writing *Presidential Power* was to show what was *not* a source of presidential power. Presidents could not command others to support their initiatives. In his words, "'powers' are no guarantee of power"[2] and "[t]he probabilities of power do not derive from the literary theory of the Constitution."[3]

Although presidents do have important unilateral powers,[4] there is no question that the negative side of Neustadt's argument—what power is not—made a valuable contribution to understanding presidential leadership. Presidents frequently fail to get their way with the public and Congress, not to speak of other nations and private interests. They cannot command success, and we must look elsewhere to explain the success and failure of leadership in the White House.

In Neustadt's view, power is a function of personal politics rather than of formal authority or position. The subtitle of *Presidential Power* is *The Politics of Leadership*. In essence, Neustadt argued that presidential leadership is the power to persuade. The implication underlying the affirmative side of Neustadt's argument—that effective presidential leadership requires persuasion—is that presidents can succeed in persuading others if they are skilled enough at recognizing and protecting their interests and exploiting critical resources.

Although Neustadt encouraged the belief that presidential persuasion was possible, he began with the premise that presidents would have to struggle to get their way. As he put it, "The power to persuade is the power to bargain."[5] Indeed, it was the inherent weakness of the presidency that made it necessary for presidents to understand how to use their resources most effectively.

Few are blessed with Neustadt's penetrating and nuanced understanding of the presidency. Many political commentators suggest that all the president has to do to obtain the support of the public or Congress is to reach into his inventory of leadership skills and employ the appropriate means of persuasion. Such a view is naïve, however. There is no silver bullet. We now know that even the most skilled presidents have great difficulty in persuading others to support them and that they typically bring about change by exploiting existing opportunities rather than creating them.[6]

Successful leadership is not the result of the dominant chief executive of political folklore who reshapes the contours of the political landscape, altering his strategic position to pave the way for change. Rather than creating the conditions for important shifts in public policy, such as attracting bipartisan support or moving public opinion in their direction, effective leaders are facilitators who work at the margins of coalition building to recognize and exploit opportunities in their environments. Barack Obama is no exception.

Strategies for governing based on the premise of creating opportunities for change are prone to failure. Moreover, they often lead to overreach and wasting the opportunities that do exist. The Obama administration overestimated the opportunities for change in its environment and the president's ability to create new opportunities. As a result, it advanced a large, liberal agenda. Yet the White House could not obtain public support for many of its most visible proposals, nor could it attract Republican votes in Congress. These failures were inevitable, and demonstrate the importance of making clear-eyed strategic assessments of the opportunity structure of a new administration.

Failure is one thing, overreach is much more serious. The Obama administration's advocacy of unpopular policies alienated much of the public, especially those in the middle of the ideological and partisan spectrums. The large Democratic losses in the 2010 midterm elections cost Obama the opportunity to exploit his party's majority in the House and the Democrat's near filibuster-proof majority in the Senate, undermining his ability to govern for the rest of his term. Moreover, the Republican gains in state legislatures, where in 2011 they held the most seats since the Great Depression, increased the probability of redistricting that would favor the GOP and thus increase the probability of Republican majorities in Congress for the next decade.

The view that effective leadership involves exploiting rather than creating opportunities is consistent with recent work on the private sector. New studies are challenging conventional views of the nature of successful entrepreneurship. They find that rather than being visionaries and catalysts for change who sell their ideas and reshape their organizations, successful entrepreneurs are typically not great risk takers who stand ahead of the pack and convince others to follow their visions. Instead, they are insightful analysts who have unique perspectives on particular markets and thus identify existing opportunities. They then strike repeatedly to exploit the opportunities until others catch on and the window of opportunity closes. All the while, they incur the least possible risk, often little risk at all. It is failed entrepreneurs who take risks.[7]

Sources of Overreach

Given the high stakes for understanding the possibilities for change, it is ironic that presidents, all of them successful politicians, so often fail at the task. We have seen that it is natural, and thus common, for presidents, basking in the glow of their electoral successes, to focus on creating, rather than evaluating and exploiting, opportunities for change. They are accustomed to making their cases—they have been doing it for years—and their victories reinforce their proclivities for believing in their persuasiveness. Presidents want to believe the people have chosen them, not that the public rejected the other contenders or simply voted a party line.

Campaigning is not governing, however. To win an election requires beating one (or perhaps two) alternatives at a specific time in a contest in which there will be a positive decision—one of the options must win. It usually does not require focusing attention on the details of a specific policy initiative, easing the path to attracting a majority. Enacting policy changes requires many victories over a sustained period of time in a context in which no action may be the preferred option and gridlock the common result. Moreover, policy debates, unlike elections, focus on the specifics of proposals, making it more difficult to garner majority support.

Other politicians, who also obtain their jobs by campaigning, reinforce the tendency of presidents to believe in the power of persuasion. One of the most common criticisms of Barack Obama in his first two years in office, including among Democrats, was for failing to offer a convincing narrative of his administration.[8] These critics often referred wistfully to the success of Ronald Reagan in doing so and thus weathering the recession at the beginning of his tenure.

Misremembering the past is a common malady for politicians, especially those who see themselves in electoral trouble and are eager for a political lifeline. In fact, Reagan did not fare well with the public during the recession. He first fell below 50 percent approval in mid-November 1981, his first year in office. Except for a late-November 1981 poll, he remained below 50 percent for the next two years, until November 1983. His approval reached a nadir of 35 percent in January 1983.[9]

Similarly, when legislation stalled in the 111th Congress, there were frequent calls for Obama to be more aggressive in his attempts to persuade Congress to support his proposals. Evocations of the last great Democratic legislative leader, Lyndon Johnson, and the famous Johnson Treatment implied that a president who pressured members of Congress could convince them to support the White House's initiatives.

Once again, such a view represents a myopic image of history. Interviews with the former Speaker of the House Carl Albert are instructive regarding the nature of LBJ's influence in Congress. Albert argued that Johnson's tenaciousness and intensity in pushing legislation were his great talents. Although pressed by the interviewer for specifics on Johnson's legislative skills, Albert responded only that the president just kept pushing.[10] The White House did not even red-flag signature Great Society legislation such as the Civil Rights Act of 1964, the Voting Rights Act of 1965, Medicare, or the Elementary and Secondary Education Act of 1965 for special presidential efforts as they came to the House floor. The president's intervention was not needed.[11] It is revealing that the tape recordings of his White House conversations show Johnson pleading, thanking, complimenting, and consulting but rarely trying directly to persuade a legislator. Even when he did, he employed a light touch.[12]

Presidents may overreach for other reasons, of course. They are in office for such a short time that it is difficult to think about husbanding resources or sequencing proposals. There may be no tomorrow. Moreover, they have campaigned promising action, and their supporters expect them to keep their promises.

Exploiting Opportunities

Exploiting opportunities requires that the president possess the analytical insight necessary to identify opportunities for change and the skills necessary to take advantage of them. As Edgar declared in *King Lear*, "Ripeness is all."[13]

Some in the Obama White House came to understand the limitations of persuasive leadership. One presidential advisor complained, "There is this sense on Capitol Hill that somehow the president can go out and make a speech and everything just magically becomes better."[14] David Axelrod added, "I would love to live in a world where the president could snap his fingers or even twist arms and make change happen, but in this great democracy of ours, that's not the way it is."[15]

Maintaining Coalitions

If exploiting opportunities to steer true believers is more critical to engendering change than persuading the skeptical, much less converting the opposition, it follows that they should focus more on maintaining and managing coalitions and less on the verbal dexterity or interpersonal persuasiveness that is hypothetically necessary to expand coalitions and thus transform the political landscape. The president focused on exploiting the advantage provided by the large Democratic majorities in Congress in 2009 and 2010 to enact a number of major changes in public policy. Working closely with congressional leaders, he probably squeezed as much as possible out of the 111th Congress. Moreover, he kept up the pressure in the lame-duck session at the end of 2010, pushing through the repeal of "don't ask, don't tell," ratification of the New START treaty, and a compromise on taxes and unemployment insurance. Obama helped to transform policy without performing transformational leadership.

Not all of the White House's public relations efforts are designed to alter opinions. Instead, the audience for much of presidential rhetoric is those who already agree with the White House. Preaching to the converted by definition does not change opinions and is not what most political commentators have in mind when they advocate that the White House employ the bully pulpit. Yet perhaps the most important function of a coalition builder, in an election or in dealing with a legislature, is consolidating one's core supporters. This may require reassuring them as to one's fundamental principles, strengthening their resolve to persist in a political battle, or encouraging them to become more active on behalf of a candidacy or policy proposal.

Maintaining preexisting support or activating those predisposed to back him can be crucial to a president's success. Important policies usually face substantial opposition. Often opponents are virulent in their criticism. No president will unilaterally disarm and remain quiet in the face of such antagonism. They feel they must engage in a permanent campaign just to maintain the status quo. When offered competing views, people are likely to respond according to their predispositions. Thus, the White House must act to reinforce the predispositions of its supporters.

Presidents also go public to demonstrate preexisting public support when that support lies in the constituencies of members of Congress who are potential swing votes. George W. Bush's travels early in his tenure seemed motivated more by demonstrating his support in states where he ran well in the election than in convincing more skeptical voters of the soundness of his proposals.

Preaching to the converted may have an additional advantage. Sometimes new policies arise on which there is little or no existing opinion. President Reagan's proposal for a defensive missile shield is an example. If the president is able to activate latent policy views by linking his initiative to existing views, such as support for a strong national defense, he may be able to obtain rapidly a sizable core of supporters for his program.

More broadly, public opinion about matters of politics and policy is often amorphous. It lacks articulation and structure. It requires leadership to tap into it effectively, give it direction, and use it to bring about policy change. The president must sense the nature of the opportunity at hand, clearly associate himself and his policies with favorable public opinion in the minds of political elites, and approach Congress when conditions are most favorable for passing legislation. As Richard Hofstadter said of Franklin D. Roosevelt, he was not able to move the public, but "he was able to give it that necessary additional impetus of leadership which can translate desires into policies."[16]

Persistence

Successful leadership also requires that the president have the commitment, resolution, and adaptability to take full advantage of opportunities that arise. Obama had the energy, perseverance, and resiliency to make the most of the

Democrats' majorities. Early on, he told a journalist, "That whole philosophy of persistence is one that I'm going to be emphasizing again and again as long as I'm in office. I'm a big believer in persistence."[17]

He was true to his word. When all seemed lost on health care reform, the president made a strategic decision to persist in trying to pass it. According to David Axelrod, "If the president weren't tough, if the president weren't committed, if the president didn't believe that this was an imperative for the future of American families, businesses and the sustainability of our budget, this thing would have been dead six months ago."[18] At the end of the lame-duck congressional session in 2010, the president reflected, "One thing I hope people have seen during this lame-duck—I am persistent. If I believe in something strongly, I stay on it."[19]

Long-Term Complications

To complicate matters, however, fully exploiting short-term opportunities may undermine an administration in the longer run. When the president thought he could create opportunities for change by expanding his supportive coalition, promoting a large agenda appeared, at least to the White House, to pose little political risk. As one White House official put it, the administration would use 2009 to restructure the nation's health care system, energy industry, and financial-regulatory regime "and then use 2010 to explain what we did."[20]

The rub came when, as another presidential aide declared about the strategy, "it didn't work."[21] When he could not create opportunities for change, Obama faced a dilemma. If he pushed hard to exploit existing opportunities, he would win important victories. Yet he could also lose the war by winning these battles. The midterm elections showed just how ephemeral the large Democratic majorities were. Would it have been prudent to have moved more slowly and with a narrower focus, nurtured his electoral majority, built greater public confidence around his leadership, and emerged with a stronger mandate to pursue his postponed campaign agenda?

We may never have a definitive answer. Much depends on the success of the Republicans' efforts to undo the initiatives passed in the 111th Congress, especially health care reform. It is possible that Democrats could not have passed an overhaul of health care at any other time, but in any case, the White House's pursuit of health care reform may have undermined its ability to govern in the remainder of the president's term. The protracted focus on this unpopular legislation helped energize the right and kept the administration from focusing on the economy, the public's highest priority.[22] As one freshman Democrat who captured a Republican seat in 2008 put it, "if I had known that it [health care reform] was going to take up all the oxygen, then I'm not sure whether we should have done exactly as we did. The economy is the most important thing."[23]

In a nationally televised interview shortly after the 2010 midterm elections, the president acknowledged that one major contributor to the "big government Obama" narrative was the health care reform law. "At the time, we knew that it probably wasn't great politics," Obama reflected, "I made the decision to go ahead and do it. And it proved as costly politically, as we expected. Probably actually a little more costly than we expected, politically." The president added, "We thought that if we shaped a bill that wasn't that different from bills that had previously been introduced by Republicans, including a Republican Governor in Massachusetts who's now running for president, we would be able to find some common ground there. And we just couldn't." In addition, the debate over health care "created the kind of partisanship and bickering that really turn people off. Partly because the economy was still on the mend. And the entire focus on health care for so many months meant that people thought we were distracted and weren't paying attention to ... the key thing that was on their minds." In the end, the president concluded that, "There's no doubt that it hurt us politically."[24]

The president was correct. There was an extraordinarily strong cross-sectional relationship between opinions of Obama's job performance and his health care reforms. On average during 2010, 88 percent of respondents offered consistent opinions of Obama and the legislation, approving of both or disapproving of both. Opinions on Obama's handling of the issue were also more closely related to his overall job performance rating than were his ratings on the handling of any other issue. Although there is causation in both directions, we can see that health care was a source of the highly polarized response to the Obama presidency.[25]

In an Election Day survey by Republican pollster Bill McInturff among respondents in the one hundred most targeted House districts, 51 percent called their vote a message of opposition to the health care reform law, while just one in five said it was a sign of support for it. A majority of Independent voters also said that their vote was in opposition to the law. A senior Democratic strategist who worked closely with the White House and congressional races agreed that although health care reform was not the entire electoral puzzle, it clearly was a piece. "The successful Republican national narrative was one of overspending, overreaching Democrats. The election wasn't a referendum on health care reform, per se. But there is no question it played a role in the overarching narrative."[26]

It is not surprising, then, that a poll of one thousand Obama voters from 2008 who abandoned Democrats in the 2010 midterm elections, either by staying home ("droppers") or by voting Republican ("switchers"), found the health care bill to be a major catalyst for not supporting Democrats. Sixty-six percent of the switchers said President Obama and Democrats in Congress "tried to have government do too much," and the same percentage said "too much government spending" was a major reason for their decision not to vote Democratic. Fifty-two percent said a lack of focus on jobs was a major reason for their defections, and 51 percent said the same thing about the health care reform bill.[27] Another poll found that 57 percent of Independent voters said they favored repealing the new health care law, while only 31 percent said they opposed repeal.[28] A post-election poll by the Kaiser Family Foundation found that 56 percent of midterm voters said they wanted to see some or all of the of the health care law repealed, including eight in ten people who voted for Republican candidates. Those for whom health care mattered were more likely to vote Republican.[29]

Analyst Nate Silver concluded that Democrats performed somewhat worse than might be expected based on the performance of the economy alone and that their losses were higher than would be expected based on President Obama's approval ratings. The most reasonable explanation for the Democrats losing additional seats, he argued, was that voters punished Democrats for their votes for extending the TARP bailout and health care reform. Individual Democrats who voted against the health care bill and the bailout extension overperformed those who did in otherwise similar districts who voted for them, and it seems probable that these votes also damaged the electoral standing of Democrats overall.[30]

Brady, Fiorina, and Wilkins concluded that Democratic votes for health care and the economic stimulus cost the Democrats between twenty-two and forty seats in the House.[31] Similarly, Gary Jacobson found that, controlling for district presidential and congressional votes in 2008, a vote for health care reform cost a House Democrat about 5 percentage points in the 2010 midterm elections. (Some of the electoral effect worked through their impact on campaign fund-raising, stimulating contributions to Democrats' opponents.)[32]

There were fourteen Democratic incumbents who voted for health care reform and lost by less than 10 percentage points in the 2010 midterm elections. (A five-percentage point increase for the Democrat typically translates into a five-percentage point decrease for the Republican candidate, closing a ten-percentage point gap.) Thus, the five-percentage point decline in the vote resulting from supporting health care translates into a loss of fourteen seats for the Democrats. Winning these seats would have taken the Democrats more than halfway toward retaining their House majority.

Losing the seats, on the other hand, put the president on the defensive. The new House Republican majority took the lead opposing the White House and displayed impressive unity on the big issues, including blocking implementation of the health care reform law, prohibiting the Environmental Protection Agency from regulating carbon emissions linked to global climate change, cutting off funding for Planned Parenthood, and supporting final passage of the continuing resolution to fund the government, which imposed the largest one-year cuts in domestic discretionary spending in recent times. In April, just four

House Republicans (three for idiosyncratic reasons) voted against Paul Ryan's ambitious budget plan.

The 112th Congress was deeply polarized. In mid-April, *Congressional Quarterly* reported that almost 80 percent of House roll call votes in 2011—by far the highest percentage on record and double the figure from 2010—pitted the parties against each other. Moreover, representatives supported their party's majority position on average at least 90 percent of the time. The Senate was relying upon a "gentlemen's agreement" to avoid filibusters and contentious cloture fights and waiting for a "Gang of Six" to write a bipartisan debt-control bill. Nevertheless, on votes on which the parties split, members voted with their party's majority at least 90 percent of the time.[33] The president could succeed in passing policy changes in a context of polarization when he had the votes in the 111th Congress, but there was little probability of success when the opposition was large and disdainful of compromise.

The issue of raising the debt ceiling was a prime example of the challenge facing the president. Republicans recognized that the need to raise the debt ceiling offered them leverage to reduce the size of government, and many of them were willing to let the nation default on its obligations rather than increase federal revenues. These views placed severe constraints on the negotiations of their own leaders.

President Obama, Vice President Biden, and other White House officials believed that it would be easier to sell a big deal than to try to persuade members of Congress to vote for spending cuts that were both politically painful and too modest to solve the problem. Many in the administration concluded that it would be possible to strike a bipartisan grand bargain that raised tax revenues and cut Medicare costs. Nevertheless, when Democrats raised the matter of new tax revenue, the Republicans kept backing away. A spokesman for Speaker John Boehner reported that the Republican leadership drove a hard bargain out of necessity, knowing that anything less would not stand a chance of passing the House.[34] It is not surprising that to obtain final passage, Boehner had to delay the vote for two days and add provisions to appease Tea Party lawmakers.

In the end, Republicans won most of what they wanted and gave little ground. The White House backed off its demand for new tax revenue, despite the president's months-long insistence on a "balanced" approach to deficit reduction, and agreed to a multiphase deal that may produce only spending cuts. In return, Congress gave the Treasury sufficient borrowing power to pay the government's bills through the 2012 election.

For Democrats, the deal's lack of new tax revenue was hard to swallow, leading half the House Democrats to oppose the bill. Moreover, even as the president attempted to pivot to a focus on job creation, he was presiding over a series of cuts to federal agencies that limited his ability to pursue his "win the future" agenda. One possible upside for Democrats was the inclusion of a trigger that will force Congress to pass another $1.2 trillion in deficit reduction or face serious automatic cuts to domestic and defense programs alike, providing an opportunity to force Republicans to accept tax increases lest they be charged with ignoring the needs of the military.

Politically, no one came out ahead on the debt-ceiling showdown. The public was split on approving the ultimate deal,[35] with most polls finding at least pluralities opposing it. The public reported it was more likely to feel more negative than positive about Obama as a result of the debt agreement,[36] and pluralities disapproved of the president's handling of the debt ceiling issue.[37] The only good news for the White House was that the public evaluated congressional Republicans even more negatively than it evaluated the president.

Such findings were of little comfort to a White House that once again tried and failed to rally the public to its side and to obtain bipartisan support in Congress. With Republicans in control of the House and a narrow Democratic majority in the Senate, the president faced continued frustration as he sought to pass legislation focused on job creation.

At the midpoint of the president's term, White House advisors conceded that their greatest miscalculation was the assumption that the president could bridge a polarized capital and forge genuinely bipartisan coalitions. "Perhaps we were naïve," senior aide David Axelrod reflected, but Obama "believed that in the midst of a crisis you could find partners on the other side of the aisle to help deal with it. I don't think anyone here expected the degree of partisanship that we confronted." Another aide added, "It's not that we believed our own press or press releases, but there was definitely a sense at the beginning that we could really change Washington. 'Arrogance' isn't the right word, but we were overconfident."[38]

Obama recognized that "this is a big country . . . and . . . there are conservatives . . . that I'm never gonna persuade on some issues."[39] Nevertheless, the president persisted in the belief that leadership was "a matter of persuading people."[40] The conventional wisdom regarding the nature of presidential leadership is difficult to change. It is very difficult for presidents to reexamine their premises, even in the face of sustained failure. If they do not reevaluate the power of persuasion and ask the right questions about their opportunities, however, they are unlikely to arrive at the right answers.

NOTES

Introduction

1. See, for example, George C. Edwards III, *The Strategic President: Persuasion and Opportunity in Presidential Leadership* (Princeton, NJ: Princeton University Press, 2009); George C. Edwards III, *On Deaf Ears; The Limits of the Bully Pulpit* (New Haven, CT: Yale University Press, 2003); George C. Edwards III, *At the Margins: Presidential Leadership of Congress* (New Haven, CT: Yale University Press, 1989); Richard Fleisher, Jon R. Bond, and B. Dan Wood, "Which Presidents Are Uncommonly Successful in Congress?" in *Presidential Leadership: The Vortex of Presidential Power,* ed. Bert Rockman and Richard W. Waterman (New York: Oxford University Press, 2007); George C. Edwards III, *Governing by Campaigning: The Politics of the Bush Presidency,* 2nd ed. (New York: Longman, 2007), chap. 3.

2. Edwards, *The Strategic President.*

3. Ibid.

4. Michael Nelson, "The President and the Court: Reinterpreting the Court-packing Episode of 1937," *Political Science Quarterly* 103 (Summer 1988): 277–278.

5. Useful sources of the battle over the court-packing bill include William E. Leuchtenburg, *The Supreme Court Reborn: The Constitutional Revolution in the Age of Roosevelt* (New York: Oxford University Press, 1995); William E. Leuchtenburg, *Franklin D. Roosevelt and the New Deal, 1932–1940* (New York: Harper & Row, 1963); James T. Patterson, *Congressional Conservatism and the New Deal* (Lexington: University of Kentucky Press, 1967; James MacGregor Burns, *Roosevelt: The Lion and the Fox* (New York: Harcourt, Brace and World, 1956; George Tindall, *The Emergence of the New South, 1913–1945* (Baton Rouge: Louisiana State University Press, 1967).

6. Leuchtenburg, *The Supreme Court Reborn,* p. 156.

7. Ibid., pp. 157–158; Leuchtenburg, *Franklin D. Roosevelt and the New Deal, 1932–1940,* pp. 250–251, chap. 11.

8. Edwards, *On Deaf Ears,* pp. 35–37.

9. Lawrence R. Jacobs and Robert Y. Shapiro, *Politicians Don't Pander* (Chicago: University of Chicago Press, 2000), pp. 76, 81–83, 105, 115–16, 136, 149, 152.

10. Ibid., pp. 115, 149.

11. Quoted in Elizabeth Drew, *Showdown: The Struggle between the Gingrich Congress and the Clinton White House* (New York: Simon & Schuster, 1996), p. 66.

12. Jacobs and Shapiro, *Politicians Don't Pander,* p. 115.

13. Quoted in Jim VandeHei and Mike Allen, "Bush Rejects Delay, Prepares Escalated Social Security Push," *Washington Post,* March 3, 2005, p. A4. See also Mike Allen and Jim VandeHei, "Social Security Push to Tap the GOP Faithful: Campaign's Tactics Will Drive Appeal," *Washington Post,* January 14, 2005, p. A6; and Thomas B. Edsall, "Conservatives Join Forces for Bush Plans; Social Security, Tort Limits Spur Alliance," *Washington Post,* February 13, 2005, p. A4.

14. Allen and VandeHei, "Social Security Push to Tap the GOP Faithful."

15. www.strengtheningsocialsecurity.gov/60stops/accomplishments_042705.pdf.

16. See Edwards, *Governing by Campaigning*, chap. 7.

17. Bill Clinton, *My Life* (London: Hutchinson, 2004), p. 514.

18. Edwards, *The Strategic President*, chap. 6.

19. Ibid., chaps. 2–3, 6.

20. "Presidential Strategies for Governing," Regent University, February 6, 2009.

21. "Five Questions for George C. Edwards III, Author of *The Strategic President*," *CQ Weekly*, March 30, 2009, p. 703.

22. Richard E. Neustadt, *Presidential Power and the Modern Presidents* (New York: Free Press, 1990), p. 4.

Chapter 1

1. George C. Edwards III, *On Deaf Ears: The Limits of the Bully Pulpit* (New Haven, CT: Yale University Press, 2003).

2. George C. Edwards III, *The Strategic President: Persuasion and Opportunity in Presidential Leadership* (Princeton, NJ: Princeton University Press, 2009), pp. 26–34.

3. George C. Edwards III, *Governing by Campaigning: The Politics of the Bush Presidency*, 2nd ed. (New York: Longman, 2007).

4. See Edwards, *The Strategic President*, chaps. 2–3, 6.

5. Quoted in Jonathan Alter, *The Promise: President Obama, Year One* (New York: Simon & Schuster, 2010), p. 47; and Dan Balz, "He Promised Change, but Is This Too Much, Too Soon?" *Washington Post*, July 26, 2009.

6. Shailagh Murray and Paul Kane, "Obama's Ambitious Agenda Will Test Congress," *Washington Post*, February 26, 2009.

7. Transcript: "President Barack Obama," *60 Minutes*, Interview by Steve Kroft, November 4, 2010.

8. Ronald Brownstein and Alexis Simendinger, "The View from the West Wing," *National Journal*, January 16, 2010, p. 27.

9. Quoted in Alter, *The Promise*, pp. 79, 429. See also p. 188.

10. Scott Wilson, "Bruised by Stimulus Battle, Obama Changed His Approach to Washington," *Washington Post*, April 29, 2009.

11. For example, White House communications director Anita Dunn concluded that the administration failed at selling health care reform as a central part of its economic message. Dan Balz, "For Obama, a Tough Year to Get the Message Out," *Washington Post*, January 10, 2010.

12. Barack Obama, State of the Union Address, January 27, 2010.

13. David E. Sanger, "Where Clinton Turned Right, Obama Plowed Ahead," *New York Times*, January 28, 2009.

14. George C. Edwards III, *At the Margins: Presidential Leadership of Congress* (New Haven, CT: Yale University Press, 1989), chap. 8; Lawrence J. Grossback, David A. M. Peterson, and James A. Stimson, *Mandate Politics* (New York: Cambridge University Press, 2006).

15. For more on the conditions that encourage perceptions of a mandate, see Edwards, *At the Margins*, chap. 8; and Grossback, Peterson, and Stimson, *Mandate Politics*, chap. 2.

16. Transcript of press conference on November 25, 2008.

17. ABC News/*Washington Post* poll, January 13–16, 2009.

18. Barack Obama, Inaugural Address, January 20, 2009.

19. Quoted in John Harwood, "'Partisan' Seeks a Prefix: Bi- or Post-" *New York Times*, December 7, 2008.

20. Ibid.

21. Gallup Poll daily tracking polls, throughout 2009. The sample includes 291,152 U.S. adults. The margin of sampling error for most states is ±2 percentage points, but is as high as ±5 percentage points for the District of Columbia.

22. Gallup Poll surveys conducted January–September 2009.

23. Shawn Treier and D. Sunshine Hillygus, "The Nature of Political Ideology in the Contemporary Electorate," *Public Opinion Quarterly* 73 (Winter 2009): 679–703; Christopher Ellis and James A. Stimson, "Symbolic Ideology in the American Electorate," *Electoral Studies* 28 (September 2009): 388–402; William G. Jacoby, "Policy Attitudes, Ideology, and Voting Behavior in the 2008 Election," paper presented at the Annual Meeting of the American Political Science Association, 2009; James A. Stimson, *Tides of Consent: How Public Opinion Shapes American Politics* (New York: Cambridge University Press, 2004); Pamela J. Conover and Stanley Feldman, "The Origins and Meaning of Liberal/Conservative Identifications," *American Journal of Political Science* 25 (October 1981): 617–645; David O. Sears, Richard L. Lau, Tom R. Tyler, and Harris M. Allen, "Self-Interest vs. Symbolic Politics in Policy Attitudes and Presidential Voting," *American Political Science Review* 74 (September 1980): 670–684.

24. Philip E. Converse, "The Nature of Belief Systems in Mass Publics," in *Ideology and Discontent*, ed. David E. Apter (New York: Free Press, 1964), pp. 206–261.

25. Teresa E. Levitin and Warren E. Miller, "Ideological Interpretations of Presidential Elections," *American Political Science Review* 73 (September 1979): 751–771.

26. Robert Huckfeldt, Jeffrey Levine, William Morgan, and John Sprague, "Accessibility and the Political Utility of Partisan and Ideological Orientations," *American Journal of Political Science* 43 (July 1999): 888–911; Kathleen Knight, "Ideology in the 1980 Election: Ideological Sophistication Does Matter," *Journal of Politics* 47 (July 1985): 828–853; Levitin and Miller, "Ideological Interpretations of Presidential Elections"; James A. Stimson, "Belief Systems: Constraint, Complexity, and the 1972 Election," *American Journal of Political Science* 19 (July 1975): 393–417.

27. Paul Goren, Christopher M. Federico, and Miki Caul Kittilson, "Source Cues, Partisan Identities, and Political Value Expression," *American Journal of Political Science* 53 (October 2009): 805–820; Christopher M. Federico and Monica C. Schneider, "Political Expertise and the Use of Ideology: Moderating the Effects of Evaluative Motivation," *Public Opinion Quarterly* 71(Summer 2007): 221–252; William G. Jacoby, "Value Choices and American Public Opinion," *American Journal of Political Science* 50 (July 2006): 706–723; Paul Goren, "Political Sophistication and Policy Reasoning: A Reconsideration," *American Journal of Political Science* 48 (July 2004): 462–478; Paul Goren, "Core Principles and Policy Reasoning in Mass Publics: A Test of Two Theories," *British Journal of Political Science* 31(January 2001): 159–177; Huckfeldt, Levine, Morgan, and Sprague, "Accessibility and the Political Utility of Partisan and Ideological Orientations"; William G. Jacoby, "The Structure of Ideological Thinking in the American Electorate," *American Journal of Political Science* 39 (April 1995): 314–335; William G. Jacoby, "Ideo-

logical Identification and Issue Attitudes," *American Journal of Political Science* 35 (January 1991): 178–205; Stanley Feldman, "Structure and Consistency in Public Opinion: The Role of Core Beliefs and Attitudes," *American Journal of Political Science* 32 (May 1988): 416–440; Sears, Lau, Tyler, and Allen, "Self-Interest vs. Symbolic Politics in Policy Attitudes and Presidential Voting."

28. Thomas J. Rudolph and Jillian Evans, "Political Trust, Ideology, and Public Support for Government Spending," *American Journal of Political Science* 49 (July 2005): 660–671; William G. Jacoby, "Issue Framing and Government Spending," *American Journal of Political Science* 44 (October 2000): 750–767; William G. Jacoby, "Public Attitudes toward Government Spending," *American Journal of Political Science* 38 (April 1994): 336–361.

29. Andrew Kohut, "Obama's 2010 Challenge: Wake Up Liberals, Calm Down Independents," Pew Research Center for the People and the Press, December 17, 2009.

30. Gallup poll, August 31–September 2, 2009.

31. Gallup polls, November 13–16, 2008, and November 5–8, 2009.

32. See also *New York Times*/CBS News poll, February 5–10, 2010.

33. Phil Mattingly, "Debt Takes a Holiday," *CQ Weekly*, December 28, 2009, pp. 2934–2941.

34. Robert H. Durr, "What Moves Policy Sentiment?" *American Political Science Review* 87 (March 1993): 158–170; Suzanna De Boef and Paul M. Kellstedt, "The Political (and Economic) Origins of Consumer Confidence," *American Journal of Political Science* 48 (October 2004): 633–649.

35. *USA Today*/Gallup polls of March 27–29, 2009.

36. Gallup poll, July 17–19, 2009.

37. *Washington Post*-ABC News poll, July 15–18, 2009.

38. Gallup poll, August 6–9, 2009.

39. Gallup poll, August 31–September 2, 2009.

40. Robert S. Erikson, Michael B. MacKuen, and James A. Stimson, *The Macro Polity* (New York: Cambridge University Press, 2002), chap. 9.

41. Ibid., pp. 344, 374.

42. See also Stuart N. Soroka and Christopher Wlezien, *Degress of Democracy* (New York: Cambridge University Press, 2010).

43. See Gary C. Jacobson, *A Divider, Not a Uniter: George W. Bush and the American Public*, 3rd ed. (New York: Longman, 2011).

44. If independent leaners are included as partisans, the figure rises to 8.0 percent; only John F. Kennedy attracted fewer (7.1 percent). These figures are from Gary C. Jacobson, "Legislative Success and Political Failure: The Public's Reaction to Barack Obama's Early Presidency," *Presidential Studies Quarterly* 41 (June 2011), p. 221.

45. Ibid, pp. 221–222.

46. Kate Kenski, Bruce W. Hardy, and Kathleen Hall Jamieson, *The Obama Victory: How Media, Money, and Message Shaped the 2008 Election* (New York: Oxford University Press, 2010).

47. Spencer Piston, "How Explicit Racial Prejudice Hurt Obama in the 2008 Election," *Political Behavior* 32 (December 2010): 431–451; Michael Lewis-Beck, Charles Tien, and Richard Nadeau, "Obama's Missed Landslide: A Racial Cost?" *PS: Political Science and Politics* 43 (January 2010): 69–76; Benjamin Highton, "Prejudice Rivals Par-

tisanship and Ideology When Explaining the 2008 Presidential Vote across the States," *PS: Political Science and Politics* 44 (July 2011): 6530–535.

48. Jay Cost, "Electoral Polarization Continues Under Obama," RealClearPolitics HorseRaceBlog, November 20, 2008.

49. Ibid.

50. See Jacobson, *A Divider, Not a Uniter*.

51. Nolan McCarty, Keith T. Poole, and Howard Rosenthal, *Polarized America: The Dance of Ideology and Unequal Riches* (Cambridge, MA: MIT Press, 2006).

52. Bill Bishop, *The Big Sort: Why the Clustering of Like-Minded America Is Tearing Us Apart* (Boston: Houghton Mifflin, 2008).

53. Ian McDonald, "Migration and Sorting in the American Electorate: Evidence From the 2006 Cooperative Congressional Election Study," *American Politics Research* 39 (May 2011): 512–533.

54. 2000 Exit Polls.

55. Alan I. Abramowitz, *The Disappearing Center* (New Haven, CT: Yale University Press, 2010).

56. Andrew Garner and Harvey Palmer, "Polarization and Issue Consistency Over Time," *Political Behavior* 33 (June 2011): 225–246.

57. Gallup Daily tracking averages for February 9–15, 2009.

58. Gallup Daily tracking averages for April 20–26, 2009.

59. Gallup Poll, News Release, January 5, 2001.

60. Gary C. Jacobson, "The Bush Presidency and the American Electorate," *Presidential Studies Quarterly* 33 (December 2003): 701–729.

61. See, for example, Jeffrey M. Jones, "Bush Ratings Show Historical Levels of Polarization," *Gallup News Service*, June 4, 2004.

62. This point is nicely illustrated in Jacobson, *A Divider, Not a Uniter*, chap. 1.

63. Jones, "Bush Ratings Show Historical Levels of Polarization."

64. Jeffrey M. Jones, "Obama's Approval Most Polarized for First-Year President," Gallup Poll, January 25, 2010.

65. Jeffrey M. Jones, "Obama's Approval Ratings More Polarized in Year 2 Than Year 1," Gallup Poll, February 4, 2011.

66. Gallup Daily tracking polls from July to mid-August 2009, including more than 47,000 interviews.

67. Spee Kosloff, Jeff Greenberg, Toni Schmader, Mark Dechesne, and David Weise, "Smearing the Opposition: Implicit and Explicit Stigmatization of the 2008 U.S. Presidential Candidates and the Current U.S. President," *Journal of Experimental Psychology* 139 (August 2010): 383–398.

68. Piston, "How Explicit Racial Prejudice Hurt Obama in the 2008 Election," 431–451.

69. Alan I. Abramowitz, "The Race Factor: White Racial Attitudes and Opinions of Obama," *Sabato's Crystal Ball*, May 12th, 2011.

70. Charlie Cook, "Intensity Matters," *National Journal*, October 24, 2009.

71. Democracy Corps poll, June 19–22, 2010.

72. CNN poll conducted by Opinion Research Corporation, July 16–21, 2010. See also *Adam J. Berinsky,* Pollster.com September 13, 2010, www.pollster.com/blogs/poll _shows_false_obama_beliefs.php.

73. Pew Research Center for the People and the Press poll, July 21–August 5, 2010.

74. *Newsweek* poll, August 25–26, 2010.

75. As Gary Jacobson points out, some of the mistaken views about Obama were probably driven by opinions about Obama more generally. See "Legislative Success and Political Failure," pp. 229–230.

76. Pew Research Media Attitudes Survey, July 22–26, 2009.

77. Logan Dancey and Paul Goren, "Party Identification, Issue Attitudes, and the Dynamics of Political Debate," *American Journal of Political Science* 54 (July 2010): 686–699; Michael Bang Petersen, Rune Slothuus, and Lise Togeby, "Political Parties and Value Consistency in Public Opinion Formation," *Public Opinion Quarterly* 74 (Fall 2010): 530–550; Matthew Levendusky, *The Partisan Sort* (Chicago: University of Chicago Press, 2009); Adam J. Berinsky, *In Time of War: Understanding American Public Opinion from World War II to Iraq* (Chicago: University of Chicago Press, 2009). See also Abramowitz, *The Disappearing Center*; Morris P. Fiorina, with Samuel J. Abrams and Jeremy C. Pope, *Culture Wars? The Myth of Polarized America*, 3rd ed. (New York: Pearson Longman, 2011); Joseph Bafumi and Robert Y. Shapiro, "A New Partisan Voter," *Journal of Politics* 71 (January 2009): 1–24; Geoffrey C. Layman, Thomas M. Carsey, and Juliana Menasce Horowitz, "Party Polarization in American Politics: Characteristics, Causes, and Consequences," *Annual Review of Political Science* 9 (2006): 83–110; Jacobson, *A Divider, Not a Uniter*.

78. Gallup poll, June 11–13, 2010.

79. Gallup poll, June 23–24, 2009.

80. Gallup poll, May 24–25, 2010.

81. See, for example, the *New York Times/CBS News* poll, June 12–16, 2009; *New York Times/CBS News* poll, September 19–23, 2009.

82. Ceci Connolly and Jon Cohen, "Most Want Health Reform But Fear Its Side Effects," *Washington Post*, June 24, 2009. These comments are based on a *Washington Post-ABC News* poll, June 18–21, 2009.

83. *Washington Post-ABC News* poll, June 18–21, 2009; CNN/Opinion Research Corp. poll, July 31–August 3, 2009; *USA Today/Gallup* poll, September 11–13, 2009; Gallup poll, November 4–7, 2010.

84. Gallup poll, July 24–25, 2009. See also *Wall Street Journal/NBC News* poll, July 24–27, 2009; *Time* poll, July 27–28, 2009; *New York Times/CBS News* poll, July 24–28, 2009; CNN/Opinion Research Corp. poll, July 31–August 3, 2009; and Kaiser Health Tracking Poll, July 7–14, 2009.

85. *Washington Post-ABC News* poll, August 13–17, 2009.

86. NBC News/*Wall Street Journal* poll, August 15–17, 2009.

87. *Washington Post-ABC News* poll, December 10–13, 2009. See also *Washington Post-ABC News* poll, November 12–15, 2009; Gallup poll, November 5–8, 2009.

88. Gallup poll, July 24–25, 2009.

89. *New York Times/CBS News* poll, July 24–28, 2009.

90. *USA Today/Gallup* poll, July 10–12, 2009; *New York Times/CBS News* poll, September 19–23, 2009.

91. Pew Research Center for the People and the Press poll, June 10–14, 2009.

92. *New York Times/CBS News* poll, July 24–28, 2009; CBS News poll, August 27–31, 2009; *New York Times/CBS News* poll, September 19–23, 2009.

93. *New York Times*/CBS News poll, July 24–28, 2009. See also CNN/Opinion Research Corp. poll, July 31–August 3, 2009.

94. Frank Newport, "Americans on Healthcare Reform: Top 10 Takeaways," Gallup Poll, July 31, 2009.

95. Pew Research Center for the People and the Press poll, July 23–26, 2009. See also poll of December 9–13, 2009.

96. Robert Pear, "House Committee Approves Health Care Bill," *New York Times*, July 16, 2009.

97. *Washington Post*-ABC News poll, December 10–13, 2009.

98. This discussion is based on Edwards, *On Deaf Ears*, chaps. 4–9.

99. See Brian J. Gaines, James H. Kuklinski, Paul J. Quirk, Buddy Peyton, and Jay Verkuilen, "Same Facts, Different Interpretations: Partisan Motivation and Opinion on Iraq," *Journal of Politics* 69 (November 2007): 957–974; Edwards, *On Deaf Ears*, chap. 9; Larry Bartels, "Beyond the Running Tally: Partisan Bias in Political Perceptions," *Political Behavior* 24 (June 2002): 117–150.

100. James N. Druckman, "Using Credible Advice to Overcome Framing Effects," *Journal of Law, Economics, and Organization* 17, no. 1(2001): 62–82; James N. Druckman, "On the Limits of Framing Effects: Who Can Frame?" *Journal of Politics* 63 (November 2001): 1041–1066; Joanne M. Miller and Jon A. Krosnick, "News Media Impact on the Ingredients of Presidential Evaluations: Politically Knowledgeable Citizens Are Guided by a Trusted Source," *American Journal of Political Science* 44 (April 2000): 301–315.

101. Rune Slothuus and Claes H. de Vreese, "Political Parties, Motivated Reasoning, and Issue Framing Effects," *Journal of Politics* (July 2010): 630–645; Charles S. Taber, Damon Cann, and Simona Kucsova, "The Motivated Processing of Political Arguments," *Political Behavior* 31 (June 2009): 137–155; Charles S. Taber and Milton Lodge, "Motivated Skepticism in the Evaluation of Political Beliefs," *American Journal of Political Science* 50 (July 2006): 755–769; John T. Jost, "The End of the End of Ideology," *American Psychologist* 61, no. 7 (2006): 651–670; Richard R. Lau and David P. Redlawsk, *How Voters Decide: Information Processing in Election Campaigns* (New York: Cambridge University Press, 2006); Milton Lodge and Charles S. Taber, "The Automaticity of Affect for Political Leaders, Groups, and Issues: An Experimental Test of the Hot Cognition Hypothesis," *Political Psychology* 26 (June 2005): 455–482; David P. Redlawsk, "Hot Cognition or Cool Consideration: Testing the Effects of Motivated Reasoning on Political Decision Making," *Journal of Politics* 64 (November 2002): 1021–1044; Milton Lodge and Ruth Hamill, "A Partisan Schema for Political Information Processing," *American Political Science Review* 80 (June 1986): 505–519; Charles Lord, Lee Ross, and Mark R. Lepper, "Biased Assimilation and Attitude Polarization: The Effects of Prior Theories on Subsequently Considered Evidence," *Journal of Personality and Social Psychology* 37 (November 1979): 2098–2109.

102. John R. Zaller, *The Nature and Origins of Mass Opinion* (New York: Cambridge University Press, 1992), pp. 102–113; Danielle Shani, "Knowing Your Colors: Can Knowledge Correct for Partisan Bias in Political Perceptions?" paper presented at the annual meeting of the Midwest Political Science Association, Chicago, 2006.

103. Larry M. Bartels, "Beyond the Running Tally: Partisan Bias in Political Perceptions," *Political Behavior* 24 (June 2002): 117–150.

104. Christopher H. Achen and Larry M. Bartels, "It Feels Like We're Thinking: The Rationalizing Voter and Electoral Democracy," paper delivered at the Annual Meeting of the American Political Science Association, Philadelphia, 2006. See also Larry M. Bartels, *Unequal Democracy* (Princeton, NJ: Princeton University Press, 2008), chap. 5; Mathew J. Lebo and Daniel Cassino, "The Aggregated Consequences of Motivated Reasoning and the Dynamics of Partisan Presidential Approval," *Political Psychology* 28 (December 2007): 719–746; Jacobson, *A Divider, Not a Uniter*; DeBoef and Kellstedt, "The Political (and Economic) Origins of Consumer Confidence."

105. Steven Kull, Clay Ramsay, and Evan Lewis, "Misperceptions, the Media, and the Iraq War," *Political Science Quarterly* 118 (Winter 2003–2004): 569–598; Edwards, *Governing by Campaigning*, chap. 3; Jacobson, *A Divider, Not a Uniter*, chaps. 5–6; Gaines, Kuklinski, Quirk, Peyton, and Verkuilen, "Same Facts, Different Interpretations: Partisan Motivation and Opinion on Iraq," 957–974.

106. Gary C. Jacobson, "The Public, the President, and the War in Iraq," paper presented at the annual meeting of the American Political Science Association, Washington, DC, September 1–4, 2005, p. 35.

107. Paul D. Sweeney and Kathy L. Gruber, "Selective Exposure: Voter Information Preferences and the Watergate Affair," *Journal of Personality and Social Psychology* 46, no. 6 (1984): 1208–1221.

108. Mark Fischle, "Mass Response to the Lewinsky Scandal: Motivated Reasoning or Bayesian Updating?" *Political Psychology* 21 (March 2000): 135–159.

109. Edwards, *On Deaf Ears*, chap. 9.

110. Zaller, *The Nature and Origins of Mass Opinion*, p. 48; William G. Jacoby, "The Sources of Liberal–Conservative Thinking: Education and Conceptualization," *Political Behavior* 10 (December 1988): 316–332; Robert C. Luskin, "Measuring Political Sophistication," *American Journal of Political Science* 31 (November 1987): 856–899; W. Russell Neuman, *The Paradox of Mass Politics; Knowledge and Opinion in the American Electorate* (Cambridge, MA: Harvard University Press, 1986); Edward G. Carmines and James A. Stimson, "The Two Faces of Issue Voting," *American Political Science Review* 74 (March 1980): 78–91; Philip E. Converse, "The Nature of Belief Systems in Mass Publics," in *Ideology and Discontent*, ed. David E. Apter (New York: Free Press, 1964).

111. James H. Kuklinski, Paul J. Quirk, Jennifer Jerit, David Schwieder, and Robert F. Rich, "Misinformation and the Currency of Democratic Citizenship," *Journal of Politics* 62 (August 2000): 790–816. See also Brendan Nyhan, "Why the 'Death Panel' Myth Wouldn't Die: Misinformation in the Health Care Reform Debate," *The Forum* 8, no. 1 (2010). Accessed at www.bepress.com/forum/vol8/iss1/art5.

112. Brendan Nyhan and Jason Reifler, "When Corrections Fail: The Persistence of Political Misperceptions," *Political Behavior* 32 (June 2010): 303–330; David P. Redlawsk, Andrew J. W. Civettini, and Karen M. Emmerson, "The Affective Tipping Point: Do Motivated Reasoners Ever 'Get It'?" *Political Psychology* 31 (August 2010): 563–593.

113. Ruth Mayo, Yaacov Schul, and Eugene Burnstein, "'I Am Not Guilty' vs 'I Am Innocent': Successful Negation May Depend on the Schema Used for Its Encoding," *Journal of Experimental Social Psychology* 40 (July 2004): 433–449.

114. Norbert Schwarz, Lawrence J. Sanna, Ian Skurnik, and Carolyn Yoon, "Metacognitive Experiences and the Intricacies of Setting People Straight: Implications for Debi-

asing and Public Information Campaigns," *Advances in Experimental Social Psychology* 39 (2007): 127–161; Ian Skurnik, Carolyn Yoon, Denise C. Park, and Norbert Schwarz, "How Warnings about False Claims Become Recommendations," *Journal of Consumer Research* 31(March 2005): 713–724.

115. John Bullock, "Experiments on Partisanship and Public Opinion: Party Cues, False Beliefs, and Bayesian Updating," Ph.D. dissertation, Stanford University, 2007.

116. John R. Zaller, "Elite Leadership of Mass Opinion: New Evidence from the Gulf War," in *Taken by Storm: The Media, Public Opinion, and U.S. Foreign Policy in the Gulf War*, ed. W. Lance Bennett and David L. Paletz (Chicago: University of Chicago Press, 1994); Zaller, *The Nature and Origins of Mass Opinion*.

117. Robert Y. Shapiro and Lawrence R. Jacobs, "The Democratic Paradox: The Waning of Popular Sovereignty and the Pathologies of American Politics," in *The Oxford Handbook of American Public Opinion and the Media*, ed. Robert Y. Shapiro and Lawrence R. Jacobs (Oxford, UK: Oxford University Press, 2011).

118. David Kahneman and Amos Tversky, "Choices, Values, and Frames," *American Psychologist* 39 (April 1984): 341–350; David Kahneman and Amos Tversky, "Prospect Theory: An Analysis of Decision under Risk," *Econometrica* 47 (March 1979): 263–292.

119. Susan T. Fiske, "Attention and Weight in Person Perception: The Impact of Negative and Extreme Behavior," *Journal of Personality and Social Psychology* 38, no. 6 (1980): 889–906; David L. Hamilton and Mark P. Zanna, "Differential Weighting of Favorable and Unfavorable Attributes in Impressions of Personality," *Journal of Experimental Research in Personality* 6, nos. 2–3 (1972): 204–212.

120. Richard Lau, "Two Explanations for Negativity Effects in Political Behavior," *American Journal of Political Science* 29 (February 1985): 119–138.

121. See, for example, David W. Brady and Daniel P. Kessler, "Who Supports Health Reform? *PS: Political Science and Politics* 43 (January 2010): 1–5.

122. Michael D. Cobb and James H. Kuklinski, "Changing Minds: Political Arguments and Political Persuasion," *American Journal of Political Science* 41 (January 1997): 88–121. On the role of emotion in political decision making, see Joanne M. Miller, "Examining the Mediators of Agenda Setting: A New Experimental Paradigm Reveals the Role of Emotions," *Political Psychology* 28 (December 2007): 689–717; George E. Marcus, W. Russell Neuman, and Michael MacKuen, *Affective Intelligence and Political Judgment* (Chicago: University of Chicago Press, 2000); George E. Marcus, *The Sentimental Citizen* (University Park: Pennsylvania State University Press, 2002); Michael MacKuen, Jennifer Wolak, Luke Keele, and George E. Marcus, " Civic Engagements: Resolute Partisanship or Reflective Deliberation," *American Journal of Political Science* 54 (April 2010): 440–458.

123. Gallup Poll, "Majorities in U.S. View Gov't as Too Intrusive and Powerful," October 13, 2010.

124. Charlie Cook, "Colossal Miscalculation on Health Care," *National Journal*, January 16, 2010.

125. Charlie Cook, "Too Much All At Once," *Off to the Races*, February 2, 2010.

126. *Washington Post*-ABC News poll, January 12–15, 2010.

127. Quoted in Peter Baker, "Education of a President," *New York Times Magazine*, October 17, 2010. See also Transcript: "President Barack Obama," *60 Minutes*, Interview by Steve Kroft, November 4, 2010.

Chapter 2

1. Barack Obama, *Dreams from My Father* (New York: Crown Publishers, 1995), p. 106.

2. Jonathan Alter, *The Promise: President Obama, Year One* (New York: Simon & Schuster, 2010), p. 46.

3. Ken Auletta, "Non-Stop News," *New Yorker*, January 25, 2010, p. 43.

4. These figures are updates of the Postscript of Martha Joynt Kumar, *Managing the President's Message: The White House Communications Operation* (Baltimore, MD: Johns Hopkins University Press, 2010), pp. 314–319, provided by Professor Kumar.

5. Mark Knoller, CBS News.

6. Jeff Zeleny, "Obama Returning to Trail to Sell Stimulus Plan," *New York Times*, February 9, 2009.

7. Alter, *The Promise*, pp. 126–127.

8. Mark Leibovich, "Between Barack Obama and the Press—Robert Gibbs," *New York Times*, December 21, 2008; Auletta, "Non-Stop News," p. 43.

9. Auletta, "Non-Stop News," pp. 41–42.

10. Rachel L. Swarns, "Obama Brings Flush Times for Black News Media," *New York Times*, March 28, 2009.

11. These figures are updates of the Postscript of Kumar, *Managing the President's Message*, provided by Professor Kumar.

12. Brian Stelter, "Obama to Field Questions Posted by YouTube Users," *New York Times*, February 1, 2010.

13. Dana Milbank, "Stay Tuned for More of 'The Obama Show,'" *Washington Post*, June 24, 2009.

14. These figures are updates of the Postscript of Kumar, *Managing the President's Message*, provided by Professor Kumar.

15. Ibid.

16. Auletta, "Non-Stop News," p. 41.

17. Glenn Thrush, "Obama Makes the Sale," Politico.com, December 17, 2010.

18. Mark and Helene Cooper, "White House Eager to Project Image of Competence in Relief Efforts," *New York Times*, January 22, 2010.

19. Brian Stelter, "Fox's Volley with Obama Intensifying," *New York Times*, October 12, 2009; Jim Rutenberg, "Behind the War between White House and Fox," *New York Times*, October 23, 2009.

20. Auletta, "Non-Stop News," p. 47.

21. Alter, *The Promise*, p. 46.

22. Quoted in Dan Balz, "For Obama, a Tough Year To Get the Message Out," *Washington Post*, January 10, 2010.

23. See Charles O. Jones, *The Presidency in a Separated System*, 2nd ed. (Washington, DC: Brookings Institution, 2005), chap. 5.

24. On continuity in foreign policy despite changes in the occupant of the presidency, see William J. Dixon and Stephen M. Gardner, "Presidential Succession and the Cold War: An Analysis of Soviet American Relations, 1948–1988," *Journal of Politics* 54 (February 1992): 156–175.

25. Quoted in John C. Donovan, *The Politics of Poverty*, 2nd ed. (Indianapolis, IN: Pegasus, 1973), p. 111.

26. See an interview with Bill Clinton by Jack Nelson and Robert J. Donovan, "The Education of a President," *Los Angeles Times Magazine*, August 1, 1993, p. 39. See also Bill Clinton, *My Life* (New York: Knopf, 2004), p. 556.

27. Quoted in Balz, "For Obama, a Tough Year to Get the Message Out."

28. George Packer, "Obama's Lost Year," *New Yorker*, March 15, 2010, p. 46.

29. Pew Project for Excellence in Journalism News Coverage Index for September 21–27, 2009.

30. Michael D. Shear, "Times Square Bomb, Oil Spill Complicate White House Agenda," *Washington Post*, May 3, 2010.

31. See George C. Edwards III, *The Strategic President: Persuasion and Opportunity in Presidential Leadership* (Princeton, NJ: Princeton University Press, 2009), pp. 96–104.

32. Quoted in Michael D. Shear, "White House Revamps Communications Strategy," *Washington Post*, February 15, 2010.

33. Mark Hertsgaard, *On Bended Knee: The Press and the Reagan Presidency* (New York: Farrar, Straus, and Giroux, 1988), pp. 107–108; Larry Speakes, *Speaking Out* (New York: Scribner's, 1988), p. 301.

34. Quoted in Balz, "For Obama, a Tough Year to Get the Message Out."

35. Sheryl Gay Stolberg, "On Abortion, Obama Is Drawn Into Debate He Hoped to Avoid," *New York Times*, May 15, 2009.

36. Pew Research Center for the People and the Press poll, July 24–27, 2009; Pew Research Center for the People and the Press News Interest survey, July 20–26, 2009.

37. "Statement by the President," White House Transcript, July 24, 2009.

38. Pew Research Center for the People and the Press News Interest survey, July 31–August 1, 2009.

39. David M. Herszenhorn and Sheryl Gay Stolberg, "Health Plan Opponents Make Voices Heard," *New York Times*, August 4, 2009.

40. Howard Kurtz, "Journalists, Left Out of the Debate: Few Americans Seem to Hear Health Care Facts," *Washington Post*, August 24, 2009.

41. Pew Research Center for the People and the Press poll, August 11–17, 2009.

42. Shear, "White House Revamps Communications Strategy."

43. Pew Research Center for the People and the Press News Interest Survey, February 26–March 1, 2010.

44. Peter Baker, "Obama Reverses Rules on U.S. Abortion Aid," *New York Times*, January 24, 2009; Howard Kurtz, "Obama Attempts to Manage His Media Presence," *Washington Post*, February 9, 2009.

45. Quoted in Jason Horowitz, "Obama Speechwriter Ben Rhodes Is Penning a Different Script for the World Stage," *Washington Post*, January 12, 2010.

46. Michael D. Shear, "Riding Herd on the Message: White House Guides Fervent Sotomayor Supporters," *Washington Post*, June 15, 2009.

47. Quoted in Balz, "For Obama, a Tough Year to Get the Message Out."

48. Ceci Connolly, "Obama Trims Sails on Health Reform," *Washington Post*, August 2, 2009.

49. Lawrence R. Jacobs and Robert Y. Shapiro, *Politicians Don't Pander* (Chicago: University of Chicago Press, 2000), p. 140, agree with this point.

50. Quoted in Balz, "For Obama, a Tough Year to Get the Message Out."

51. Michael D. Shear and Ceci Connolly, "Debate's Path Caught Obama by Surprise; Public Option Wasn't Intended as Major Focus," *Washington Post*, August 19, 2009; Dan Balz, "Concern, Doubts from the Left on Obama's Health-Care Plan," *Washington Post*, August 23, 2009; Alter, *The Promise*, 295.

52. "Remarks by President Bush in a Conversation on Strengthening Social Security," Greece, New York, March 24, 2005.

53. David Gergen, *Eyewitness to Power: The Essence of Leadership* (New York: Simon & Schuster 2000), pp. 54, 186. Also see Kumar, *Managing the President's Message*, chaps. 2–3.

54. Philip E. Converse, "The Nature of Belief Systems in Mass Publics," in *Ideology and Discontent*, ed. David E. Apter (New York: Free Press, 1964), pp. 206–261.

55. Charles W. Ostrom, Jr. and Dennis M. Simon, "The President's Public," *American Journal of Political Science* 32 (November 1988): 1096–1119.

56. Joe S. Foote, "Ratings Decline of Presidential Television," *Journal of Broadcasting and Electronic Media* 32 (Spring 1988): 225–230; A. C. Nielsen, *Nielsen Newscast* (Northbrook, IL: Nielson, 1975); Edwards, *On Deaf Ears*, chap. 8; George C. Edwards III, *Governing by Campaigning*, 2nd ed. (New York: Longman, 2007), pp. 86–94.

57. Matthew A. Baum and Samuel Kernell, "Has Cable Ended the Golden Age of Presidential Television?" *American Political Science Review* 93 (March 1999): 99–114.

58. Nielsen Company.

59. Peter Baker, "Obama Selling His Economic Plan on the Airwaves, Again," *New York Times*, March 24, 2009.

60. Benjamin Toff, "Viewers Pass on Obama," *New York Times*, June 25, 2009; Tobin Harshaw, "Hawking Health Care in Prime Time," *New York Times*, June 26, 2009.

61. "TV Ratings: President Obama Pulls in Record 'View' Audience," July 31, 2010.

62. Transcript: "President Barack Obama," *60 Minutes*, Interview by Steve Kroft, November 4, 2010.

63. Gergen, *Eyewitness to Power*, p. 54. See also Kumar, *Managing the President's Message*, chap. 1.

64. Gergen, *Eyewitness to Power*, p. 54.

65. CBS News/*New York Times* poll, February 5–10, 2010.

66. Bloomberg Poll conducted by Selzer & Co., July 9–12, 2010.

67. CBS News/*New York Times* poll, September 10–14, 2010.

68. Bloomberg News National Poll, October 24–26, 2010.

69. Pew Research Center for the People and the Press poll, July 1–5, 2010.

70. Bloomberg News National Poll, October 24–26, 2010.

71. Quoted in Mark Leibovich, "Obama's Message Maven Finds Fingers Pointing at Him," *New York Times*, March 6, 2010.

72. Pew Research Center for the People and the Press and the Pew Forum on Religion & Public Life polls, March 9–12, 2009, and July 21–August 5, 2010. See also *Newsweek* poll of August 25–26, 2010, taken by Princeton Survey Research Associates International; and *Time* poll, August 16–17, 2010.

73. See, for example, Elizabeth McCaughey, *The Kudlow Report*, CNBC, June 16, 2009; Elizabeth McCaughey, "Dissecting the Kennedy Health Bill," *Wall Street Journal*, June 19, 2009; Elizabeth McCaughey, "How Health Care 'Reforms' Will Mess with Your Coverage," *New York Daily News*, June 23, 2009. For detailed coverage of the conserva-

tive propagation of the claim, see Brendan Nyhan, "Why the 'Death Panel' Myth Wouldn't Die: Misinformation in the Health Care Reform Debate," *The Forum* 8, no. 1 (2010). Accessed at www.bepress.com/forum/vol8/iss1/art5.

74. Howard Kurtz, "Death Panels Smite Journalism," *Washington Post*, August 24, 2009.

75. Auletta, "Non-Stop News," pp. 44–46.

76. Pew Research Center for the People and the Press, News Interest Index survey, conducted August 14–17, 2009. See also Pew Research Center for the People and the Press poll, August 11–17, 2009.

77. NBC News/*Wall Street Journal* poll, August 15–17, 2009.

78. Mark Knoller, "Obama's First Year: By the Numbers," CBS News, January 21, 2009.

79. Sheryl Gay Stolberg, "Obama to Forge a Greater Role on Health Care," *New York Times*, June 7, 2009.

80. Tobin Harshaw, "Hawking Health Care in Prime Time," *New York Times*, June 26, 2009.

81. Quoted in Michael D. Shear and Shailagh Murray, "President Is Set to 'Take the Baton': As Skepticism on Health Reform Mounts, He Will Intensify His Efforts," *Washington Post*, July 20, 2009.

82. Jim Rutenberg and Jackie Calmes, "White House Adapts to New Playbook in Health Care Debate," *New York Times*, August 11, 2009.

83. Balz, "Concern, Doubts from the Left on Obama's Health-Care Plan."

84. Anne E. Kornblut, "Obama to Push Health Care Reform in Town Hall Meetings," *Washington Post*, August 11, 2009.

85. Ben Pershing, "Groups Take Health-Reform Debate to Airwaves," *Washington Post*, August 5, 2009; Emily Cadei, "Health Care Ad Wars Heat Up as Recess Begins," *CQ Daily*, August 4, 2009.

86. See Edwards, *On Deaf Ears*, pp. 130–131, 140–142; Edwards, *Governing by Campaigning*, pp. 82–84.

87. Nielsen Wire, September 10, 2009.

88. Quoted in Mark Leibovich, "Obama the Omnipresent," *New York Times*, September 18, 2009. See also, Auletta, "Non-Stop News," p. 44; and Peter Baker, "Obama Complains About the News Cycle but Manipulates It, Worrying Some," *New York Times*, July 24, 2009.

89. Sheryl Gay Stolberg, "Obama Takes a Health Care Hiatus," *New York Times*, October 21, 2009.

90. See also Gallup poll, March 17, 2010; CBS News/*New York Times* poll, March 18–21, 2010.

91. CBS News/*New York Times* poll, September 19–23, 2009.

92. Pew Research Center for the People and the Press News Interest survey, September 3–6, 2009. See also Pew Research Center for the People and the Press News Interest survey, September 30–October 4, 2009; and CBS News/*New York Times* poll, September 19–23, 2009.

93. ABC News, *This Week* Transcript: "President Barack Obama," accessed on September 20, 2009, at abcnews.go.com/ThisWeek/Politics/transcript-president-barack-obama/story?id=8618937. See also Alter, *The Promise*, pp. 262, 420, 424.

94. Kaiser Health Tracking Poll, July 8–13, 2010.

95. Kaiser Health Tracking Poll, January 7–12, 2010.

96. Kaiser Health Tracking Poll, January 7–12, 2010. Based on a partial sample (N=511).

97. Alter, *The Promise*, p. 420.

98. Kaiser Health Tracking Poll, June 9–14, 2011.

99. Sheryl Gay Stolberg, "A Rewired Bully Pulpit: Big, Bold and Unproven," *New York Times*, November 22, 2008.

100. Helene Cooper, "The Direct Approach," *New York Times*, December 18, 2008.

101. Quoted in Stolberg, "A Rewired Bully Pulpit."

102. Chris Cillizza, "Obama Makes a Point of Speaking of the People, to the People," *Washington Post*, December 14, 2008, p. A05.

103. Elham Khatami, "Who listens to Obama's addresses?" Congress.org, November 8, 2010.

104. Virginia Heffernan, "The YouTube Presidency—Why the Obama Administration Uploads so Much Video," *New York Times*, April 12, 2009.

105. Brian Stelter, "Obama to Field Questions Posted by YouTube Users," *New York Times*, February 1, 2010.

106. Alter, *The Promise*, p. 278.

107. Auletta, "Non-Stop News," p. 45.

108. Kate Phillips, "Obama Rallies the Base on His Supreme Court Choice," *CQ Today*, May 27, 2009.

109. Auletta, "Non-Stop News," p. 44.

110. People typically turn to the Web sites of traditional news sources for their news, however. See blog.nielsen.com/nielsenwire/online_mobile/election-gives-online-news -sites-major-traffic-boost/; and Pew

111. Pew Internet & American Life Project, *Understanding the Participatory News Consumer*, March 2010; Pew Research Center for the People and the Press poll, December 1–5, 2010.

112. Michael A. Fletcher and Jose Antonio Vargas, "The White House, Open for Questions," *Washington Post*, March 27, 2009, p. A02; Sheryl Gay Stolberg, "Obama Makes History in Live Internet Video Chat," *New York Times*, March 27, 2009.

113. Stolberg, "A Rewired Bully Pulpit."

114. Michael D. Shear, "Campaign Urges Reinstating Ban on Offshore Oil Drilling," *Washington Post*, April 30, 2010.

115. Quoted in Stolberg, "A Rewired Bully Pulpit."

116. Pew Internet & American Life Project 2008 Post-Election Survey, November 20–December 4, 2008.

117. Lois Romano, "'08 Campaign Guru Focuses on Grass Roots," *Washington Post*, January 13, 2009, p. A13.

118. Peter Wallsten, "Retooling Obama's Campaign Machine for the Long Haul," *Los Angeles Times*, January 14, 2009; Associated Press, "Obama Launches Grass-Roots Campaign," January 17, 2009.

119. Matt Bai, "Democrat in Chief?" *New York Times Sunday Magazine*, June 13, 2010.

120. Ceci Connolly, "Obama Policymakers Turn to Campaign Tools; Network of Supporters Tapped on Health-Care Issues," *Washington Post*, December 4, 2008, p. A1.

121. Quoted in ibid.

122. Quoted in Cillizza, "Obama Makes a Point of Speaking of the People, to the People."

123. Quoted in Wallsten, "Retooling Obama's Campaign Machine for the Long Haul."

124. Jose Antonio Vargas, "Obama Team Finds It Hard to Adapt Its Web Savvy to Government," *Washington Post*, March 2, 2009, p. A3.

125. Chris Cillizza, "Obama Enlists Campaign Army in Budget Fight," *Washington Post*, March 16, 2009, p. A1.

126. Dan Eggen, "Obama's Machine Sputters in Effort to Push Budget; Grass-Roots Campaign Has Little Effect," *Washington Post*, April 6, 2009, p. A3.

127. Peter Slevin, "Obama Turns to Grass Roots to Push Health Reform," *Washington Post*, June 24, 2009.

128. Slevin, "Obama Turns to Grass Roots to Push Health Reform"; and Eli Saslow, "Grass-Roots Battle Tests the Obama Movement," *Washington Post*, August 23, 2009.

129. Saslow, "Grass-Roots Battle Tests the Obama Movement."

130. Jeff Zeleny, "Health Debate Fails to Ignite Obama's Grass Roots," *New York Times*, August 15, 2009.

131. Alter, *The Promise*, pp. 252, 398.

132. Amy Gardner, "Midterms Pose Major Challenge for Obama's Grass-Roots Political Organization," *Washington Post*, March 28, 2010.

133. Philip Rucker, "Obama Mobilizes Volunteers to Urge Repeal of 'Don't Ask, Don't Tell,'" *Washington Post*, December 17, 2009.

134. Rucker, "Obama Mobilizes Volunteers to Urge Repeal of 'Don't Ask, Don't Tell.'"

135. Slevin, "Obama Turns to Grass Roots to Push Health Reform."

136. See, for example, William A. Gamson and Andre Modigliani, "The Changing Culture of Affirmative Action," in *Research in Political Sociology*, vol. 3, ed. Richard D. Braungart (Greenwich, CT: JAI Press, 1987), p. 143; William A. Gamson and Andre Modigliani, "Media Discourse and Public Opinion on Nuclear Power: A Constructionist Approach," *American Journal of Sociology* 95 (July 1989): 1–37; William A. Gamson, *Talking Politics* (Cambridge, UK: Cambridge University Press, 1992); Donald R. Kinder and Lynn M. Sanders, *Divided by Color: Racial Politics and Democratic Ideals* (Chicago: University of Chicago Press, 1996); and Zhongdang Pan and Gerald M. Kosicki, "Framing Analysis: An Approach to News Discourse," *Political Communication* 10, no. 1 (1993): 55–75.

137. Quoted in Gerald M. Boyd, "'General Contractor' of the White House Staff," *New York Times*, March 4, 1986, sec. A, p. 22.

138. Converse, "The Nature of Belief Systems in Mass Publics."

139. John R. Zaller, *The Nature and Origins of Mass Opinion* (New York: Cambridge University Press, 1992), pp. 42–48; James H. Kuklinski and Norman Hurley, "On Hearing and Interpreting Messages: A Cautionary Tale of Citizen Cue-Taking," *Journal of Politics* 56 (August 1994): 729–751; Jeffrey Mondak, "Source Cues and Policy Approval: The Cognitive Dynamics of Public Support for the Reagan Agenda," *American Journal of Political Science* 37 (February 1993): 186–212.

140. There is some evidence that the president's rhetoric can prime the criteria on

which the public evaluates him. See James N. Druckman and Justin W. Holmes, "Does Presidential Rhetoric Matter? Priming and Presidential Approval," *Presidential Studies Quarterly* 34 (December 2004): 755–778.

141. "Remarks by the President on the Importance of Passing a Historic Energy Bill," White House Transcript, June 25, 2009.

142. For a good discussion of this point, see Jacobs and Shapiro, *Politicians Don't Pander*, pp. 49–52.

143. See, for example, William B. Riker, *The Art of Political Manipulation* (New Haven, CT: Yale University Press, 1986); William B. Riker, *The Strategy of Rhetoric: Campaigning for the American Constitution* (New Haven, CT: Yale University Press, 1996); William B. Riker, "The Heresthetics of Constitution Making: The Presidency in 1787, with Comments on Determinism and Rational Choice," *American Political Science Review* 78 (March 1984): 1–6.

144. Byron E. Shafer and William J. M. Claggett, *The Two Majorities: The Issue Context of Modern American Politics* (Baltimore, MD: Johns Hopkins University Press, 1995). See also James N. Druckman, Lawrence R. Jacobs, and Eric Ostermeier, "Candidate Strategies to Prime Issues and Image," *Journal of Politics* 66 (November 2004): 1180–1202.

145. John R. Petrocik, "Divided Government: Is It All in the Campaigns," in *The Politics of Divided Government*, ed. Gary W. Cox and Samuel Kernell (Boulder, CO: Westview Press, 1991); John R. Petrocik, "Issue Ownership in Presidential Elections, with a 1980 Case Study," *American Journal of Political Science* (August 1996): 825–850.

146. Andrew Gelman and Gary King, "Why Are American Presidential Election Campaign Polls So Variable When Votes Are So Predictable"? *British Journal of Political Science* 23 (Part 4, 1993): 409–451.

147. See Stephen Skowronek, "Leadership by Definition: First Term Reflections on George W. Bush's Political Stance," *Perspectives on Politics* 3 (December 2005): 818.

148. An exception to the experimental nature of framing studies is William G. Jacoby, "Issue Framing and Public Opinion on Government Spending," *American Journal of Political Science* 44 (October 2000): 750–767. He employed NES data to present both frames to the same sample. Even here, however, the framing occurred in the context of an interview in which different frames were presented at different times.

149. James N. Druckman and Kjersten R. Nelson, "Framing and Deliberation: How Citizens' Conversations Limit Elite Influence," *American Journal of Political Science* 47 (October 2003): 729–745.

150. James N. Druckman, "Using Credible Advice to Overcome Framing Effects," *Journal of Law, Economics, and Organization* 17 (April 2001): 62–82.

151. Donald P. Haider-Markel and Mark R. Joslyn, "Gun Policy, Opinion, Tragedy, and Blame Attribution: The Conditional Influence of Issue Frames," *Journal of Politics* 63 (May 2001): 520–543.

152. Gregory A. Huber and John S. Lapinski, "The 'Race Card' Revisited: Assessing Racial Priming in Policy Contests," *American Journal of Political Science* 50 (April 2006): 421–440.

153. Druckman and Nelson, "Framing and Deliberation."

154. Zaller, *The Nature and Origins of Mass Opinion*, p. 99, chap. 9. See also Adam J.

Berinsky, "Assuming the Costs of War: Events, Elites, and American Public Support for Military Conflict," *Journal of Politics* 69 (November 2007): 975–997.

155. See Paul M. Sniderman and Sean M. Theriault, "The Structure of Political Argument and the Logic of Issue Framing," in *Studies in Public Opinion: Attitudes, Nonattitudes, Measurement Error and Change*, ed. Willem E. Saris and Paul M. Sniderman (Princeton, NJ: Princeton University Press, 2004). Also see Paul M. Sniderman, "Taking Sides: A Fixed Choice Theory of Political Reasoning," in *Elements of Reason: Understanding and Expanding the Limits of Political Rationality*, ed. Arthur Lupia, Mathew D. McCubbins, and Samuel L. Popkin (New York: Cambridge University Press, 2000); James N. Druckman, "Political Preference Formation: Competition, Deliberation, and the (Ir)relevance of Framing Effects," *American Political Science Review* 98 (November 2004): 671–686.

156. John Zaller, "Elite Leadership of Mass Opinion: New Evidence from the Gulf War," in *Taken by Storm: The Media, Public Opinion, and U.S. Foreign Policy in the Gulf War*, ed. W. Lance Bennett and David L. Paletz (Chicago: University of Chicago Press, 1994), pp. 186–209.

157. See Brian J. Gaines, James H. Kuklinski, Paul J. Quirk, Buddy Peyton, and Jay Verkuilen, "Same Facts, Different Interpretations: Partisan Motivation and Opinion on Iraq," *Journal of Politics* 69 (November 2007): 957–974; Edwards, *On Deaf Ears*, chap. 9; Larry Bartels, "Beyond the Running Tally: Partisan Bias in Political Perceptions," *Political Behavior* 24 (June 2002): 117–150.

158. Carl Hulse, "'Recovery' Is In; 'Stimulus' Is So Seven Months Ago," *New York Times*, November 26, 2008.

159. Peter Baker, "The Words Have Changed, but Have the Policies?" *New York Times*, April 3, 2009.

160. Jonathan Weisman, "Obama Allies Find Words Fail Them," *Wall Street Journal*, August 25, 2009, p. A4.

161. Drew Armstrong, "Axelrod Fuels Democratic Message Machine for Health Care Overhaul," *CQ Today*, May 13, 2009; Robert Pear, "Democrats to Develop Plan to Sell Health Care," *New York Times*, May 13, 2009.

162. Quoted in Perry Bacon Jr., "Language Lessons for Democrats, from the Political Brain of Drew Westen," *Washington Post*, May 18, 2010.

163. Alter, *The Promise*, pp. 272–274.

164. Peter Baker, "Familiar Obama Phrase Being Groomed as a Slogan," *New York Times*, May 16, 2009.

165. Shear, "White House Revamps Communications Strategy."

166. White House Transcript, "Remarks by the President at GOP House Issues Conference," January 29, 2010.

167. Alessandra Stanley, "The News Conference: The Same, and Different," *New York Times*, February 10, 2009.

168. Quoted in Ronald Brownstein, "The Solvency Solution, *National Journal*, February 7, 2009.

169. Nate Silver, "The Proliferation of 'Pork,'" *FiveThirtyEight*, February 4, 2009.

170. Pew Research Center's News Index Survey, February 6–9, 2009.

171. Alter, *The Promise*, p. 131.

172. Slevin, "Obama Turns to Grass Roots to Push Health Reform."

173. Jonathan Alter, *The Promise*, p. 33.

174. Michael D. Shear, "Poll Results Drive Rhetoric of Obama's Health-Care Message," *Washington Post*, July 30, 2009.

175. Sheryl Gay Stolberg, Jeff Zeleny, and Carl Hulse, "The Long Road Back," *New York Times*, March 21, 2010.

176. Ibid.

177. Interview with George Stephanopoulos on of ABC, January 20, 2010.

178. "Remarks by the President on Financial Reform," White House, January 21, 2010.

179. Sheryl Gay Stolberg, "White House and Allies Set to Build Up Health Law," *New York Times*, June 6, 2010.

180. Ibid.

181. Frank Newport, "Wall Street Reform from the People's Perspective," *Polling Matters*, April 23, 2010.

182. Gallup poll, April 17–18, 2010, using a split national sample.

183. White House Transcript, "Remarks by the President on Wall Street Reform," April 22, 2010.

184. Mark Jurkowitz, "Terrorism Tops Disasters," Pew Research Center's Project for Excellence in Journalism, May 11, 2010.

185. Anne E. Kornblut, "As Right Jabs Continue, White House Debates a Counterpunching Strategy," *Washington Post*, September 16, 2009.

186. Shear, "White House Revamps Communications Strategy."

187. Quoted in Kornblut, "As Right Jabs Continue, White House Debates a Counterpunching Strategy."

188. Alter, *The Promise*, pp. 272–274.

189. Karen Tumulty and Juliet Eilperin, "With Oil Spill, White House Struggles to Assert Control of the Unknown," *Washington Post*, June 6, 2010.

Chapter 3

1. Quoted in Ken Auletta, "Non-Stop News," *New Yorker*, January 25, 2010, p. 44. See also Jonathan Alter, *The Promise: President Obama, Year One* (New York: Simon & Schuster, 2010), p. 125.

2. Matt Bai, "Democrat in Chief?" *New York Times Sunday Magazine*, June 13, 2010.

3. Alter, *The Promise*, p. 126.

4. Scott Wilson, "Bruised by Stimulus Battle, Obama Changed His Approach to Washington," *Washington Post*, April 29, 2009.

5. Quoted in Dan Balz, "Testing the Promise of Pragmatism," *Washington Post*, January 17, 2010, p. A1. See also George Packer, "Obama's Lost Year," *New Yorker*, March 15, 2010, p. 46.

6. Quoted in Mark Leibovich, "Obama's Message Maven Finds Fingers Pointing at Him," *New York Times*, March 6, 2010.

7. Gallup poll, January 13, 2009.

8. Gallup poll, February 20–22, 2009.

9. CNN/Opinion Research poll, March 12–15, 2009.

10. Pew Research Center for the People and the Press poll, April 21–26, 2010.

11. Alter, *The Promise*, 262.

12. *Time* poll conducted by Abt SRBI, October 26–27; 2009; Bloomberg Poll conducted by Selzer & Co., December 3–7, 2009; Pew Research/National Journal Congressional Connection Poll, sponsored by the Society for Human Resource Management polls, April 21–26 and June 17–20, 2010; CBS News poll, May 20–24, 2010.

13. See Pew Research Center for the People and the Press polls of March 31–April 6 and September 30–October 4, 2009, and February 3–9 and March 11–21, 2010; *Washington Post*-ABC News polls, February 1–22, 2009, and February 4–8 and April 22–25, 2010; CBS News polls, February 2–5 and May 20–24, 2010; Gallup poll, April 17–18, 2010; ABC News/*Washington Post* poll, April 22–25, 2010; *USA Today*/Gallup poll, June 11–13, 2010. But also see Pew Research Center for the People and the Press, Congressional Connection Poll, June 3–6, 2010, which found only plurality support.

14. FOX News/Opinion Dynamics poll, May 4–5, 2010; CNN/Opinion Research Corporation polls, May 21–23 and July 16–21, 2010 (the latter poll used a half sample on the question).

15. Bloomberg Poll conducted by Selzer & Co, July 9–12, 2010.

16. ABC News/*Washington Post* poll, July 7–11, 2010.

17. Gallup poll, January 27, 2009.

18. Gallup poll, January 6–7, 2009. The question did not specifically mention President Obama.

19. *USA Today*/Gallup poll, February 4, 2009. The question did not specifically mention President Obama.

20. Gallup poll, January 30–February 1, 2009.

21. Pew Research Center for the People and the Press polls, January 7–11, and February 4–8, 2009.

22. CBS News/*New York Times* polls of January 11–15, and February 2–4, 2009.

23. Lydia Saad, "Stimulus Support Edges Higher, Now 59%," Gallup poll, February 11, 2009.

24. The *Washington Post*-ABC News poll of February 19–22, 2009, found that 64 percent of the public supported the bill shortly after it was passed. In this case, the question included reference to tax cuts and aid to states and individuals but did not mention Obama or the Democrats.

25. *USA Today*/Gallup poll, August 6–9, 2009.

26. CNN/Opinion Research Corp. poll, January 8–10, 2010.

27. Pew Research Center for the People and the Press poll, April 21–26, 2010. See also CBS News/*New York Times* poll, April 5–12, 2010.

28. CBS News/*New York Times* poll, September 10–14, 2010. See also ABC News/*Washington Post* poll, September 30–October 3, 2010.

29. Quoted in Dan Balz, "For Obama, a Tough Year to Get the Message Out," *Washington Post*, January 10, 2010.

30. Peter Baker, "The President Whose Words Once Soared," *New York Times*, November 8, 2009.

31. *Wall Street Journal*/NBC News poll, June 12 –15.

32. CBS News poll, May 20–24, 2010. See also Bloomberg poll conducted by Selzer & Co, July 9–12, 2010.

33. *Wall Street Journal*/NBC News poll June 12–15, 2009; CBS News/*New York Times* polls, June 12–16, July 9–12, and July 24–28, 2009; *Washington Post*-ABC News poll, July 15–18, 2009. An exception to these findings was the Pew Research Center for the People and the Press poll, July 22–26, 2009.

34. Gallup poll, June 13–14, 2009.

35. See, for example, *Washington Post*-ABC News polls of March 26–29, July 15–18, and September 10–12, 2009; AP-GfK poll, September 3–8, 2009, conducted by GfK Roper Public Affairs & Media poll; CBS News/*New York Times* polls, April 1–5, and July 24–28, 2009, and February 5–10, April 5–12, and September 10–14, 2010, and April 15–20 and June 24–28, 2011; *USA Today*/Gallup poll, July 17–19, 2009; Quinnipiac University poll, January 5–11, 2010; Gallup polls, March 26–28 and August 27–30, 2010.

36. CBS News/*New York Times* poll, June 12–16, 2009. Fifty percent said they heard or read "some," 23 percent "not much," and 5 percent "nothing."

37. Pew Research Center for the People and the Press poll, July 24–27, 2009. See also Pew News Interest Index, September 3–6, 2009, which found 40 percent of the public following health care reform very closely.

38. Pew Research Center for the People and the Press poll, July 20–26, 2009.

39. See, for example, *Washington Post*-ABC News poll, October 15–19, 2009; *USA Today*/Gallup poll, October 16–19, 2009; *Washington Post*-ABC News poll, November 12–15, 2009; CBS News/*New York Times* poll, March 18–21, 2010.

40. Gary C. Jacobson, "Barack Obama and the American Public: From Candidate to President," paper presented at the Conference on the Early Obama Presidency, Centre for the Study of Democracy, University of Westminster, London, May 14, 2010, pp. 19–21.

41. Frank Newport, "Americans on Healthcare Reform: Top 10 Takeaways," Gallup Poll, July 31, 2009; *Time* magazine poll, July 27–28, 2009; Pew Research Center for the People and the Press poll, July 23–26, 2009; CBS News/*New York Times* poll, September 19–23, 2009; Pew Research Center for the People and the Press News Interest survey, September 30–October 4, 2009; *Washington Post*-ABC News poll, October 15–19, 2009; *USA Today*/Gallup poll, October 16–19, 2009; and *Washington Post*-ABC News poll, November 12–15, 2009.

42. Gallup polls, July 17–19, August 6–9, and November 20–22, 2009; and *USA Today*/Gallup poll, September 11–13.

43. The lower level of no opinion in the March 2010 poll is likely the result of the absence of a prompt for "or do you not have an opinion" in the earlier polls.

44. Gallup poll, September 11–13, 2009.

45. Frank Newport, Jeffrey M. Jones, and Lydia Saad, "Americans on Healthcare Reform: Five Key Realties," Gallup Poll, October 30, 2009.

46. Peter Baker, "The Limits of Rahmism," *New York Times Magazine*, March 14, 2010.

47. CNN/Opinion Research Corp. poll, September 9, 2009. The sample size was 427.

48. Gallup poll August 6–9, 2009; and *USA Today*/Gallup poll, September 11–13.

49. *Washington Post*-ABC News poll, September 10–12, 2009.

50. NBC News/*Wall Street Journal* poll, September 17–20, 2009.

51. *Washington Post*-ABC News poll, September 10–12, 2009.

52. CBS News/*New York Times* poll, September 19–23, 2009.

53. *Washington Post*-ABC News poll, September 10–12, 2009. See also Pew Research

Center for the People and the Press News Interest survey, September 30–October 4, 2009.

54. *USA Today*/Gallup poll, September 11–13, 2009; CBS News/*New York Times* poll, September 19–23, 2009.

55. See also CBS News/*New York Times* poll, September 19–23, 2009; *Washington Post*-ABC News poll, November 12–15, 2009; Pew Research Center for the People and the Press poll, January 6–10, 2010.

56. *USA Today*/Gallup poll, January 20, 2010. See also Pew Research Center for the People and the Press poll, January 6–10, 2010.

57. Gallup poll, February 23, 2010.

58. David Brady, Daniel Kessler, and Douglas Rivers, "ObamaCare and the Independent Vote," *Wall Street Journal*, June 19, 2010; Kaiser Family Foundation tracking poll, June 17–22, 2010.

59. Gallup poll, June 11–13, 2010.

60. CBS News/*New York Times* poll, July 9–12, 2010. The Kaiser Family Foundation poll in July found that favorable views of the bill increased to 50 percent while opposition decreased to 35 percent. The Kaiser Poll regularly found more support for health care reform than other national polls.

61. CNN/Opinion Research Corp. poll, August 6–10, 2010. The Kaiser Health Tracking Poll, August 16–22, 2010, found a plurality with an unfavorable opinion of the bill.

62. CBS News/*New York Times* poll, September 10–14, 2010.

63. Gallup poll, January 4–5, 2011.

64. Gallup poll, March 18–19, 2011.

65. ABC News/*Washington Post* poll, July 7–11, 2010.

66. CBS News/*New York Times* poll, July 9–12, 2010.

67. See, for example, ABC News/*Washington Post* polls, April 21–24, June 18–21, and December 10–13, 2009, and June 3–6, 2010. Half samples were used on this question.

68. Pew Research Center for the People and the Press poll, September 30–October 4, 2009.

69. Gallup poll, March 4–7, 2010. See also Gallup poll, March 5–8, 2009.

70. Pew Research Center for the People and the Press polls, June 14–19 and September 30–October 4, 2009.

71. See, for example, the Civitas Poll, July 19–21, 2010, of 600 likely voters in North Carolina by Tel Opinion Research.

72. Lydia Saad, "Americans Firm in Prioritizing Economy Over Environment," Gallup Poll, March 18, 2010. Gallup polls, March 5–8, 2009, and March 4–7, 2010.

73. Gallup poll, May 24–25, 2010. See also Pew Research Center for the People and the Press poll, June 10–13, 2010.

74. Gallup poll, March 3–6, 2011.

75. *USA Today*/Gallup poll, February 20–22, 2009. See also *Washington Post*-ABC News poll, February 19–22, 2009.

76. Pew Research Center for the People and the Press poll, March 9–12, 2009.

77. Gallup polls, November 5–8 and 20–22, 2009.

78. Gallup poll, December 2, 2009.

79. CBS News/*New York Times* poll, December 4–8, 2009. See also Pew Research Center for the People and the Press poll, December 9–13, 2009; and *Washington Post*-ABC News poll, December 10–13, 2009.

80. Gallup poll, December 2, 2009.

81. Pew Research Center for the People and the Press poll, December 9–13, 2009.

82. CBS News/*New York Times* poll, December 4–8, 2009.

83. Gallup poll, June 25–26, 2010.

84. CBS News/*New York Times* polls, September 10–14, 2010, and February 11–14, March 18–21, and June 3–7, 2011.

85. Pew Research Center for the People and the Press poll, June 15-19, 2011. See also See also *New York Times*/CBS News poll, June 24–28, 2011.

86. Gallup poll, June 25–26, 2011.

87. See also *New York Times*/CBS News poll, June 12–16; and *Wall Street Journal*/NBC News poll June 12–15.

88. Gallup poll, November 20–22, 2009.

89. Gallup poll, May 29–31, 2009.

90. Gallup poll, June 22, 2011.

91. *New York Times*/CBS News polls, June 3–7 and June 24–28, 2011.

92. *New York Times*/CBS News poll, June 24–28, 2011.

93. Gary C. Jacobson, "The Effects of the George W. Bush Presidency on Partisan Attitudes," *Presidential Studies Quarterly* 39 (June 2009): 172–209; Robert S. Erikson, Michael MacKuen, and James A. Stimson, "What Moves Macropartisanship? A Response to Green, Palmquist, and Schickler," *American Political Science Review* 92 (December 1998): 901–921; Donald Green, Bradley Palmquist, and Eric Schickler, "Macropartisanship: A Replication and Critique," *American Political Science Review* 92 (December 1998): 883–899; Michael MacKuen, Robert S. Erikson, and James A. Stimson, "Macropartisanship," *American Political Science Review* 83 (December 1989): 1125–1142.

94. Jacobson, "Legislative Success and Political Failure," pp. 237–238.

95. Gallup poll, September 13–16, 2010, 2010.

96. Jeffrey M. Jones, "Democratic Party ID Drops in 2010, Tying 22-Year Low," Gallup Poll, January 5, 2011.

97. Gallup Daily tracking polls, January 1–December 31, 2010.

98. *USA Today*/Gallup poll, May 24–25, 2010.

99. *USA Today*/Gallup poll, August 27–30, 2010. See also Gallup poll, September 30–October 3, 2010.

100. Pew Research Center for the People and the Press poll, October 27–30, 2010. See also Gallup poll, October 28–31, 2010.

101. Gary C. Jacobson, "The Republican Resurgence in 2010," *Political Science Quarterly* 127 (Spring 2011): 35–36.

102. National House Exit Poll, accessed at www.cnn.com/ELECTION/2010/results/polls/#USH00p1.

103. David R. Jones and Monika L. McDermott, "The Salience of the Democratic Congress and the 2010 Elections," *PS: Political Science and Politics* 44 (April 2011), p. 299.

104. Gallup poll, October 28–31, 2010. See also Pew Research Center for the People and the Press poll, October 27–30, 2010. The Gallup results on how voters viewed their votes as support or opposition to the president were very similar to those of the National House Exit Poll, accessed at www.cnn.com/ELECTION/2010/results/polls/#USH00p1.

105. National House Exit Poll, accessed at www.cnn.com/ELECTION/2010/results/polls/#USH00p1.

106. Pew Research Center for the People and the Press poll, August 25–September 6, 2010, among 2,816 registered voters, including 2,053 voters considered the most likely to vote on November 2.

107. See also Pew Research Center for the People and the Press poll, December 1–5, 2010.

108. Lymari Morales, "In U.S., 67% Support Repealing 'Don't Ask, Don't Tell,'" Gallup poll, December 9, 2010.

109. *USA Today*/Gallup polls, August 27–30, November 19–21, and December 10–12, 2010; Pew Research Center for the People and the Press poll, December 9–12, 2010; ABC News/*Washington Post* poll, December 9–12, 2010; CBS News polls, August 20–24, 2010, and November 29–December 1, 2010; CNN/Opinion Research Corp. poll, November 11–14, 2010; NBC News/*Wall Street Journal* poll conducted by the polling organizations of Peter Hart and Bill McInturff, August 5–8, and September 22–26, 2010; CNN/Opinion Research Corp. poll, September 10–14, September 21–23, October 21–26, and November 11–14, 2010; Bloomberg National poll, December 4–7.

110. See also Pew Research Center for the People and the Press poll, December 1–5, 2010.

111. Andrew Kohut, "Obama's 2010 Challenge: Wake Up Liberals, Calm Down Independents," Pew Research Center for the People and the Press poll, December 17, 2009.

112. Quoted in Elizabeth Drew, *Showdown: The Struggle Between the Gingrich Congress and the Clinton White House* (New York: Simon & Schuster, 1996), p. 66.

113. Quoted in Bob Woodward, *The Choice* (New York: Simon & Schuster, 1996), p. 22.

114. Quoted in Karen Travers, "Exclusive: President Obama: We Lost Touch with American People Last Year," *ABC World News with Diane Sawyer*, January 20, 2010.

115. Quoted in Peter Baker, "Education of a President," *New York Times Magazine*, October 17, 2010. See also the president's remarks in Ron Fournier, "Obama 2.0," *National Journal*, October 23, 2010, pp. 27–28. See also, Transcript: "President Barack Obama," *60 Minutes*, Interview by Steve Kroft, November 4, 2010.

116. Quoted in Glenn Thrush, "Obama Makes the Sale," Politico.com, December 17, 2010.

117. Elting E. Morison, ed., *The Letters of Theodore Roosevelt* (Cambridge, MA: Harvard University Press, 1951–54), vol. 3, p. 23.

Chapter 4

1. George C. Edwards III, *The Strategic President: Persuasion and Opportunity in Presidential Leadership* (Princeton, NJ: Princeton University Press), chaps. 4–5; George C. Edwards III, *At the Margins: Presidential Leadership of Congress* (New Haven, CT: Yale University Press, 1989), chaps. 9–10; Jon R. Bond and Richard Fleisher, *The President in the Legislative Arena* (Chicago: University of Chicago Press, 1990), chap. 8; Richard Fleisher, Jon R. Bond, and B. Dan Wood, "Which Presidents Are Uncommonly Suc-

cessful in Congress?" in *Presidential Leadership: The Vortex of Presidential Power*, ed. Bert Rockman and Richard W. Waterman (New York: Oxford University Press, 2007).

2. Keith Krehbiel, *Pivotal Politics: A Theory of U.S. Lawmaking* (Chicago: University of Chicago Press, 1998), chaps. 7–8.

3. Paul C. Light, "Less Room for Breakthrough Ideas," *Washington Post*, November 11, 2008.

4. White House Transcript, "Remarks by the President to the Business Roundtable," March 12, 2009.

5. Peter Baker, "Obama Defends Agenda as More Than Recession," *New York Times*, March 13, 2009.

6. Quoted in Helene Cooper, "Some Obama Enemies Are Made Totally of Straw," *New York Times*, May 24, 2009. See also Peter Baker, "The Limits of Rahmism," *New York Times Magazine*, March 14, 2010.

7. Dan Balz, "With New Priorities, Obama and Democrats Can Recover in 2010," *Washington Post*, December 27, 2009; Jonathan Alter, *The Promise: President Obama, Year One* (New York: Simon & Schuster, 2010), pp. 244, 246.

8. Baker, "The Limits of Rahmism"; Alter, *The Promise*, p. 245.

9. Alter, *The Promise*, pp. 79, 246; Michael D. Shear and Shailagh Murray, "President Is Set to 'Take the Baton': As Skepticism on Health Reform Mounts, He Will Intensify His Efforts," *Washington Post*, July 20, 2009; Baker, "The Limits of Rahmism;" and Scott Wilson, "Bruised by Stimulus Battle, Obama Changed His Approach to Washington," *Washington Post*, April 29, 2009.

10. Brian Friel, "Democrats Face Daunting Legislative Agenda," *National Journal Online*, May 9, 2009.

11. Alter, *The Promise*, p. 79.

12. Ibid., p. 32.

13. Edwards, *At the Margins*, chap. 8; David Peterson, Lawrence J. Grossback, James A. Stimson, and Amy Gangl, "Congressional Response to Mandate Elections," *American Journal of Political Science* 47 (June 2003): 411–426.

14. David R. Mayhew, *Congress: The Electoral Connection* (New Haven, CT: Yale University Press, 1974), 70–71.

15. Patricia Heidotting Conley, *Presidential Mandates* (Chicago: University of Chicago Press, 2001).

16. For an analysis of the perceptions of mandates, see Edwards, *At the Margins*, chap. 8; Peterson, Grossback, Stimson, and Gangl, "Congressional Response to Mandate Elections."

17. Quoted in Everett Carll Ladd, *The Ladd Report #1* (New York: W. W. Norton, 1985), p. 3.

18. Edwards, *At the Margins*, chap. 8.

19. Carl Hulse, "Not All New Democrats Rode an Obama Tide," *New York Times*, December 7, 2008.

20. George C. Edwards III and Andrew Barrett, "Presidential Agenda Setting in Congress," in *Polarized Politics: Congress and the President in a Partisan Era*, ed. Jon R. Bond and Richard Fleisher (Washington, DC: CQ Press, 2000).

21. Alan D. Rozzi, "Defining Debates from the Outside Looking In: How Presidents Affect the Decisions of the House Rules Committee," *Congress & the Presidency* 37 (January 2010): 64–91.

22. David R. Mayhew, *Divided We Govern*, 2nd ed. (New Haven, CT: Yale University Press, 2005).

23. Sarah A. Binder, *Stalemate* (Washington, DC: Brookings Institute Press, 2003); William G. Howell, Scott Adler, Charles Cameron, and Charles Riemann, "Divided Government and the Legislative Productivity of Congress," *Legislative Studies Quarterly* 25 (May 2000): 285–311; John J. Coleman, "Unified Government, Divided Government, and Party Responsiveness," *American Political Science Review* 93 (December 1999): 821–835; Sarah A. Binder, "The Dynamics of Legislative Gridlock, 1947–96," *American Political Science Review* 93 (September 1999): 519–533; George C. Edwards III, Andrew Barrett, and Jeffrey Peake, "The Legislative Impact of Divided Government," *American Journal of Political Science* 41 (April 1997): 545–563.

24. Edwards, Barrett, and Peake, "The Legislative Impact of Divided Government."

25. Ibid.

26. See Peter Trubowitz and Nicole Mellow, "Going Bipartisan: Politics by Other Means," *Political Science Quarterly* 120 (Fall 2005): 433–455, for an interesting discussion of the conditions under which bipartisanship is most likely to occur.

27. Shailagh Murray, Michael D. Shear, and Paul Kane, "2009 Democratic Agenda Severely Weakened by Republicans' United Opposition," *Washington Post*, January 24, 2010.

28. Keith Poole, "Party Polarization: 1879–2009," voteview.com/Polarized_America. htm#POLITICALPOLARIZATION. See also Nolan McCarty, Keith T. Poole, and Howard Rosenthal, *Polarized America: The Dance of Ideology and Unequal Riches* (Cambridge, MA: MIT Press, 2006).

29. Shawn Zeller, "Party Unity—Parties Dig In Deep on a Fractured Hill," *CQ Weekly*, December 15, 2008, pp. 3332–3341.

30. Gary C. Jacobson, "Barack Obama and the American Public: From Candidate to President," *Presidential Studies Quarterly* 41 (June 2011): 220–243.

31. See, for example, Gallup polls, December 4–7, 2010, and January 7–9, 2011; and Pew Research Center for the People and the Press poll, January 5–9, 2011.

32. Quoted in Peter Baker, "Bipartisanship Isn't So Easy, Obama Sees," *New York Times*, February 13, 2009.

33. Ronald Brownstein, "For GOP, A Southern Exposure," *National Journal*, May 23, 2009.

34. Nate Silver, "Popularity of 'Don't Ask' Repeal May Have Drawn Republican Votes," *New York Times*, December 19, 2010.

35. Quoted in Alter, *The Promise*, pp. 256–257.

36. Ibid., p. 129.

37. Bruce Smith, "Graham Censured by Charleston County GOP," *The State*, November 12, 2009.

38. The Lexington County Republican Party, "Lexington County Party Passes Resolution of Censure for Lindsey Graham," accessed at http.lcrp-online.com/1.html.

39. Robert Draper, "Lindsey Graham, This Year's Maverick," *New York Times*, July 4, 2010.

40. Pew Research Center for the People and the Press poll, January 6–10, 2010.

41. Alan K. Ota, "GOP Moderates See Political Benefits in Opposing Obama's Economic Agenda," *CQ Today*, February 6, 2009.

42. Frances E. Lee, *Beyond Ideology: Politics, Principles, and Partisanship in the U.S. Senate* (Chicago: University of Chicago Press, 2009), chap. 4.

43. Quoted in Carl Hulse, "Legislative Hurdles in an Era of Conflict, Not Compromise," *New York Times*, June 19, 2010.

44. Shailagh Murray and Paul Kane, "Democratic Congress Shows Signs It Will Not Bow to Obama," *Washington Post*, January 11, 2009, p. A5.

45. Quoted in Carl Hulse and David M. Herszenhorn, "New White House and Congress Hope to Have Bills Ready by Inauguration," *New York Times*, November 26, 2008.

46. John M. Broder, "Climate Bill Is Threatened by Senators," *New York Times*, August 7, 2009.

47. Quoted in John M. Broder, "Obama Opposes Trade Sanctions in Climate Bill," *New York Times*, June 29, 2009.

48. Stephen Labaton, "Ailing, Banks Still Field Strong Lobby at Capitol," *New York Times*, June 5, 2009.

49. Jodi Kantor, "Abortion Foe Defies Party on Health Care Bill," *New York Times*, January 7, 2010.

50. "2009 Vote Ratings," *National Journal*, February 27, 2009.

51. Charlie Cook, "Senate's Power Rests with Centrists: Democrats Can't Overcome Filibusters without Help from the Middle," *National Journal, December 13, 2008.*

52. Robert Pear, "2 Democrats Spearheading Health Bill Are Split," *New York Times*, May 30, 2009.

53. Steven Greenhouse, "Democrats Drop Key Part of Bill to Assist Unions," *New York Times*, July 17, 2009.

54. Peter H. Stone, "Lobbyists Go Full Tilt In Health Fight," *National Journal*, March 13, 2010; Jeff Zeleny, "Millions Spent to Sway Democrats on Health Care," *New York Times*, March 14, 2010; Sheryl Gay Stolberg, Jeff Zeleny, and Carl Hulse, "The Long Road Back," *New York Times*, March 21, 2010.

55. Peter Wallsten, "Retooling Obama's Campaign Machine for the Long Haul," *Los Angeles Times*, January 14, 2009.

56. Jim Rutenberg, "Bloggers and Unions Join Forces to Push Democrats," *New York Times*, February 27, 2009.

57. Jeff Zeleny, "Budget Has Obama Courting Fellow Democrats," *New York Times*, March 26, 2009.

58. Peter Baker and David M. Herszenhorn, "Senate Allies Fault Obama on Stimulus," *New York Times*, January 9, 2009.

59. Peter Baker and Adam Nagourney, "Sotomayor Pick a Product of Lessons From Past Battles, *New York Times*, May 28, 2009.

60. Pew Research Center for the People and the Press poll, March 9–12, 2009.

61. *USA Today*/Gallup poll, October 6, 2009.

62. Paul Kane, "Pelosi Says Rallying Votes for Troop Surge in Afghanistan Will Be Obama's Job," *Washington Post*, December 17, 2009, p. A4.

63. Perry Bacon Jr., "Liberal Group Blasts Obama for Considering Tax Compromise," *Washington Post*, December 2, 2010; Jennifer Epstein, "Liberal Group's New Ad Blasts Obama," Politico.com, December 20, 2010.

64. Sam Graham-Felsen, "Why Is Obama Leaving the Grass Roots on the Sidelines?" *Washington Post*, December 17, 2010.

65. Remarks of the president, White House, December 7, 2010.

66. Ibid.

Chapter 5

1. Carl Hulse and David M. Herszenhorn, "New White House and Congress Hope to Have Bills Ready by Inauguration," *New York Times*, November 26, 2008.

2. For more background on the staff of the Office of Legislative Affairs, see Jonathan Alter, *The Promise: President Obama, Year One* (New York: Simon & Schuster, 2010), pp. 78–79.

3. Quoted in Matt Bai, "Taking the Hill," *New York Times Magazine*, June 7, 2009.

4. Carl Hulse and Jeff Zeleny, "Stimulus Offers Glimpse of Obama's Battle Plan," *New York Times*, February 13, 2009.

5. Quoted in Janet Hook and Christi Parsons, "Barack Obama Has a Head Start Working with Congress," *New York Times*, November 27, 2008.

6. Hulse and Herszenhorn, "New White House and Congress Hope to Have Bills Ready by Inauguration."

7. Peter Baker and Adam Nagourney, "Sotomayor Pick a Product of Lessons from Past Battles, *New York Times*, May 28, 2009.

8. Transcript of press conference on November 25, 2008.

9. Scott Wilson, "Bruised by Stimulus Battle, Obama Changed His Approach to Washington," *Washington Post*, April 29, 2009.

10. John Harwood, "'Partisan' Seeks a Prefix: Bi- or Post-," *New York Times*, December 7, 2008.

11. Quoted in ibid.

12. Quoted in Ronald Brownstein, *The Second Civil War* (New York: Penguin Press, 2007), pp. 240–248, 252, 287.

13. Ibid., pp. 229–230, 249–252, 287–296.

14. Quoted in Robert Draper, *Dead Certain: The Presidency of George W. Bush* (New York: Free Press, 2007), p. 230.

15. Quotes from David D. Kirkpatrick, "Obama Reaches Out for McCain's Counsel," *New York Times*, January 19, 2009; Jeff Zeleny and David M. Herszenhorn, "Obama Seeks Wide Support in Congress for Stimulus," *New York Times*, January 6, 2009.

16. Jonathan Weisman and Laura Meckler, "Obama Reaches Out to Republicans," *Wall Street Journal*, December 15, 2008, p. 10; Jeff Zeleny, "Initial Steps by Obama Suggest a Bipartisan Flair," *New York Times*, November 24, 2008.

17. Ronald Brownstein, "Two Visions of Leadership," *National Journal*, January 17, 2009.

18. Howard Kurtz, "Obama Charms Even a Night's Grand Ol' Party," *Washington Post*, January 15, 2009, p. C1.

19. Kirkpatrick, "Obama Reaches Out for McCain's Counsel."

20. Quotes from Carl Hulse, "Obama Team Makes Early Efforts to Show Willingness to Reach Out to Republicans," *New York Times*, January 19, 2009; David M. Herszenhorn, "Obama Officials Ask Senate G.O.P. to Back Release of Bailout Money," *New York Times*, January 15, 2009.

21. Jackie Calmes and David M. Herszenhorn, "Obama Presses for Quick Jolt to the Economy," *New York Times*, January 24, 2009.

22. See Dana Milbank, "The Republicans Are Smiling, but They're Not Buying," *Washington Post*, January 28, 2009, p. A3; Jackie Calmes and Carl Hulse, "Obama, Visiting G.O.P. Lawmakers, Is Open to Some Compromise on Stimulus," *New York Times*, January 28, 2009; Jackie Calmes, "House Passes Stimulus Plan Despite G.O.P. Opposition," *New York Times*, January 29, 2009.

23. Calmes, "House Passes Stimulus Plan Despite G.O.P. Opposition."

24. Alter, *The Promise*, p. 127.

25. Carl Hulse, "Short-Circuiting Bipartisanship Is Nothing New for Congress," *New York Times*, February 14, 2009.

26. Alter, *The Promise*, p. 130.

27. Peter Baker, "Taking on Critics, Obama Puts Aside Talk of Unity," *New York Times*, February 10, 2009.

28. Wilson, "Bruised by Stimulus Battle, Obama Changed His Approach to Washington"; Alter, *The Promise*, p. 130.

29. Mark Leibovich, "Missing Element in Obama's Ties With G.O.P. Leaders: Good Chemistry," *New York Times*, February 24, 2010.

30. Quoted in Peter Baker, "The Limits of Rahmism," *New York Times Magazine*, March 14, 2010.

31. See, for example, John Harwood, "The President's Best Hope in the G.O.P.," *New York Times*, September 20, 2009; Sheryl Gay Stolberg, "Taking Health Care Courtship Up Another Notch," *New York Times*, September 27, 2009.

32. Quoted in Kathleen Hunter, "GOP Lawmakers Unmoved by Obama Overtures of Bipartisanship," *CQ Daily News*, April 23, 2009.

33. Quoted in Baker and Nagourney, "Sotomayor Pick a Product of Lessons from Past Battles."

34. Sheryl Gay Stolberg, "A Brisk First Round on Supreme Court Search," *New York Times*, April 22, 2010.

35. Michael D. Shear and Ceci Connolly, "Reform Gets Conditional GOP Support: Urged by the White House, Republicans Speak Up for Bipartisan Health Fix," *Washington Post*, October 7, 2009.

36. Sheryl Gay Stolberg, Jeff Zeleny, and Carl Hulse, "The Long Road Back," *New York Times*, March 21, 2010; Ceci Connolly, "How Obama Revived His Health-care Bill," *Washington Post*, March 23, 2010.

37. Connolly, "How Obama Revived His Health-care Bill."

38. David M. Herszenhorn and Robert Pear, "Obama Offers to Use Some GOP Health Proposals," *New York Times*, March 2, 1010.

39. Connolly, "How Obama Revived His Health-care Bill"; Alter, *The Promise*, p. 415.

40. Brian Friel and Kerry Young, "A Trying Relationship," *CQ Weekly*, September 3, 2010, p. 2082.

41. "Remarks by the President to the House Democratic Caucus," White House Transcript, March 20, 2010.

42. Sheryl Gay Stolberg and David M. Herszenhorn, "Obama Finds G.O.P. Resistance in Meeting on Financial Bill," *New York Times*, April 14, 2010.

43. Carl Hulse, "Republican Senators' Lunch With Obama Is Marked by Spirited Confrontations," *New York Times*, May 25, 2010.

44. Peter Baker, "Obama Gamble Pays Off With Approval of Arms Pact," *New York Times*, December 22, 2010.

45. Robert Draper, "Lindsey Graham, This Year's Maverick," *New York Times*, July 4, 2010.

46. Quoted in Juliet Eilperin, "On Climate Bill, Democrats Work to Overcome Graham's Objections," *Washington Post*, April 26, 2010.

47. Interview with Ezra Klein, "Sen. Lindsey Graham: 'I Care Equally about Immigration and Climate Change,'" *Washington Post*, April 29, 2010.

48. Quoted in John M. Broder, "White House Energy Session Changes No Minds," *New York Times*, June 29, 2010.

49. Josh Gerstein, "Graham: W.H. Talks Just Went 'Dead,'" Politico.com, September 20, 2010.

50. For a discussion of presidential party leadership in Congress, see George C. Edwards III, *At the Margins: Presidential Leadership of Congress* (New Haven, CT: Yale University Press, 1989), chaps. 3–5.

51. Quoted in Bai, "Taking the Hill."

52. Ibid.

53. Carl Hulse and Jeff Zeleny, "Stimulus Offers Glimpse of Obama's Battle Plan," *New York Times*, February 13, 2009.

54. Jeff Zeleny, "Budget Has Obama Courting Fellow Democrats," *New York Times*, March 26, 2009.

55. Keith Koffler, "The Oval Office: Obama's Lobbying Turf," *CQ Today Online News*, December 7, 2009; Stolberg, "Taking Health Care Courtship Up Another Notch."

56. Glenn Thrush, "Obama Makes the Sale," Politico.com, December 17, 2010.

57. Koffler, "The Oval Office: Obama's Lobbying Turf;" Alter, *The Promise*, pp. 327, 409.

58. Quoted in Sheryl Gay Stolberg, "Obama to Forge a Greater Role on Health Care," *New York Times*, June 7, 2009. See also Alter, *The Promise*, pp. 127, 327.

59. Sandhya Somashekhar and Paul Kane, "Democrats Yet to Decide on Health-care Bill Bear the Weight of Washington," *Washington Post*, March 18, 2010; Stolberg, Zeleny, and Hulse, "The Long Road Back"; Alter, *The Promise*, pp. 409, 432.

60. Brian Friel et al., "So, Who Won?" *National Journal*, March 27, 2010, p. 20.

61. These examples come from Connolly, "How Obama Revived His Health-care Bill."

62. Bai, "Taking the Hill."

63. Shailagh Murray, "Obama's Chief of Staff Grants Access, Gets Results," *Washington Post*, April 13, 2009.

64. Coral Davenport and Avery Palmer, "Climate Bill Rides Last-Minute Blitz," *CQ Today Online News*, June 25, 2009; Alter, *The Promise*, 260.

65. Connolly, "How Obama Revived His Health-care Bill."

66. Carl Hulse and Robert Pear, "Obama Weighs in as House Debates Health Overhaul," *New York Times*, November 8, 2009.

67. "Remarks by the President to the House Democratic Caucus," White House Transcript, March 20, 2010.

68. Bai, "Taking the Hill."

69. Nevertheless, some House Democrats complained that the White House routinely showed them disrespect. For example, there were complaints that administration aides would wait until the last minute to inform them when a cabinet official would be traveling to their districts to give a speech or announce a government grant. Lawmakers love these events, which let them take advantage of local press coverage. Paul Kane, "House Democrats Hit Boiling Point Over Perceived Lack of White House Support," *Washington Post*, July 15, 2010.

70. Mike Allen and Jim VandeHei, "Obama Isolated Ahead of 2012," Politico.com, November 8, 2010.

71. Murray, "Obama's Chief of Staff Grants Access, Gets Results."

72. John M. Broder, "With Something for Everyone, Climate Bill Passed," *New York Times*, July 1, 2009.

73. Alter, *The Promise*, p. 411.

74. Quoted in Stolberg, "Obama to Forge a Greater Role on Health Care."

75. Quoted in *Brian Friel, "The Middle Wants In," National Journal, March 28, 2009, p. 43.*

76. Quoted in Carl Hulse, "Obama Goes to Lawmakers on Budget," *New York Times*, March 31, 2009.

77. Quoted in Jackie Calmes, "Clinton's Health Defeat Sways Obama's Tactics," *New York Times*, September 6, 2009.

78. Quoted in Stolberg, Zeleny, and Hulse, "The Long Road Back." See also Alter, *The Promise*, p. 432.

79. Connolly, "How Obama Revived His Health-care Bill."

80. Quoted in Sheryl Gay Stolberg, "White House and Allies Set to Build Up Health Law," *New York Times*, June 6, 2010.

81. Jeff Zeleny, "Millions Spent to Sway Democrats on Health Care," *New York Times*, March 14, 2010.

82. Kane, "House Democrats Hit Boiling Point Over Perceived Lack of White House Support." See also Friel and Young, "A Trying Relationship," p. 2084.

83. Friel and Young, "A Trying Relationship," pp. 2077, 2082.

84. Quoted in Bai, "Taking the Hill."

85. Quoted in Shailagh Murray, Michael D. Shear, and Paul Kane, "2009 Democratic Agenda Severely Weakened by Republicans' United Opposition," *Washington Post*, January 24, 2010. See also David M. Herszenhorn, "Democrats See Progress on Proposal for Economy," *New York Times*, January 13, 2009.

86. Quoted in Bai, "Taking the Hill."

87. Quoted in Peter Baker, "Obama Defends Agenda as More Than Recession," *New York Times*, March 13, 2009.

88. Hulse and Zeleny, "Stimulus Offers Glimpse of Obama's Battle Plan."

89. Ibid.; Wilson, "Bruised by Stimulus Battle, Obama Changed His Approach to Washington."

90. Bai, "Taking the Hill"; Hulse and Zeleny, "Stimulus Offers Glimpse of Obama's Battle Plan."

91. Stephen Labaton, "Ailing, Banks Still Field Strong Lobby at Capitol," *New York Times*, June 5, 2009; Stolberg, "Obama to Forge a Greater Role on Health Care."

92. Richard E. Cohen, "Can the Committee System Handle Obama's Ambitious Agenda?" *National Journal*, May 2, 2009; Adriel Bettelheim, "Overhaul Hard to Steer Using Hands-Off Approach," *CQ Weekly*, August 10, 2009, pp. 1894–1895; *Washington Post, Landmark: The Inside Story of America's New Health-Care Law and What It Means for Us All* (New York: Public Affairs, 2010), pp. 15–16.

93. Quoted in Cohen, "Can the Committee System Handle Obama's Ambitious Agenda?"

94. Quoted in Michael D. Shear and Shailagh Murray, "President Is Set to 'Take the Baton,'" *Washington Post*, July 20, 2009. See also Alter, *The Promise*, p. 249.

95. Alter, *The Promise*, pp. 249, 254.

96. Bettelheim, "Overhaul Hard to Steer Using Hands-Off Approach," p. 1894.

97. Bai, "Taking the Hill."

98. Alter, *The Promise*, p. 396.

99. Ibid., p. 260.

100. Sheryl Gay Stolberg, "White House Nudges Test the Power of Persuasion," *New York Times*, February 24, 2010; Murray, Shear, and Kane, "2009 Democratic Agenda Severely Weakened by Republicans' United Opposition"; Richard E. Cohen, "Pelosi's Bill: How She Did It," *National Journal*, November 14, 2009, p. 32; Jackie Calmes, "Clinton's Defeat Sways Obama's Tactics," *New York Times*, September 6, 2009.

101. Connolly, "How Obama Revived His Health-care Bill"; *Washington Post, Landmark*, pp. 50–51; Alter, *The Promise*, pp. 265–266.

102. Cohen, "Pelosi's Bill," p. 32.

103. David D. Kirkpatrick, "Obama Is Taking an Active Role in Talks on Health Care Plan," *New York Times*, August 13, 2009.

104. Sheryl Gay Stolberg and David M. Herszenhorn, "In Health Talks, President Is Hands-Off No More," *New York Times*, January 16, 2010; Alter, *The Promise*, p. 417.

105. Stolberg, Zeleny, and Hulse, "The Long Road Back."

106. Michael D. Shear, "Obama to Ask CEOs to Abandon 'Furious Efforts' to Block Financial Overhaul," *Washington Post*, April 22, 2010; Anne E. Kornblut and Michael D. Shear, "Obama Makes a Strong Case for Financial Reform," *Washington Post*, April 23, 2010.

107. Edward Epstein, "Pelosi's Action Plan for Party Unity," *CQ Weekly*, March 30, 2009, p. 707.

108. For an overview of her role, see *Washington Post, Landmark*, chap. 2.

109. Cohen, "Pelosi's Bill," p. 32.

110. Ibid., p. 28.

111. Quoted in Stolberg, Zeleny, and Hulse, "The Long Road Back."

112. Connolly, "How Obama Revived His Health-care Bill"; Stolberg, Zeleny, and Hulse, "The Long Road Back."

113. Stolberg, Zeleny, and Hulse, "The Long Road Back."

114. Quoted in *Congressional Quarterly*, "Biden Declares Pelosi More Powerful than Obama, VP," Roll Call, July 19, 2010.

115. Cohen, "Can the Committee System Handle Obama's Ambitious Agenda?"

116. Carl Hulse and Jackie Calmes, "Biden and G.O.P. Leader Helped Hammer Out Bipartisan Tax Accord," *New York Times*, December 7, 2010; Glenn Thrush, "For W.H., Upside in Fighting Hill Dems," Politico.com, December 8, 2010.

117. Joe Eaton and M. B. Pell, "Lobbyists Swarm Capitol to Influence Health Reform," The Center for Public Integrity, February 23, 2010; Dan Eggen, "Expecting Final Push on Health-care Reform, Interest Groups Rally for Big Finish," *Washington Post*, February 28, 2010.

118. John Harwood, "New Business Group Forms to Promote Obama Agenda," *New York Times*, May 20, 2009.

119. Stolberg, Zeleny, and Hulse, "The Long Road Back."

120. Allen and VandeHei, "Obama Isolated Ahead of 2012."

Chapter 6

1. Quoted in George Packer, "Obama's Lost Year," *New Yorker*, March 15, 2010.

2. Jonathan Alter, *The Promise: President Obama, Year One* (New York: Simon & Schuster, 2010), pp. 118, 246.

3. The first round of the "cash for clunkers" program was part of a much larger supplemental appropriations bill. Thus, I have used the second round, passed shortly after the first, which focused entirely on the vehicle trade-in program.

4. Perry Bacon Jr., "House Passes War Funds As 51 Democrats Dissent," *Washington Post*, May 15, 2009.

5. Paul Kane, "Pelosi Says Rallying Votes for Troop Surge in Afghanistan Will Be Obama's Job," *Washington Post*, December 17, 2009, p. A4.

6. Some of the Democratic opposition may have stemmed from the decision by party leaders to strip from the bill money that had been included in the original House version to help address the weak economy at home, including funds to help preserve teachers' jobs.

7. Jeff Zeleny, "Gregg Ends Bid for Commerce Job," *New York Times*, February 13, 2009.

8. Alter, *The Promise*, p. 424.

9. Richard Rubin, "Party Unity: An Ever Thicker Dividing Line," *CQ Weekly*, January 11, 2010, pp. 122–131; Shawn Zeller, "The Staying Power of Partisanship," *CQ Weekly*, January 3, 2011, pp. 30–40.

10. voteview.com/Polarized_America.htm#POLITICALPOLARIZATION

11. See voteview.com/houserank.asp; voteview.com/senrank.asp; jackman.stanford.edu/ideal/s111/x1.pdf; and jackman.stanford.edu/ideal/h111/x2.pdf. *National Journal* found a very slight overlap. See Ronald Brownstein, "Pulling Apart," *National Journal*, February 26, 2010.

12. Carl Hulse and Jeff Zeleny, "Stimulus Offers Glimpse of Obama's Battle Plan," *New York Times*, February 13, 2009.

13. Quoted in Alter, *The Promise*, p. 129.

14. Scott Wilson, "Bruised by Stimulus Battle, Obama Changed His Approach to Washington," *Washington Post*, April 29, 2009.

15. Quoted in Peter Baker, "Education of a President," *New York Times Magazine*, October 17, 2010.

16. Peter Baker, "The Limits of Rahmism," *New York Times Magazine*, March 14, 2010.

17. See, for example, Pew Research Center for the People and the Press poll, July 31–August 5, 2010.

18. Ronald Brownstein, "Dems' Governing Core Stays Intact," *National Journal*, April 3, 2010.

19. Greg Giroux, "Breaking Down the House Vote to Increase Federal Debt Limit," *CQ Daily*, December 17, 2009. The figures do not include Bill Owens, who won a special election in November 2009 in a district the GOP was defending.

20. Alexis Simendinger and Brian Friel, "A Hard Sell for Congressional Democrats," *National Journal*, January 16, 2010, p. 25.

21. Charlie Cook, "The Health Bill Could Have Foundered in So Many Places, but the Speaker and Chief of Staff Muscled It Through," *National Journal*, November 14, 2009.

22. Ibid.

23. Richard E. Cohen and Brian Friel, "Serving a District that Went for the Other Party's Presidential Nominee Can Force Congressmen to Make Tough Choices," *National Journal*, April 18, 2009.

24. Quoted in Simendinger and Friel, "A Hard Sell for Congressional Democrats."

25. Rubin, "Party Unity: An Ever Thicker Dividing Line"; Zeller, "The Staying Power of Partisanship."

26. Ben Pershing, "Critical Ads to Follow Obama on Vacation," *Washington Post*, August 23, 2009; Katherine Q. Seelye, "Competing Ads on Health Care Plan Swamp the Airwaves," *New York Times*, August 16, 2009; Katherine Q. Seelye, "Ad Campaign Counterattacks Against Overhaul's Critics," *New York Times*, August 14, 2009; and Ceci Connolly, "Health-Care Activists Targeting Democrats," *Washington Post*, June 28, 2009.

27. Baker, "The Limits of Rahmism."

28. Peter H. Stone, "Lobbyists Go Full Tilt in Health Fight," *National Journal*, March 13, 2010; Jeff Zeleny, "Millions Spent to Sway Democrats on Health Care," *New York Times*, March 14, 2010; Sheryl Gay Stolberg, Jeff Zeleny, and Carl Hulse, "The Long Road Back," *New York Times*, March 21, 2010.

29. Nate Silver, "Obama's Share Determined Dems' Votes on ObamaCare," *538*, March 22, 2010.

30. Silver, "Obama's Share Determined Dems' Votes on ObamaCare." Ideology is measured by DW-Nominate scores.

31. See, for example, Keith Koffler, "The Oval Office: Obama's Lobbying Turf," *CQ Today Online News*, December 7, 2009.

32. Matthew Watkins, "Edwards Bucked Pressure on Vote," *Bryan-College Station Eagle*, November 10, 2009.

33. These examples come from Connolly, "How Obama Revived His Health-care Bill."

Chapter 7

1. Richard E. Neustadt, *Presidential Power and the Modern Presidents* (New York: Free Press, 1990), p. 11.

2. Ibid., p. 10.

3. Ibid., p. 37. Italics in original.

4. See, for example, Kenneth R. Mayer, *With the Stroke of a Pen, Executive Orders and Presidential Power* (Princeton, NJ: Princeton University Press, 2001); Phillip J. Cooper, *By Order of the President: The Use and Abuse of Executive Direct Action* (Lawrence: University Press of Kansas, 2002); William G. Howell, *Power without Persuasion* (Princeton, NJ: Princeton University Press, 2003); Adam L. Warber, *Executive Orders and the Modern Presidency: Legislating from the Oval Office* (Boulder, CO: Lynne Rienner, 2006).

5. Neustadt, *Presidential Power and the Modern Presidents*, p. 32.

6. See George C. Edwards III, *The Strategic President: Persuasion and Opportunity in Presidential Leadership* (Princeton, NJ: Princeton University Press, 2009).

7. See, for example, Michel Villette and Catherine Vuillermot, *From Predators to Icons; Exposing the Myth of the Business Hero* (Ithaca, NY: ILR Press, 2009); and Scott A. Shane, *The Illusions of Entrepreneurship* (New Haven, CT: Yale University Press, 2008).

8. One example is George Packer, "Obama's Lost Year," *New Yorker*, March 15, 2010.

9. George C. Edwards III, *Presidential Approval* (Baltimore, MD: Johns Hopkins University Press, 1990), pp. 93–100. Reagan obtained majority approval in the November 20–23, 1981 Gallup poll.

10. Carl Albert, interview by Dorothy Pierce McSweeny, July 9, 1969, interview 3, transcript, pp. 7, 11, Lyndon Baines Johnson Library, Austin, TX; Carl Albert, interview by Dorothy Pierce McSweeny, August 13, 1969, interview 4, transcript, pp. 22, 25, Lyndon Baines Johnson Library; Carl Albert, interview by Dorothy Pierce McSweeny, April 28, 1969, interview 1, transcript, pp. 22–23, Lyndon Baines Johnson Library; Carl Albert, interview by Dorothy Pierce McSweeny, June 10, 1969, interview 2, transcript, p. 14, Lyndon Baines Johnson Library.

11. Russell Renka, "Comparing Presidents Kennedy and Johnson as Legislative Leaders," paper presented at the annual meeting of the Southern Political Science Association, Savannah, GA, November 1984, p. 26. See also Carl Albert, interview by Dorothy Pierce McSweeny, July 9, 1969, interview 3, transcript, p. 3.

12. Michael R. Beschloss, *Taking Charge: The Johnson White House Tapes, 1963–1964* (New York: Simon & Schuster, 1997); Michael R. Beschloss, *Reaching for Glory: Lyndon Johnson's Secret White House Tapes, 1964–1965* (New York: Simon & Schuster, 2001).

13. Act V, Scene 2.

14. Quoted in Shailagh Murray, Michael D. Shear, and Paul Kane, "2009 Democratic Agenda Severely Weakened by Republicans' United Opposition," *Washington Post*, January 24, 2010.

15. Quoted in Sheryl Gay Stolberg, "White House Nudges Test the Power of Persuasion," *New York Times*, February 24, 2010.

16. Richard Hofstadter, *The American Political Tradition* (New York: Vintage, 1954), p. 316.

17. Quoted in Jonathan Alter, *The Promise: President Obama, Year One* (New York: Simon & Schuster, 2010), p. 344. See also p. 421.

18. Quoted in Stolberg, "White House Nudges Test the Power of Persuasion."

19. Barack Obama, News Conference, White House, December 22, 2010.

20. Quoted in Peter Baker, "The Limits of Rahmism," *New York Times Magazine*, March 14, 2010.

21. Quoted in Baker, "The Limits of Rahmism."

22. See, for example, Gallup poll of September 13–16, 2010.

23. Quoted in Brian Friel and Kerry Young, "A Trying Relationship," *CQ Weekly*, September 3, 2010, p. 2083.

24. Transcript: "President Barack Obama," *60 Minutes*, Interview by Steve Kroft, November 4, 2010.

25. Gary C. Jacobson, "Legislative Success and Political Failure: The Public's Reaction to Barack Obama's Early Presidency," *Presidential Studies Quarterly* 41 (June 2011), pp. 231–232. Jacobson found that an average of 90 percent of Republicans, 88 percent of Democrats, and 82 percent of independents offered consistent evaluations; analysis is based on 10 surveys by Gallup, NBC News/*Wall Street Journal*, and CNN taken between February and August and available for secondary analysis from the Roper Center, University of Connecticut. In the June 2010 Pew survey, 88 percent of respondents gave consistent evaluations of Obama's performance on health care and his overall job performance; on eight other issues, including the economy, the deficit, and the Iraq and Afghan wars, consistency ranged from 69 percent to 85 percent.

26. Chris Cillizza, "What Effect Did Health-care Reform Have on Election?" *Washington Post*, November 7, 2010.

27. Lincoln Park Strategies conducted the poll for The Third Way, contacting households in 10 battleground states with contested races on November 4–12, 2010. There were 1,000 respondents, half of which were "switchers" and the other half, "droppers."

28. Survey conducted jointly by Resurgent Republic and Democracy Corps on behalf of the Bipartisan Policy Center, November 2–3, 2010, among 886 voters in the midterm election.

29. Kaiser Health Tracking Poll, November 3–6, 2010.

30. Nate Silver, "Health Care and Bailout Votes May Have Hurt Democrats," *New York Times*, November 16, 2010. See also Eric McGhee, "Did Controversial Roll Call Votes Doom the Democrats?" *The Monkey Cage*, November 4, 2010; and Eric McGhee, "Which Roll Call Votes Hurt the Democrats?" *The Monkey Cage*, November 9, 2010.

31. David W. Brady, Morris P. Fiorina, and Arjun S. Wilkins, "The 2010 Elections: Why did Political Science Forecasts Go Awry?" *PS: Political Science and Politics* 44 (April 2011): 247-250.

32. Gary C. Jacobson, "The Republican Resurgence in 2010," *Political Science Quarterly* 127 (Spring 2011): 35–66.

33. John Cranford, "The Partisanship Pendulum," *CQ Weekly* (April 18, 2011): 845.

34. Lori Montgomery, Paul Kane, Brady Dennis, Alec MacGillis, David Fahrenthold, Rosalind Helderman, Felicia Sonmez, and Dan Balz, "Origins of the Debt Showdown," *Washington Post*, August 6, 2011.

35. *USA Today*/Gallup poll, August 2, 2011; CNN/ORC poll conducted by Opinion Research Corporation, August 5–7, 2011; Reuters/Ipsos poll conducted by Ipsos Public Affairs, August 4–8, 2011. But see CBS News/*New York Times* poll, August 2–3, 2011.

36. Reuters/Ipsos poll conducted by Ipsos Public Affairs, August 4–8, 2011.

37. CBS News/*New York Times* poll, August 2–3, 2011; *USA Today*/Gallup poll, August 2, 2011.

38. Quoted in Baker, "Education of a President," *New York Times Magazine*, October 17, 2010.

39. Transcript: "President Barack Obama," *60 Minutes*, Interview by Steve Kroft, November 4, 2010.

40. Ibid.

INDEX

CPSIA information can be obtained at www.ICGtesting.com
Printed in the USA
BVOW08s1530230416

445213BV00011B/15/P